Self Help Workbook

for Woman

3 books in 1

Rediscover your life without limits through the art of Self-Love, Rebuild your Self-Confidence and Increase your Self-Esteem to change your life and finally achieve happiness

Marie Grey

© Copyright 2021 by Marie Grey

Copyright: The content contained within this book should not be reproduced, duplicated, or transmitted without direct written permission from the author or the publisher.

Under no circumstances should any blame or legal responsibility be held against the publisher, or author, for any damages, reparation, or monetary loss due to the information contained within this book, either directly or indirectly.

Disclaimer Notice: Please, note that the information contained within this book is for educational and entertainment purposes only. All effort has been executed to present accurate, up to date, complete, and reliable information. No warranty of any kind is expressed or implied. Readers should acknowledge that the author is not engaging in the rendering of legal, financial, medical, or professional advice. The content within this book has been derived from various sources. Please, consult a licensed professional before attempting any technique outlined in this book.

By reading this document, the reader agrees that under no circumstances is the author responsible for any losses, direct or indirect, which are incurred as a result of the use of information contained within this document, including, but not limited to, — errors, omissions, or inaccuracies.

Table of Contents

Book 1 Self Confidence: *Increase your self-Confidence by overcoming doubts and uncertainties to create a better future*   5

Introduction   6

What is self-confidence?   11

How To Overcome Self Doubt   31

Creating Real Self-Confidence   58

What does self-confidence have to do with Forgiveness?   103

Why Self-confidence Is Vital in Sports   111

Conclusion   127

Book 2 Self Esteem: *Gain Confidence, free yourself from negative thoughts, and enjoy the benefits of self-esteem to change your life*   130

Introduction   131

Lack of Self-Esteem in women   134

How to Evade Low Self-Esteem   159

Women's self-esteem For Stress Reduction, Balance, and Autonomy   171

Steps to Build Self-Confidence   186

Ways to Help Females Overcome Lack of Confidence   194

Self Esteem in Teenage Girls   196

Self Esteem for Immigrant Women Who Wants to Achieve Their Goals	205
Relationship between self-esteem and eating disorders	214
Why Counseling Could Help Women Achieve More Positive Self-Confidence	226
Challenging your internal criticism	239
Conclusion	247
Book 3 Self Love: Find your inner love, increase your self-esteem and confidence, and practice self-care	252
Introduction	253
Self-Love: A very crucial issue for women	256
Self-Love Principles	271
The Power of Self-Love	284
Simple Practices of Self-Love to Love Yourself More	297
Simple Steps to Enhance Your Self-Love Using Self-Hypnosis	313
For Self-Love, Let go of Mother, Sister, Daughter position holding you back	325
Welcome Success With self-love and self-acceptance	336
Self-care, self-love-Two directions to joy	342
Challenges of Developing Self-love in women	354
Bulimia Recovery: 3 Strategies for How to Achieve Self-Love	362
Conclusion	374

Book 1

Self Confidence: *Increase your Self-Confidence by overcoming doubts and uncertainties to create a better future*

Introduction

Confidence in yourself is all about the view of yourself. It reveals your sense of value. Yet, in truth, there is more to it than possessing the greatest ability to believe, to live with the everyday trials and challenges of life, and to realize that you are most likely to have fun, prosperity, and satisfaction, of course.

Typically, multiple factors affect confidence levels, whether they are internal or external factors. This only means that things inside and outside of you can have a serious impact on your view of yourself. Low self-confidence can therefore have a major impact on all aspects of a person's life-whether it's your family, career, or health. That's why you need to learn how to cope with all of these variables to broaden your confidence and preserve your sense of value. The true essence of self-confidence is to trust in yourself and know that you are deserving of consideration.

But the question is how low self-confidence can affect the life of somebody? Because self-esteem is all about how you view yourself, it is exactly the opposite of low self-confidence. When he feels good about himself, a man is said to be optimistic. Nonetheless, low self-confidence occurs if you feel bad about yourself with something or a specific circumstance. This may be rejection, anxiety, loss, ridicule, or deprivation. The issues that make you feel bad most of the time are the main reasons that your self-confidence seems to be weak.

In particular, three fundamental factors affect an individual's level of trust. Furthermore, these considerations apply to the following:

- Values-It is a must that you learn to live life with your highest values to appreciate your existence. If what you really believe in is clear to you, then you are most likely able to appreciate your life. And only people who respect themselves know how to appreciate themselves and who are sure of who they are.

- Mastery–This factor refers to the state of self-confidence and comfort in your life and work. You become more successful in anything you do by being in control of yourself. It gives you the feeling that you are good and important. And whenever you feel you are effective in whatever you do, your level of trust is increased and your sense of value is also improved.

- Plans–It's very important to know what you're searching for to improve your self-confidence. In whatever task you take, you have to set your targets. Once you think you're doing something you want or you believe in, you feel much better. It allows you to perform better because you realize you have a goal to achieve.

Self-confidence is something to put in plain words that is quite complex. This is because there are several factors to consider and understand how it can seriously affect the life of a person. Nonetheless, if you only learn how to make the most of all the good things in your life and focus on the positive side, you will find that your confidence and self-worth will immediately start to improve.

Low self-confidence can emerge from many aspects, impacting both adults and kids alike. In adolescents, reasons for low self-esteem are usually caused by social situations such as establishing school friendships or how they interact with their families. At a young age, kids assign themselves respect and importance based on how they think other people value them, so they are unable to consider themselves because they believe other people don't rate them.

Self-confidence in adulthood comes largely from within as the ability to self-assess one's success improves. Issues such as work problems, contrasting one's achievements in life such as marriage, having a family or buying a house for one's friends, or financial success can all relate positively and negatively to the self-confidence of an individual. External factors can also impair the self-confidence of an individual, and failure circumstances such as breaking up and death may drastically reduce self-esteem.

Low self-confidence can be very detrimental as it causes a downward spiral that, even in young children, may lead to depression. We think that they have no worth, and therefore they are not looking for opportunities to excel or gain value, which makes them feel even worse about themselves.

During moments like this, a person with low self-esteem can only be supported by outside support. Time spent with one's close friends and working through the problems can aid with mild cases, as it is often overlooked that others keep them in much higher esteem than they do.

Professional therapy may be needed in more severe cases to help discover the causes of low self-confidence and provide assistance and advice on how to improve it. Getting the most of the resources that will help build self-esteem requires a great deal of determination and commitment, but the positive benefits of doing this greatly exceed the anxiety experienced before the opportunities.

Confidence in oneself is an essential part of life. It's leading us to success. Anyone who thinks of himself poorly in life will not achieve his target. Believing in oneself is crucial to our positive life while doing something.

We should have a positive and friendly mind to achieve self-confidence. We should be serving others and respecting the emotions of others. Refrain from being a selfish person. Then you can value others and recover other people's love. The devotion is the moral support that must be a trustworthy person. Always feel there's anything you can get or can't do. Do not be mean to others; hold warmth on your mind and smile in your eyes. Then everybody's response in your life will be constructive and your trust will be improved.

Lack of trust makes people introvert, harming their lives. They'll turn morose and slow, even though they've had a lot of qualities before. Be mindful of your strengths and weaknesses and try to compensate for your deficiencies. Only think of your strengths, and keep your head straight.

The main reason people lack confidence in themselves is an unwillingness to see their abilities. Everyone has advantages of their own. We must consider them. Most people don't think about their strengths, but about certain attributes and how they don't fit.

Another reason people lose confidence in themselves can be in their relationships through a traumatic event. From such an event, many people can grow; others will focus on it and become terrified. The upbringing of one often influences one's faith. A conflict between parents, the desire of a mother may cause problems of self-confidence in the mind of a child. Families should share their issues with their children and give them relevant advice to help them build trust.

What is self-confidence?

Confidence in oneself is a deep and rational faith in oneself, abilities, and capabilities. This includes being mindful of one's weaknesses and being conscious of one's skills. It is a positive attitude that leads to the idea that one is armed with the necessary resources to respond positively to all of life's challenges.

The degree of confidence is the product of your view of yourself. This has an impact on how you are viewed by men. Whether people interrelate with each other and react to you is a representation of how you think. Therefore, if you don't have high self-esteem, people will usually find it difficult to trust your skills.

The degree of trust is the product of your view of yourself. This has an impact on how you are viewed by men. Whether people interrelate with each other and react to you is a representation of how you think. Furthermore, if you don't have high self-esteem, people will usually find it difficult to accept your talents.

Low self-esteem is a commodity that relies too much on your negative characteristics and what you do wrong. In other words, you are the worst adversary of your own!

Individuals that exude self-confidence do not necessarily rely on others ' approval. They listen and value others ' opinions; however, at the end of the day, they judge for themselves.

Like most individuals, optimistic people have realistic goals, follow concrete objectives, and pursue their dreams. We are also facing challenges. What do self-confident people do if things are not going their way? To evaluate the situation, confident people take a step back to seek the best options available.

When things didn't go as planned, through these attempts, they come to a point when they know that they can't always get what they want.

We step on from this point and take the experiences learned from previous practice with them. We are excited to come to grips with fresh goals and dreams. The strong belief in their ability remains unchanged, realizing they are now older, more knowledgeable, and better equipped with experience.

Let's get straight to the point: with self-confidence, we're not raised. Simply put, there's nothing inherent about self-confidence. Self-confidence takes time to develop and demands that the same be nurtured. However, honesty is no one's private possession. Trust and mindset are open to everyone. Determining the criteria is up to you.

People's obsession with self-confidence makes it look like a magic potion. That characteristic tends to be the be-all- and - end-all that will allow all issues to vanish. Trust alone will not take you to the dream life for which you strive. You need to take action in the first place. To succeed, you need perseverance, persistence, logical reasoning, trustworthy advisors, and a whole host of others. Trust is the first crucial step.

When we see a self-confident person, we always feel he is comfortable in ALL of his abilities. Confidence doesn't protect anything. Let's take an example. Robert Kiyosaki, Poor Dad's writer, exudes confidence in his company and entrepreneurial skills. Yet he's honest enough to admit he's been failing at college in academic subjects.

A friend of mine trusts in her ability as a writer. Yet tell her to add up figures and she transfers herself automatically to the farthest known world, where percentages, quantities, amounts, disparities, products, and quotients cannot enter here! Confidence doesn't embrace everything. It's not daunting.

Three Pillars of Self-confidence

The quest for true self-confidence takes us all in different directions. We all want the magic pill that will immediately give us somebody with true self-confidence's attributes and personality. Trust is not something that can be achieved easily from reading books with various self-help. Through taking action every day, it can't be gained and then finding it didn't work. Sitting about seeing yourself with it will never gain it. True self-confidence will become the substance only by constant learning, practice, and belief.

Education is the first pillar of self-confidence. My first instinct to gain self-confidence was reading books about it and listening to CDs. Through telling professionals in their professions where they obtained it, I received the best self-confidence training. I find the basis instantly to teach myself through books, CDs, and other personal experiences. The most significant step in the process of training was to extend my knowledge only to one area of my life. For instance, in my career, which was sales and marketing, I needed self-confidence. I've read books about opportunities and contract termination. I have told the most effective sales and marketing leaders how they were coping with certain circumstances. Be precise as you begin the process of reading. In every aspect of our lives, self-confidence is something we want. Surprisingly, when you start to teach yourself in a particular context, you will see that it can be extended to all areas of your life.

Self-confidence's second ingredient is knowledge by practice. Take action is a more straightforward way of saying it. We were all accused of teaching ourselves and discovering how unexpectedly we made a great discovery. The problem most of us have is that once we get the data we don't take action on it. I'm going to be the first to confess. Do the behavior that brings you confidence. If you're in marketing and you're having a problem with your outlook, inquire about the deal. If on a date you want to ask for one, just ask for the day. Note, what's relevant isn't the outcome. It doesn't matter if the person says yes or no in the short term. If you get a response, you can automatically get a lift from your self-confidence. If you receive a no, the next time you ask, you will gain valuable experience that will help you. Failure is the experience's most important element. Write this expression again. Those with the greatest self-confidence in their lives are still more likely to fail than succeed. Consider disappointment as a stepping stone for unwavering confidence in oneself. When true self-confidence is achieved, the explanation being; once one is confident with loss, the brain may continue to pursue the potential in all matters.

Trust is the third pillar. Belief is the force that cannot be measured in terms of education and experience. Faith is an ingredient that, if accepted, will take you to unimagined higher levels. I don't speak of blind faith. I'm thinking about the confidence that is trained, ready, and optimistic. If you take action against your doubts, true faith will be attained. You will realize when you have true faith because the knowledge, encounters, and circumstances you once feared will thirst you. You'll be master of feelings that don't dread disappointment anymore. Your faith will drive you through the thoughts of fear. They will no longer be seen as barriers, but as simple challenges that will only improve you in the long run.

Note that all three self-confidence principles must be regularly exercised and implemented. Belief brings in change. Faith is a need for consistent action. Learning without practice is worse than not reading first. You won't learn if you don't take action. Focus on all three foundations in your daily life now concurrently to take the first step towards true self-confidence.

How Our Early Years Shaped Us

Social Sciences have invented a special term that is often connected with how our parents educated us. They're considering it training.

Psychologists concluded, "Parents ' behaviors are crucial to how children feel about themselves, particularly throughout their adolescence." Parents play an important role in the early years' growth of self-confidence as this forms the basis for raising well-rounded teenagers and mature adults.

Consider living in a household of perfectionist relatives, living with unrealistic expectations, as a child. They're so harsh on themselves that they're asking you to hold expectations that can't be high. It seems that you are already set to fail at this early stage of our life. Consider the negative effect on your faith that it would have. If you use unrealistic standards established by parents or members of society, you will certainly still experience fear that will prevent you from reaching your full potential.

See yourself in another situation where your parents in their careers are well-known. They're nurses, for example; they're asking you to follow their footsteps. The idea of pursuing a different profession, like that of a painter or chef, is brought up, and an argument follows. They discourage you from exploring your talents, assert your independence, and dissuade you from finding faults by saying, "You're not creative enough, you're better off as a doctor!" Parents often over-protect their children. Families want to protect their children from harsh realities as much as possible. We love them as their kids are life-based on them. Children raised in this manner do not make mistakes; and therefore, rarely learn from mistakes.

You can also affect your life with your choice of friends and role models. Recall how much you loved the idea of belonging to the popular group in your teenage years! You looked up at the campus ' most popular people. Do you wish you could be them! You may have even tried to copy their styling attitude and style or entered their circle of friends. You begin to realize when you grow up that "making yourself" is more rewarding than being a replica of these people.

Which part will parents and friends play in fostering confidence then? Parents and friends have to be children's models. Parents and friends must give good examples of feeling good for themselves, being independent thinkers, overcoming obstacles, and, most notably, being self-confident. They are live proofs that you can be effective.

What if I have little Confidence in myself?

Often used interchangeably with self-esteem, the idea that you can be or do certain things is self-confidence. On the other side, a lack of self-confidence relies on the idea that you can't be or do something. The defining terms low or high as in poor or high self-confidence are key to the use of this definition. It is the use of such words that can act as an advantage or disadvantage as a human trait of self-confidence.

The road to greater success is for some self-confidence, while for others it can be a life sentence of disappointment. Whether you're effective or not can rely on your self-confidence level to some degree. There is no understanding of self-confidence in solitude. It's a series of unmistakable internal and external indications that indicate certain individuals who have it or who don't. You need to realize that self-confidence is possible if you're one of the many who don't. While this book focuses on weak and low self-confidence, note, with you starts self-confidence.

What are the indicators of a lack of self-confidence in a person?

1. When you think you always have to justify after making a mistake.

2. You feel the need to answer/defend any critique that is aimed at you.

3. For your lack of self-confidence you over-compensate

4. The language of your body

5. It is a learned trait to continually aspire to become a perfectionist self-confidence.

No one is born comfortable in himself. It is the culmination of many years of learning how to respond to others around you as an individual. You are bombarded with positive messages about yourself from infancy onwards. It's how you view the signals that decide your confidence level.

One of the most hated interpersonal activities of all is a good example of this: public speaking. It would appear like this if you were to observe a person's production of self-confidence. Let us observe the growth of self-confidence in a school setting with the context of education. Something like that would go in many situations.

Many kids were eager to please from pre-school to about the 4th grade. Not because of some misplaced confidence in their base of knowledge, but because of a need to please. If the instructor asks a question about the school, the number of hands raised will be quite a few at this point in the educational process. Whether the response is right or not, it is not necessary to obtain the acknowledgment.

Attitude begins to change when the baby continues to become conscious of an identity. Generally, those with high self-confidence are the ones who lift their hand if asked to answer a query by a show of hands. It persists for much of the rest of their lives as a pattern of behavior.

The reason this book argues for self-confidence as an acquired characteristic is that, regardless of their age, even the most awkward young adults can "discover" their abilities in the right situation. Consider the true story of the football player Michael Ohr made famous by Baltimore Raven in The Blind Side's book and movie.

Ohr was seen by most as having zero faith in himself outwardly. He witnessed incidents, however, while in high school, that changed his life. It was also learned in the end how much trust he had in himself.

If you or someone you meet has a lack of self-confidence, note that it may seem hard to gain self-confidence, but it's a matter of choosing to learn how to do that. Here are a few ideas to begin with: remind yourself every day that you can do anything you want. You will begin to believe it soon and show your newly found the self-confidence to everyone.

Do those tasks you think you do well and start asking yourself, "Why am I good at this? And then try to replicate how you do that in other areas of your life. At the end of this essay, look at the five indicators of poor self-confidence and then perform in the exact opposite of each one with focused attention. Eventually, poor self-confidence is a condition that can easily respond to self-help program.

Self-Acceptance

Self-acceptance is closely linked to "self-image." That's the picture you've built up about how good, successful, talented, or how unhappy and ugly you are. It is an image that has been built up throughout your lifetime, an image that is predominantly based on your successes and failures. Therefore, the first step in improving your self-acceptance is to improve your self-image, and to do so you need to change the way you think about yourself.

Apart from enhancing your self-image, learning to accept yourself as you are now, with all your flaws, is the most important thing to do. You can change some of your faults, deficiencies, and so on, and you should try to change them, but you have to accept them for now. Some people feel that they are too thin, too overweight, too tall, not intelligent enough, or that they have too big ears, or that they don't have enough hair. If you have such flaws, it's crucial not to blame yourself—in many situations they're stuff you've been born with and can't do anything about. You don't have to be great, and no one is flawless. Explain to yourself: "I'm not fine, but so what. No one is, and I'm going to make the most of what I have." Be your own. And the main reason is that your well-being and prosperity rely on your self-acceptance to a large extent. Yes, without it, it's difficult to be content or productive. So stop trying to be perfect; look at yourself as you are. This doesn't mean that you shouldn't try to improve yourself in any way you can— you should.

Often, your friends and associates have a great impact on your self-acceptance and self-esteem. Increasing your self-acceptance and self-esteem if you think they have a high opinion of you. On the other side, when you feel people have a low opinion of you, your perception of yourself usually falls apart. Therefore, it is important to ensure that this does not occur. Yeah, don't care about what others think; you're always right in most situations. However, it is important to remember that, unless you let them, no one can make you feel bad for yourself. People often make remarks that are harmful to others without realizing it (and they do it on purpose, of course, sometimes). Don't be serious about taking them. No one has anything to do with how you think for yourself— if you permit it. Train to ignore them.

Sit down and mention your achievements is one of the easiest ways to boost your self-acceptance and confidence. You might not think you've got a ton, but you might be shocked. Consider the milestones you've reached, the honors you've got, the years you've spent in school or university. Think of your successes at school, your interests, etc. Write to them when you're finished. When you talk of them, take pride in them.

Tips on Self-Acceptance

- Change Don't try to impress others.

- Reflect on your life's positive things. They love it.

- Do not disregard our faults and shortcomings— accept them. Don't think about them, so promise yourself that you are going to work to resolve anything that can be solved.

- Choose a role model— someone you look up to and respect— and imitate their good points.

- Set targets. You still feel good at achieving goals.

- Do not apologize; do not constantly blame anyone, and do not whine.

- Know from your mistakes.

- Occasionally recover the "best moments" (in your memory). Mind your unique talents.

Note that they all have stuff in themselves that they don't like. You're not on your own.

If you start to worry about something you don't like about yourself, say to yourself, "Nobody's great. I'm not good, but neither is anyone else, and I'm a guy. Self-confidence Like I discussed at the beginning of the book, self-confidence has to do with how comfortable you're in your skill.

Sit down to mention all the stuff you truly love doing, then make a list of your weaknesses while you're at it. Do they suit the things that you love to do? You'll have to worry about how to get them back if they don't. What are you going to need? Further training? Further workout? Get that. Get it.

First, reflect on your abilities and think about your weaknesses. This doesn't imply you ought to build an unreasonable self-image; it implies you ought, to be frank to yourself. You should look at your skills and weaknesses carefully but always stress the positive.

We've also met people we respect, and often because they are so self-confident, the main reason we appreciate them. Trying to emulate them correctly is not a good idea, but you can learn to mold them and integrate some of their best features into your character.

Self-acceptance and self-confidence in the workplace is the fragile gap between shattered self-esteem and a polished ego with pride-your self-confidence; this makes a difference. My years of counseling have shown me that those who are effective feel that the specific positive actions, attitudes, and achievements of those they have interacted with or witnessed have significantly enhanced their self-confidence. If this is true, then we have an obligation as managers and leaders to manage our levels of self-confidence and to inspire others to manage theirs positively.

Experience tells me that levels of self-confidence are well below a positive mindset for many. They're probably much more delicate than we'd think. That attitude is one of "can't do" rather than "can do" and is combined with many more detrimental than positive influences, sadly. I would say that self-confidence levels are well below healthy levels in my coaching experience, in the majority of people I meet. I would also suggest that a high level of self-confidence is a cornerstone of achievement and results.

Self-confidence is usually described as a mental state of being certain or self-confident at the moment with any thought or situation. To go forward and excel, it could be described as a psychological state of mind and confidence in oneself. What self-confidence does is encourage people to control conditions or events rather than be influenced by them. It can help to alleviate depression and irrational or dangerous thoughts by doing so. Most specifically, they can create optimistic performance goals.

I give this idea-it belongs to self-confidence. The self-confidence that you have is yours and belongs to you alone.

Even if that involves a face-to-face conversation with the image you see in the mirror, you must secure and continue to build on it. I would never say that from time to time it's not going to be under extreme pressure, but the power to control it is inside you. In reality, as a way of outperforming others around you, you should learn how to use your self-confidence. Believing in oneself allows you to gain the upper hand from those who cannot follow the same optimistic values. This ensures you should feel in control in all circumstances, regardless of who's around you. This suggests, of course, that you have to be willing to take all the steps necessary to do what is put before you. The pillar of your personal and professional achievements is your self-confidence. Always encourage anyone to strip away your self-confidence. Holding on and holding on forever is yours. Yet, it is only you who can weaken your self-confidence by making others.

Individuals are at all levels of an organization. Just social rules, practice, and corporate governance has given unique benefits for entities such as specialized expertise, names, corner rooms, or employee advantages. It, in effect, offered any control, whether real or perceived or a position of authority. And, more to the point, the awareness and control which you and think give them power over you have been given to them. The truth is they come the same way into the universe and they're going to leave the same way-with a first and last breath. In their lives, how people have been subjected to, what they have encountered, and how they choose to incorporate what they have witnessed is what places them toward others. In reality, on a personal note, I recognize that irrespective of position, function, or name, I have encountered, and witnessed high and low levels of self-confidence.

I had the opportunity to get to know the company president on a personal level very early in my career. I was out with him on a boat at his summer home on a particular occasion on a river. With all my words, I wanted to be very specific. My voice was stiff and uncomfortable, stating "Yes sir, no sir, three bags full sir." He pushed me into the water as we reached the pier and he got out of the boat. When he offered his arm with a friendly smile to pull me out of the cold, he politely told me that he also liked having fun like everyone else. The lecture I have never forgotten; the talk has instilled a level of self-confidence in me for all the years that followed. I've heard how to handle older people than I do. Although I regard older people with the respect they deserve and received, the truth is that they are essentially the same as you and I are. We also receive the same degree of personal recognition and should gain it. Remember that the communication and interactions that you will have with others along the path to success could have a significant impact on your learning and self-confidence growth.

Managing Upward –A higher self-confidence will be crucial for dealing with people in higher positions. You should understand that easily, be more willing to be at home with you, and appreciate your skills, irrespective of the circumstance. It is probable that the members themselves may be uncertain about certain subjects or may not be informed. Not unexpectedly, it is not predicted that rulers will be specialists in all fields. Your level of self-confidence will allow you to continue to focus on yourself. We will come to appreciate you in the workforce for the interest you give with them. You can note that as their confidence in you grows, further responsibilities would probably be assigned to you. We may not always be able to determine and properly evaluate your skill and personal motivation for a specific task at times. Therefore, you're going to have to work to make that clear to them to complete the task. Managing is an important learning experience when you discover true confidence and understanding inside you. It will come from within you your self-confidence. Yes, it may be the key ingredient to give you the chance to succeed. At the same moment, it can also give you a role model to handle for other workers.

I've tried what I could to handle or become a mentor to my boss on many occasions. I offered them advice on how stuff could work best, for instance, and solutions that work well in similar situations previous to them. One of the easiest ways to continue is to simply ask what they feel about the outcome of something or how they might have handled something better. Sometimes I'd go straight out and ask if they're open to an alternative approach and left them with compelling ideas they could pick and choose from. Over time, and with the correct level of respect, people are often going to look for you - a satisfying experience.

Managing Downward–When you communicate with your employees, your self-confidence will be a signal of their adamant reliance on you as a manager; when your self-confidence grows on a problem, so will theirs. Let it fall and you're going to be scrutinized. An important practice is to allow and encourage your employees to come up with ideas- particularly ideas that might be better than your own. Encourage them to be their strongest and freely accept that some people can move faster than you someday. Encouraging this will allow them to see that they too can be more effective than they have ever thought. And, for promoting such a mentality, they would thank you. Don't try to guess and explain what people want, as it will close them off to a world they don't know exists yet. As a chief, you are responsible for providing an open environment and providing guidance on how to navigate the world at your fingertips. Which happens when you do that? We have faith in you, you in them, and they have trust in themselves. You've generated a positive force to fuel performance-yours and yours!

Moving Through-The same relates to interacting with your colleagues as to moving up or down. You're going to be studied and tested. The world is both social and competitive, and the person with the highest level of self-confidence will often go above their colleagues. Obtain information and data, become optimistic about the scenario, set reasonable targets for yourself and others, and solicit help from those who will have a good impact on the results. In reality, a leadership team with high self-confidence would characterize an organization's culture, a culture of self-confidence! This is a society that needs more than just saying and praising than punishing.

It can be a powerful tool to move you back to your personal and professional ambitions when you learn to accept your level of self-confidence and use it positively. A word of caution, however, make sure you don't misinterpret unchecked ego for self-confidence in yourself and others that are managed and interpreted. I discovered first-hand that administrators and leaders with self-confidence should be similarly involved in two ways; preserving and strengthening one's self-confidence and also building confidence in those you lead. Leadership performance should not be a reflection of the individual individually, but rather a measure of confidence within those for whom they are responsible.

Self-Esteem, Self-Confidence, and Self-Efficacy-Do you know the difference?

Often there is uncertainty about self-esteem and self-confidence. It's not the same. There are some good but critical differential criteria.

What is Self-Esteem

Self-esteem is unconditionally respected, you can have full self-esteem if you are healthy. Go on, you're invited. You are respected as a human being by self-esteem. When a child enters the world, nothing can be achieved. Without help, it cannot clean up after itself, feed itself, or even remain alive. Yet we value it, we're saying it's special, unique, and precious. And that's it! Once you've been a kid like this, the interest is inherent. It's all the time there, nobody can take it away from you. If you think you have low self-esteem, remember the baby and how precious and special it is, then apply to yourself that awe and gratitude. You're alive, you've got the power of thought, feeling, expression, and movement. You can do something! This is awe-inspiring as you talk about the sheer liberty of being alive and being able to think, hear, speak, and act as you like. Try to be surprised at your natural abilities and try how unique and special you are. No-one's the same as you. You should respect yourself no matter what you do or who you are.

The trust that you can do this or that stuff is self-confidence. It's about or dependent on your abilities and success. You can be confident that you can do that if you are competent in a certain skill. Trust depends on you being good at that job. There's no use feeling optimistic if you're not good at it. If you're sure you can buy skydive you've never experienced it before and know nothing about it, that's a nightmare formula. No integrity, trust can make you a fool. Your confidence should grow as your abilities improve. There's another item you can trust to help you boost your faith in any ability...

What is Self-Efficacy?

Self-efficacy is the perception or conviction that comes from having faith in several different abilities. When you practice and develop each new skill, the confidence in your ability to learn is greater and you begin to believe in your effectiveness. The thinking goes like this: "I've learned to walk, chat, think for myself, drive a vehicle, take care of myself, add other things here, so I can learn more. I may not understand how to do it right now, but I know how to find someone to show me and I know how to spend time and resources to learn a new skill, so yeah, I can do anything!

How To Overcome Self Doubt

It is clear that discovering how to resolve self-doubt and fear is one of life's most difficult challenges. how great our quality depends a lot on how much self-confidence we have because anxiety is an uncommon sort of internal torment that can quickly slip into.

So how do you resolve the fears, difficulties, and anxieties that overtake your thoughts? To order to achieve better, what can you do to trust yourself? How can you resolve the self-doubt that stops you from succeeding?

Self-doubt is a position where we were both but each one of us struggles with it differently. Doubt and anxiety are difficult to control and are usually deep in our heads. An error, a mistake, or even a minor loss, lets you doubt and challenge your ability. Next thing you know, there's a lack of trust.

Once you start a business or have a theory, self-doubt always crawls in as you continue to equate yourself to those who have been good before you and are overwhelmed by the thought of how much effort you have to put in. You're also starting to think at that stage that there's no chance you can ever make it as successful people do.

But success is the courage to move in the direction of your dreams and on the path your heart takes you. It doesn't matter if you don't do it like those before you do. You should understand that self-doubt is not a rational behavior and that you can go beyond it.

"Self-doubt ruins more illusions than ever does defeat."-Suzy Kassem None of us will ever be completely free from doubts. Everybody, no matter how successful, always struggle with it. But if you let it take hold, self-doubt can become a self-fulfilling prophecy. You may have tried to achieve an objective in the past and decided to give up when you met an obstacle that seemed difficult, but you shouldn't give up.

It's the way life is! Goals get you out of the comfort zone, put you into new territory, and with your doubts and fears, take you head-on. The question here is not how to overcome self-doubt and anxiety, but how to make constructive decisions that improve your self-confidence while there are uncertainties.

Due to self-doubt, insecurity, loss of faith, or terror, too many people give up on their aspirations.

Moving past self-doubt and fear

Essentially all successful people have admitted that every single day they have to battle self-doubt. Doubt is so harmful that countless people are discouraged from doing beautiful things. Yet anxiety is not who you are at all, but rather an event you're passing through.

It doesn't make them go away if you're trying to avoid uncertainty and anxiety. It doesn't make it any less unpleasant if you neglect certain thoughts, and if you look the other way, it doesn't help them disappear into thin air.

Now take a deep breath. Then know that you still need to take action, even if you have questions or a deep fear hits you. Avoid crippling self-doubt and take the necessary steps to achieve your goals.

Overcoming Self-Doubt

It is always easier to say than done to remove doubts on the spot. But below are ways to start conquering self-doubt, to accomplish the goals you have wanted.

Remove Wrong Words

You must remove from your vocabulary any words that seem wrong. The expressions, sentences, and verbs that you use to refer to yourself can shake off your confidence. Often these wrong words are untrue.

Instead, delete or skip terms like "never," "still," "can't," "no one," "when," and "will." Then you'll see that the frame of mind or self-doubt can change for the better.

Recognize Self-Doubt

It is necessary to identify suspicions that are not an easy task. To create a business, a website, or even an app, you might have a great idea. Yet if you think you can't just quit your job to move into something else, you could shrug it off. You've got to pay for a home and a mortgage. And who is going to pay for the bills?

There are, of course, still threats. But if you don't feel you can be good, you're not going to guess anything. And, if you force a thought away next time, wonder seriously if it's the self-doubt and truth that sneaked in.

Get Daily Dose of Inspiration

Subscribe to podcast, watch videos, read books, or watch inspiring films. It can allow you to resolve whatever doubts and fears you may have. You may also feel empowered to act.

You can also find some great conversation leaders and advisors. When you lack self-confidence, turn to these men.

Also popular was Overcome Self-Doubt Dumber men. You have to remember that you are an intelligent and capable person. The explanation is that in this universe there are individuals who have done greater things with less expertise, resources, incentives, and experience than you have.

You have to note that you've been effective for others with less benefit than you. It is difficult or even futile to handle some desire or vision of yours. The hurdle you have to conquer most of the time is self-doubt.

Reflect on previous achievements

Are you focused on the bad like the mistakes you have encountered when you wake up or during the day? Or on the better like the wins you've won?

Recent studies have shown that how you recall history determines what you feel about yourself now. Your feelings on yourself have a huge impact on any future actions you take and how well they work out for you.

Check for reviews

The quest for input from others is also great. Having a conversation about your skills and abilities with those who help you and are around you can stop self-doubt right on the spot.

However, above all, seeking input can make you see both the positive and negative aspects of your skills. As a consequence, some of the necessary skills can be improved.

Be mindful of Doubt from Others

Self-doubt is already difficult to deal with, but other people's suspicions are only frustrating. Once you know that you are starting to gain more self-confidence and ability, you may find other people around you, even nearer than you expect, who are focusing their self-doubt on you. They're going to try to shoot down your dreams or even find reasons why you shouldn't pursue them. But let me still tell you to act on your ideas.

Celebrate Small Wins

This absorbs you whenever you're caught in the pit of self-doubt. Even if it's not true in fact, you could make it accurate and make it a big deal in your head. To sink to that point, it took you a series of small acts.

Okay, to get out, it will also take small yet necessary moves. This motivates you when you enjoy small wins because you see progress being made and you create momentum that easily adds up.

More Strategies to Conquer Self Doubt

- Self-doubt is difficult to conquer, but almost anyone with the will can do it.

- Brainstorm any event, process, or initiative you feel will help you achieve success.

- Remember all the things you know to do and abilities you can learn quickly.

- Start learning and bringing these different skills and abilities into action.

- Believe that you can do better to do more.

- Draw the inspiration well from the left and focus on acts that deliver results.

- Stay away from self-doubt by taking small steps contributing to progress and working on the next.

- Activate the internal genius and disregard self-doubt or criticism.

Even when other people tell you that you can't do it, or that it's an impossible dream, or that it's impractical, it's not easy to get going and give up, but use their skepticism as a reason to prove them wrong.

A symptom of self-doubt is when you let other people's opinions and self-doubt affect you on your vision and concept to take action. You have to carefully pick your thoughts because they become your impulses which determine your actions in effect.

Undoubtedly, there will be questions in your heart. Therefore, you have to choose not to accept the feelings that offer you such suspicions to overcome self-doubt. Uncertainties, worries, and suspicions are always going to be part of your life, but you are the one who chooses to believe them or not.

This presumption of achievement is important because if you allow self-doubt (the fear of failure) to enter, you can erode the prospects of positive practice. The lack of action, not, in general, any failures, is what keeps you from moving towards your objectives.

Life is too short to allow that to happen, so let's look at why people are struggling with self-doubt and some fast actions you should take in the next ten minutes to make sure you don't get out of the stuff you want to do.

Where does self-doubt come from?

Well, this comes through two types of pessimistic anticipation- first, the assumption that it might not be possible to achieve the target itself, and second, the perception that even if the goal is possible, it will likely not be achievable for you.

Everyone daily thinks like these at some level. Let's concentrate on how to defuse their power to create self-doubt in the first place, an active two-step method.

Stage 1 — Note that it is not difficult for someone to achieve the goal itself.

There's a lot of silent "self-talk" going on every day in your mind. There's a part of you staring at the limitless possibilities before you... And then there's the other part of you that advises you to be "fair," the bar is set so low, the goal is simply not achievable.

Today, many people face the problem of not even realizing that this discussion is taking place. They're likely to just go through the motions and ponder why they're motivated to take initiative occasionally, and sometimes they're not. That may describe you (and I know it's been defining me several times in my life, so I'm speaking here from personal experience).

Nonetheless, the way to avoid self-doubt is to take full and absolute care of that interaction. To learn to listen carefully to the value of the discussion that takes place in your mind and to take command when it doesn't go the way it needs to be.

The way to start doing this is by trying to look objectively at the case-that is, by keeping oneself out of the equation. Instead of worrying about what you can and can't do, look at the target and note that a human being can't achieve it. It could certainly be done by somebody on Earth (or has already achieved this).

Rehearse a phrase that you can use to break the habit of thought which stops you from being 100% sure that you can achieve your goal is the way to do this job. Let's say your goal in the next 12 months is to become fully financially independent.

While this may appear to many to be a daunting task, it is certainly not impossible. People are doing this all the time. So maybe your answer would be something like this: "Within 12 months or less, it's not difficult to become financially independent. It's been achieved over and over again." Well, why do I choose to say "It's not unlikely..." rather than the more optimistic "It's feasible..." sound? The response is because I don't want to give you a chance to justify using the term "but." You know, they always feel "Yes, it's conceivable, however." If you reply "It's not unlikely..." you actively resist the opportunity to come up with a good argument to challenge the capacity to do it. You are forced to admit that there is no immovable, unstoppable force that stops you from achieving your goal at all times. Your focus is on the fact that at any given time the potential exists, no matter how you "feel" about it.

Do not make the mistake of taking this step as a matter of course, because it is essential. The universal assumptions that you have about life-what are likely and what is not-drive your acts on a day-to-day basis. We control where you can go, like the strings of a puppet. So you must be careful to get them right and never lose sight of the fact that you can do just about anything.

Sidebar: This is not positive thinking I'm writing about here to clarify things. I don't say you're going to succeed because you're saying "I think I can." It's realistic thinking that I'm talking about-focusing on facts, not emotions. Looking critically at stuff. Taking personal anxiety out of the equation and realizing your ability as an individual being-not as the array of skills and experiences you label "you." To sum up this first step, you need to have a strong statement (or series of them) that you can concentrate on having your head firmly rooted in a fact-the reality that your objective is by no means impossible. It may be challenging, and it may demand more of yourself than you have ever provided, but it is not impossible. In reality, it is impossible with the right commitment and strategies.

You are ready to move on to the next stage once you have presented the target logically in your head this way, and you are convinced that your aim is not impossible to achieve.

Step 2 — Note that you cannot achieve the goal itself—particularly—.

A lot of people get into trouble here. We claim, "Yes, it's conceivable, but not for me." That's where we step into the magical world of explanations, where every challenge seems to be eternal and far too difficult to overcome. To change the situation, we see ourselves as relatively powerless.

However, in reality, we have a huge amount of power. If we dwell on our shortcomings, whether it's energy, cash, ability, what ever that's when we turn over that control to the side of us thinking "you really can't do it." Its part of us concentrating on what we can't do has a long list of all the excuses why we're not up to the task, and it's pretty hard to refute it. You realize I'm thinking about the sound.

So the secret of it all is turning the tables around and making a clear list of all the benefits you should do it - and why you're the one to do it, in general. It's not the same as reading a review. You think long and hard about how you're going to verbalize why you're more than qualified to do the job when you want to apply for a new position. You mention your qualifications, training, wealth, and above all, your accomplishments and achievements.

If you give that to a hiring manager, the hope is that they will look at it and say, "Oh, this guy is the one to get the job done." In creating a resume for yourself, you will build the same feeling of confidence.

You have to put aside some time and do some hard thinking to do this and do it correctly. You need to brag about yourself and note all the knowledge you've taken for granted. You have all the tools you can manage. You have all the experience from which you can benefit.

There's so much more to it than you know right now because you've let your ambitions obstacles transform your attention to your failures and weaknesses. But it is time to strike hard now.

Now you've got to do that.

If you want to conquer self-doubt permanently, this is the important part. You need to take this advice and put it into action. Read this post and do the job, and you will immediately begin to see progress. And if you don't feel like doing it now, and think to yourself, "That may be feasible to you, but it's not for me," bookmark this post and read it every day. Ultimately, you're going to get fed up with the reasons and decide to act.

Abraham Maslow claims that raising your self-esteem is centered on the essence of psychological health, and it is achievable only when the basic heart of the individual is genuinely understood, loved, and respected by others and by himself or herself. Jack Canfield says: "Self-esteem is focused on feeling lovable and worthy."

Self-esteem is interrelated with self-image. The word self-image is used to define the self-image of a person's mind. The image of yourself leads to self-esteem. We develop mental representations of ourselves during early childhood: what we are, what we are good at, what we feel, and what our strengths and weaknesses might be. The memories and the relationships with other individuals will reinforce these mental images within us. Such mental self-images can grow our self-esteem notion over time. Self-esteem is about feelings we develop as a result of external factors within ourselves. Self-esteem is about how much other people accept, love, and appreciate us, and how much we recognize, support, and praise ourselves. Their self-esteem is formed by the synthesis of these two variables.

Generally, in terms of how we view ourselves and our attributes, self-esteem is described. According to Stanley Coppersmith, a leading scholar in the area, it is "a personal judgment of worthiness that is reflected in the individual's attitudes toward himself." Good self-esteem implies that we have enough self-confidence not to need the validation of others.

How is it Developed?

You build your self-esteem through emotions, friendships, and interactions. Self-esteem begins to form as early as adolescence, and factors that influence it to include the likes of one's feelings and beliefs, how other people react, college interactions, job and community experiences, illness, cancer, accident, history, faith, and even one's position and status in society. If the individual does not see himself as having the values he admires, low self-esteem is established. Unfortunately, people with low self-esteem typically have the things they respect, but because they conditioned their self-image this way, they can't see it. Dr. Michael Miller, editor-in-chief of the Harvard Mental Health Letter, states, "It's more possible that self-esteem can emerge from clear self-understanding, recognition of one's true talents, and the pleasure of supporting others." People close to you like family, relatives, colleagues, mates, educators, and other connections, and your relationship with those individuals will have a big impact. In your early childhood, self-esteem is developed, and it matures during late adolescence. They begin to formulate self-esteem when the person stabilizes their sense of being in control of their destiny. When deciding our self-esteem, family relationship plays a major role. It's how others view us that tell us if we are significant. Our level of self-esteem will shape the feeling of being cared for or worthwhile. This is connected to other people receiving recognition. However, women often seek approval more than men based on early life experiences and their social roles. By the age of 16, more girls start experiencing low self-esteem than children. According to Dove Research: The Real Truth regarding Beauty: 7 in 10 women feel that they are not great enough or do not measure up with their appearance, performance in school, or relationships in some way.

What is the value of self-esteem?

According to Brian Tracy: "Your self-esteem is probably the most important part of your character. This precedes and affects your success in almost everything you do. Your level of self-esteem is your degree of mental fitness. You should be in a constant state of self-esteem if you want to succeed at the highest and feel great about yourself." Self-esteem should allow the individual to be more confident and more successful in achieving their goals. Individuals with low self-esteem usually feel inadequate and under different circumstances may not perform well. They formed inaccurate feelings that they are not welcomed or appreciated by anyone. Those with a healthy self-esteem, on the other side, will feel good about their life and then about themselves. They can and do things more efficiently; they can feel proud of their achievements and themselves.

We will be able to enjoy life more and more by feeling good about ourselves. Feeling that we are welcomed, valued and respected implies that we have healthy self-esteem, and that feeling will be mirrored in our ties.

Low self-esteem is one of the main causes of broken relationships.

Developing self-esteem helps us in our lives to welcome joy. That sensation makes you believe you deserve happiness. This faith, the belief that you really ought to be happy and fulfilled, is very important to understand because with this conviction you will treat people with respect and kindness while preferring rich interpersonal relationships and preventing destructive ones. Too no self-consciousness may cause people to become unhappy, fall short of their ability, or accept abusive situations and relationships. Several findings indicate that low self-esteem contributes to stress, depression, and anxiety. Research shows a positive relationship between healthy self-esteem and many positive outcomes, including satisfaction, modesty, endurance, and confidence. In almost everything you do, self-esteem plays a role.

In "Preventing Suicide," released in 2000, the World Health Organization advises that improving the self-esteem of learners is important to shield children and adolescents from mental distress and despondency, allowing them to deal with difficult and stressful life situations adequately. In the book: Alcoholism: A False Stigma: Low Self-Esteem The Real Problem, (1996) Candito reports: "Those who have described themselves as' recovered alcoholics' suggest that low self-esteem is the most significant problem in their lives. Low self-esteem is the true problem and the real problem. Alcohol is but a result of an alcoholic's illness." According to Glenn R. Schiraldi, Ph.D., writer of The Self-Esteem Workbook and a professor at the University of Maryland School of Public Health: "Those with good self-esteem will assess their abilities, shortcomings, and ability realistically and honestly." According to Madelyn Swift, our emotional health relies on our self-esteem. The pillars on which emotional health depends are to enjoy oneself and feel capable.

Healthy self-esteem helps you to embrace yourself as it is meant to be and appreciate life.

Could you create healthy self-esteem? The fact is, there is hardly any positive self-esteem. According to a study published by the American Psychological Association, self-esteem is the lowest in young adults, but rises during puberty and peaks at age 60, just before decreasing again. Participants in the survey assessed 3,617 U.S. adults ' self-esteem. On average, during most adulthood, women had lower self-esteem than males, but self-esteem rates converged as men and women entered their 80s and 90s. During young adulthood and middle age, blacks and whites have equal levels of self-esteem. The lead author of the study, Ulrich Orth, Ph.D. said: "Self-esteem is linked to better health, reduced criminal behavior, lower levels of depression and, ultimately, greater life achievement. Thus, it is important to learn more about how the self-esteem of the average person changes over time." Your emotions are the main source of self-esteem, and these feelings are within your power. It will grow low self-esteem by dwelling on your failures and shortcomings. Through reflecting instead on the positive points and attributes, you can counteract this kind of thought.

Your self-esteem in the present is not how you feel about yourself, but how you fundamentally assume yourself over the long term. If you have low self-esteem, day-to-day activities can have a big impact on how you think. A nice smile or a better day at work, for instance, could make you feel great for a couple of days. Or even a not that great day can make you feel extremely low. And let's face it most days are uneventful and dull, so staying high can be a struggle when you have low self-esteem! good healthy self-esteem is focused on knowing what you are-know who you are and be happy, just like you are!

It's been your self-esteem. Designed and grown at this point during your entire life! And yeah, you knew right, there was a huge impact on your self-esteem of childhood. All the fun, better, poor, and unpleasant things that happened when you grew up affected how you perceive yourself today. When growing up, healthy self-esteem will be founded on affection, trust, and secure factors. Those who have been yelled at, constantly humiliated, insulted, received little positive attention, harassed, etc. will find it hard to develop healthy self-esteem. These are extreme examples and also have a great impact on subtle negative / positive experiences. Things happening that you don't recall, but you didn't think a bit could have been big influences as well.

Argue with your "inner voice" to help improve self-esteem

We all have a voice inside our heads that is continuously chatting away. Commenting about everything we've done/have/want to do. And it reassures so rewards those with healthy self-esteem. The inner voice criticizes us with poor self-esteem, sets us down, and stands in our path! Of starters, if you do anything-compete in sport or go for a job interview, and someone compliments you the inner voice might suggest something like "he was cheating, you were bad, don't bother next time." What you have to do is challenge the inner voice, then snap back with something like-" He congratulated me when I performed good, maybe I wasn't flawless, but win lose or draw I did my best and I'm proud of myself! "Arguing with your inner voice is going to improve your self-esteem, begin now! Remember, you're the manager, you're in charge, don't let the critic get you down inside!

Use Negative Affirmations To Boost Self-Esteem

A positive statement about yourself is a positive statement. Use them in a relaxation method as well as by explaining them to yourself in your head every day. Ideally, you would like to rest at least once a day and only make those positive statements to yourself softly-playing some calming music at the same time is good to help!

Definitions for positive self-esteem affirmations: Who you are- I'm great I'm good I'm unique Who you're going to be I can be a champion I can be powerful I will recover I will lose weight I'm going to do-I'm going to smile more I'm going to control my emotions by constantly repeating those stuff for yourself you have no option but to accept them profoundly! You're able to become those things, and the self-esteem increases.

Self-Nurturing To Improve Self-Esteem

To improve self-esteem, self-nurturing is important. Begin by physically taking care of yourself, eating healthy, staying in shape, and obtaining all the rest you want-not too much and not too little.

To improve your self-esteem, self-nurturing makes you feel worthwhile. Regularly reward yourself by doing pleasant and enjoyable activities-especially if something positive has been accomplished. You have to be praised for successes! Think about the things you love about yourself and note them all the time. Do not dwell or punish yourself for failure-reward yourself in the first place for trying. Try to focus on the good and learn to forgive what you feel is poor. Days ,when you don't feel good or optimistic, are important, you have to seek things that are good for yourself, no matter how small they may be! Those things will help to boost self-esteem. It can be a great help to receive encouragement from loved ones to boost self-esteem. Tell family and friends to show you what they like about you. Tell them to be your release valve when you're feeling low and upset-this can be a huge help to boosting self-esteem by listening when you let off steam.

The community is essential for enhancing self-esteem and preserving it is a huge factor of self-esteem that is surrounded by moist, loving people. Already I realize for a bit that's not true, not everybody has a loving partner or community network. Nonetheless, you have to make sure you are respected by those you have in your life, and you have to respect them for who they are. A feeling of understanding will help you realize that people's variations are all wrong. It will be easier to build relationships with others by understanding this. Bond to those you see and connect with every day, speak, contact, display love, listen, be helpful, and be honest. Understanding that those around you think the same about you is a huge boost to your self-esteem!

Criticism

You're not sorry for who you are! When and when you are questioned, make sure to "judge" what's being said to you before you reach for whatever reason. Don't apologize immediately! If the critique is valid then consider it and respond by agreeing with the critic. If unfair, then, as with your inner voice, stand up to it. A well-composed and self-possessed individual will uninterruptedly listen to feedback and then react. Make certain to critique at appropriate times, it is often more difficult for people with poor self-esteem to give than to accept. Before you "boil flat," don't let annoyances go, it's usually better to nip stuff in your bud. Be tactful and seek not to damage the self-esteem of others. Use the term "I" not "you," for instance-when that occurs, I have problems.

Environmental Factors Vs Self-esteem

Self-esteem is generally considered as a subjective self-evaluation. Self-esteem is generally believed to be nothing but your image of yourself. It's not outside of you, it's an internal thing. Self-esteem is about how we think inside and how we respond outside will be influenced by this emotion. Our self-esteem tends to define our personalities, defining our behavior, determining how we react to the stresses and challenges we face in our lives, and influencing our interaction with other people as well. Particularly residing in a healthy environment for a relatively long time, positive thinking, productive actions, and feel-good experiences not only improve our motivation and growth but also provide us with a strong foundation for our future goals and accomplishments. Thus one can tackle challenges comfortably with the requisite confidence and maintain a high level of self-esteem. As a consequence, the level of satisfaction and confidence would be so high that ambitious aspirations such as self-actualization, self-improvement, and the standard of' ideal' identity could be reached.

Self-esteem is not an individual concept; it is combined with other important concepts such as self-respect, self-pride, self-confidence, self-dignity, and so on. It was never possible to separate all these ideas from self-esteem. As when we can compose alphabets, interpret alphabets, enter them in a coherent word that we can understand what it means, we can finally say we can read and write in English to some degree or some point. Likewise, if we can make decisions, if we accomplish those goals based on our faith and commitment, if we are respected by the people we consider important, we obtain a good position in our community, we believe that we are respectable human beings. Eventually, these emotions drive us to high self-esteem. In other terms, they have a lower level of self-esteem.

In this post, we concentrate on the environmental factors that have a tremendous impact on self-esteem. Although it's practically impossible to change one's climate, it's a reality that if we go into a different situation and momentarily switch our condition, we feel different. We feel scared/composed when we're in the company of outsiders, so when we're in the company of friends, we feel safe and happy. We could easily choose a better company. Likewise, if we set achievable goals and finally achieve them, we feel confident and effective, on the other side, if we choose objectives that we cannot reach in any way, we feel discouraged, weak, and separated. It could be rightly said here that we must smartly and deliberately choose our targets. In short, the crux of the discussion is whether it's about choosing friends or setting goals, we can try our best to change our current situation to increase our self-esteem.

The problem now is why our climate should be changed? After all, only to gain higher self-esteem will we alter our thoughts and emotions. In reality, our dilemma can only be solved by shifting thoughts and feelings. We need to do something else that would be seen as a major change in our environment otherwise our overall self-esteem would never be so high to protect us. The more our environment changes (good and positive), the more our self-esteem would be.

It is also possible to discuss individually the environmental factors that could be improved by human activities. Such as personal, academic, professional, cultural, fitness, financial status, place of staying, clothes and dressing style, people we met and interact with, activities we like to do, and being happy would be known as the critical/basic levels of improvement.

Hierarchically, the most important factor in the process of change is' finance' from which you could easily change your position, company, and tasks. It's the basis of all the improvements that you might think and make. Therefore, becoming financially strong (to its basic level) is the first move in this sequence of measures, and then pursue certain moves. You may find other ways to improve the world without being financially strong, however, but this method is very difficult and time-consuming.

In the second stage of transition, if you are already able to earn good money, you have to aim for a good place where you can not only live comfortably but also interact with people you like and who value you and where you can still gain further progress and set new goals to achieve greater trust and stamina. In other words, at this point, though having enough money, proper place (in terms of weather conditions, amenities, beauty) and high status, if you don't have good friends, you'd also need to switch the position to have new friends who could appreciate/ encourage you and improve your self-esteem. To return, of course, you would also boost their self-esteem. Such a relationship is most necessary if we were not to be content with ourselves and others. Here it is important to suggest that good friends can also be made when staying in the same location when we try our best, but in most situations, it is nearly impossible because of the numerous obstacles around us. A temporary substitute for a living could also solve the problem with severe limitations.

The strongest thing we would need after having a change to our social environment is' to be accepted' or to be around loving people in our communities when we travel. It's great that everyone has a caring family who looks after them, but after a certain era when we need dignity, autonomy, and prestige, we need others (not immediate relatives) who can respect us, accept our contributions, and support them to improve our self-esteem. The "other" might be anybody, among our friends/colleges, or strangers whose names they don't even know at times. There are plenty of possibilities in the new environment to meet that' friend' more appreciative and caring than they already have. Even if we don't reach our perfect social circle, we shouldn't be anxious and push on until we consider it as we deserve it.

In the third stage of transition, if we the have first three items (good income, good place, and good company) and have no desired goal in our lives, we will also feel unhappy, insecure, lonely, boring, and boredom. Because our academic condition does not change, we would never be able to pretend/appreciate our friend /colleges ' remarks. Ultimately, these three factors/ things will give us the foundations for our self-satisfaction and are important to our self-esteem.

While it may seem crazy to take a step towards improving our world, it is a fact that sometimes things we want (loving, nice, and accepting people, good weather, new opportunities, increasing wealth, higher income, etc.) can only be done significantly and effectively by changing the environment — especially the place of different cultures (the most appropriate environment for you). It is the most important step towards high self-esteem and will also give better and more expected results, of course. Certain changes/benefits linked to your social status improvement and self-satisfaction will accompany this action and the individual environment's responses would in effect influence your behavior which would lead you to your ultimate goal of higher self-esteem.

It is very important to mention here that these judgments would also entail a profound understanding of our existence. Some people never find it necessary to move a place to get an upgrade, rather they are really satisfied with their location. Those individuals need no improvement and may need something else to boost their self-esteem (it's out of the reach of this essay to address those needs). But we don't recognize what our fundamental problem is for most of us; we need a change, not in our thinking, but our environment. We want good' others' to give us positive feedback, to make us happy and fulfilled in the manner we need. Such a move is not easy to manipulate, but a lot of confidence and decision-making capacity would be required. Realistically, they would need to be emotionally strong enough to take appropriate measures as well as mentally fit / strong enough to make our selection choices.

Under rare circumstances, if we cannot alter our position as well as our fellow beings because of our unique shortcomings, it would be strongly suggested to adjust our disposition and actions accordingly (not feeling or believing). Although it is very easy to say that improving one's self is the hardest task in our quest to achieve high self-esteem particularly for adults. Sadly, our young people don't have enough books, films, and plays to follow good examples in their lives on how to respond to other people's negative comments/attitudes. However, behaviors characteristic of low-estimated individuals are very common and valued, and those with high-estimated individuals are mostly overlooked or rare. That's why; it becomes a struggle to improve self-esteem for adults.

Realistically speaking, we need to work more on how to reach and sustain higher and higher self-esteem under current environmental conditions despite meeting the objectives mentioned above. We need to learn that in the case that something desired/required could not be achieved/changed, how to tackle this problem to preserve our self-esteem. In the books of self-esteem everywhere in the world, there is a huge literature accessible that will provide us with the laws of thought and boost our self-esteem by simply putting our best efforts at our point.

We also need to develop new ideas/concepts/ beliefs based on which we can set up television series or school curriculum to teach our children how to deal with issues of self-esteem and how to enhance self-esteem in its real sense that can guide them throughout their lives and even modify their environment instead of allowing their self-esteem to change their environment. In fact, there should be very specific examples of incidents in our daily lives in the children's education that cause low self-esteem in people and children, and then specific solutions need to be sought. Otherwise, the issue would never be addressed by only books and instructional content on increasing self-esteem.

In reality, the new change in life is a crisis in self-esteem, and as a result, through definition, we as human beings still aim for good / positive self-esteem. It's like a battle: a war between our true self, our planned selves, and our ecological observations perceptions. It is a kind of ongoing struggle that would never stop and will always drive us toward higher and higher self-esteem (provided we understand it as a good design phenomenon) until the time of death.

Creating Real Self-Confidence

Ination brings fears and anxiety. Action brings trust and bravery. If you want to overcome apprehension, don't sit back and think about it. Go out and get going."-Dale Carnegie I've been reading, researching, educating, and practicing the ideals of positive living for almost 40 years now. Those concepts are universal, changeless, and can be followed and supported by everyone. I have found that the performance criteria are often overlooked, despised, misrepresented, or misled about. Nothing more than the self-confidence principle.

The concept of self-confidence has been distorted and redefined into many things, none that are actually what honesty is. It was called "Self-Centeredness" and often turned into a narcissistic self-satisfaction search. It is seen as an over-inflated ego, and trustworthy people are the ones who walk onto others to go on. Self-confidence is viewed as a lack of real ability to replace it with a pushy and arrogant attitude that causes others to care.

Successful people need to understand that these negative self-confidence statements are false. In reality, real self-confidence is not good quality, but a necessity for success. We don't dare to move forward without this, try new things, and test our boundaries. It's a lack of self-confidence which contributes to many of today's members becoming indifferent.

Have you failed your fight to make your dream come true? Did you find that you think you can do more, have more, and excel in your goals, but can't get you to do it? Many things are going to deprive you of your ability to succeed more than a lack of self-confidence in any area of life. But you must first know what it is and how you do it to have that faith.

"Every accomplishment I've ever seen said,' My life turned around when I started to believe in myself.'"-Dr. Robert Schuller Self-confidence is the knowledge and understanding that you have unique abilities and capabilities. It's the awareness of what you can do and the desire to do it to the best of your ability with excellence. Real self-confidence is not believing that you are stronger than everyone else, rather realizing that you can do better things than anyone else.

Where some people may think you need a big ego to have faith, the fact is that true self-confidence is calm and centered. The man or woman with real self-confidence will do their work with perfection and they don't think they want to let everyone else realize they've achieved it. Those who see it always acknowledge perfection. It is the person who lacks self-confidence who thinks they have to point out to everyone around them what they are doing.

Feeling optimistic is realizing that in certain areas of life you can succeed. It also acknowledges that in some cases, others also have advantages and are stronger than you. The confident person is not threatened by this realization, but celebrated. Even as they want to do their own, they are pleased to see others do their own. It's a lack of trust that makes a man and woman feel threatened but other people's performance. Lack of self-confidence causes people to feel that they are always the best to compete with the next guy. We get upset, frustrated, and mean if they're not seen as the strongest in everything. We've seen it all before and it's never a beautiful sight.

Writer Marcus Garvey once said, "If you have no self-confidence, you will be beaten once in the pursuit of life." Believing in yourself and your ability is not prideful or self-centered. You have to work hard to be the best at what you do. Why would you like to be the best? Not to make others feel less or to show off, but to give them the best you have, you owe it to others. It's selfish and lazy on your part to give nothing less.

Dwight D. Eisenhower Helen Keller, a woman who faced more challenges and difficulties in her life than most people might even imagine, once said, "Optimism is the faith that leads to achievement. Nothing can be done without hope and trust." Why do we need to build trust in our lives? Simply put, we can do nothing without it.

You have the bravery to hit and face the challenges before you if you feel confident. The belief that you can reach your targets is self-confidence. It's realizing that even if you struggle in this effort, you're going to learn from the mistakes, step forward and ultimately win. Confident people are those who grow the ability to hold going, even in the face of great difficulties.

U.S. Chief, a man of great self-confidence became Abraham Lincoln. But in diplomacy he lost more than he achieved, it hurt if he won. He was optimistic that he had something to offer to his country, beginning with great drawbacks and many heartbreaks. He was one of the presidents ' most modest. Knowing that he couldn't do it alone, he was building his cabinet with the very best of his day's leaders. Some were his rivals, yet more than their differences, he appreciated their skills. He grew to become one of world history's most famous and revered rulers.

The confidence of Lincoln wasn't a big ego that made him think he was better than anybody else. He realized he was going to have to work hard for the things he wanted and he had the determination to keep working even when things didn't go his way. He once said, "I'm going to prepare because my The opportunity will arrive one day." You don't excel in anything because you think you're better. If you think you want it, it won't come. It's not going to come if you feel it's your time. Only when you brace for it will it arrive.

Boy Scouts of America's slogan is, "Be ready." It's not waiting for your chance, go get it or you deserve it. What was prepared for? Here's how Sir Robert Baden-Powell, father of the Boy Scouts, said it, "Be ready... the essence of the slogan is that a Scout should brace himself by thinking ahead and learning how to respond on any incident or disaster so that he will never be taken by surprise." I believe they must also be prepared to thrive. We must be ready and able to go after it when the moment comes our way. The opportunity seems to always occur to the other man for the unaware.

Confidence in ourselves allows us the confidence to think clearly and accurately. There are no endless hours spent thinking about what we're supposed to do or whether we should. It is not a matter of "if" but of "when" with self-confidence. If a person thinks of "when" they get their shot, and "if" they encounter the challenge, they'll be ready and prepared for it. Every the day they're going to think about it and always be aware of what's going on in their life so they don't forget it. Confidence in ourselves helps us ready and we feel confident if we feel prepared. You can see how all of this draws on itself, getting you stronger and stronger.

Myths About Building Self-Confidence

People who believe in themselves and feel able to achieve what they want in life or deal with any situation they may have to face. They have an aura of self-confidence and self-confidence that is visible to others. People like to spend time with them; in their company, they feel comfortable and secure.

There are many people, on the other hand, who are reasonably talented but lack confidence in themselves. Many people are victims of the numerous myths surrounding self-confidence.

1. One of the leading self-confidence misconceptions is that people are born with esteem in themselves. It's a value that can't be bought. There can be nothing further from the facts. It is possible to build self-confidence, like other abilities. All you need is a good direction and self-confidence.

2. others fault their lack of good appearance and poor education for their low self-confidence. We don't know that their features have nothing to do with self-confidence. It's a sign of

one's confidence. Only by beginning to trust in themselves will we resolve this fallacy. In reality, there is no correlation between talent and self-confidence.

There are hundreds of young actors and actresses who do very well with their careers, but whose personal lives are broken by a lack of confidence in themselves. It may sound contradictory, but that's how it is. Ability can be an important component of self-confidence, but it's certainly not a substitution for esteem. Therefore, don't think about talent shortages. Use the knowledge you have.

3. Another misconception is that self-confidence is directly proportional to an individual's appreciation and approval of his or her life; those who don't wallow in self-pity. Also, there is little question that appreciation and encouragement can make you feel better about yourself and increase confidence in yourself.

Yet you can't rely on other people's approval. You have to work hard to earn your respect, and this can only be achieved if you are sure in yourself. The same refers to the unsuccessful ones. If they work hard and win the respect of people, they too can earn praise.

Kids should be cared for by these men. Children believe in themselves, and this allows them the confidence to try to do something they've never tried before, whether they're trying to bike or swim.

In reality, no child who learns all the skills comes into the world. Yet teaching children most of the basic skills doesn't take long. Then why should learning new skills and brave new tasks be challenging for adults?

4. Another misconception is that chances can only be faced by self-confident people. That's not valid yet. Yes, self-confident people are more optimistic regarding their skills. I understand what they can and can't do. We know how to deal with losses, most specifically.

Those who lack self-confidence, on the other side, fear failure. Such uncertainty makes it impossible for them to take on new assignments. They constantly pine for others ' approval, and they end up losing their self-confidence when they don't get it.

The lack of understanding is what is evident. People have to realize that a state of mind is self-confidence. It does not rely on the attractiveness or presence of an individual. It comes from the self-belief of an individual, and it can construct that confidence.

All that a person needs to do is to debunk myths that it is impossible to acquire self-confidence or that self-confidence is a byproduct of extraordinary intelligence, abilities, and chance. They will find it easier to gain the same magnetic powers that self-confident people have once they do so.

Building Trust

Now that we have some understanding of what self-confidence is and is not; and why we need to build trust, let's talk about how to build self-confidence in our lives. I think some people have more confidence in building potential than others. Some lean toward a more self-confident attitude in their behavioral style and their nature is to build their confidence without much focus or effort. I do believe some find it very difficult in any area of life to develop self-confidence. Through nature, they are reserved, distant, and lack a true belief in their skills. Nonetheless, it is important and necessary for each person to work on their level of trust to reach the goal of their desires.

Confidence in oneself is an internal power and must therefore be managed and used. It's the same with rage, affection, hate, excitement, fear, and other emotions that can bring us great harm if not managed. Simultaneously, we cannot live with our lives without these feelings. They are like a flame, fire brings warmth, cooks meat, produces fuel, and more when used and regulated. Fire is one of the most damaging forces on the planet, out of reach and misused. Fire destroyed towns, took countless lives, and left destruction on its path. Uncontrolled and misused self-confidence will lead to selfishness, pride, and emotional destruction. Controlled and properly used self-confidence will lead to success, service, and life fulfillment.

There are two distinct areas in which we can build self-confidence intentionally and properly. These are physical and mental regions.

Building Trust: Physical

"The more we do, the more we can do."-William Hazlitt One of Tony Robbins ' best lessons I have learned is this: "Motion creates emotion." Whether we travel and behave has a lot to do with how we think and how we view ourselves. For those who understand it and use it, this is a strong reality. It will have an impact on your health, behavior, and attitudes.

Of the things I love to do, seeing people in public spaces is one of the greatest. I think God even enjoying His life must have hours and hours of fun. One of the aspects that can be easily found is how you think about how you carry yourself. People who are depressed, frustrated, and burdened by life tend to collapse, walk slowly, and look down. Many are likely to have a scowl on their mouth to avoid contact with their fellow human beings.

On the other side, with a little swagger to their move, people who are more confident and feel good tend to walk straight up. For everybody we come across, they move faster and have a smile. Such citizens give the impression they are content to be wherever they are.

Here's for you a check. Lie by yourself in a seat. Let your head slip and slow down a little bit. Enable deep and quick breathing and look down to the floor. Let your face's muscles relax and frown. Take note of these things after a few moments:

1)   How are you feeling?

2)   What do you think about things that are positive or negative?

3)   you're either happy or sad?

Second part: Sit up straight and high now. Keep your eyes at a steady pace, breath deeply. Shake your arms and put them on your hips as if you were Peter's pan and put your face with a big smile. Ask the same questions: 1) how are you feeling? 2) What do you think about things that are positive or negative? 3) you're either happy or sad?

Many people will find that when they have a good posture or behave in a friendly way, they look their best, consider their best and perform their best.

Look at the people you ever meet that are good. How are they going to move? What do they do when they speak? Note that there are indicators of progress. Through studying effective and self-confident individuals and doing what they do, you will learn a lot about achievement and self-confidence.

It won't happen to you to use movement and gestures. It is a very deliberate action that will demand that you pay close attention to what you are doing and that you are prepared to act. Ask yourself this question: "If I were the person I want to be productive, how would I move? How would I breathe, speak, look at people, and introduce myself?" Is this a fake thing until you do it? Yeah, that's it. Test it before you push. On this idea, Dale Carnegie built his entire theory of public speaking. He told his students that before they acted the part, they had to act the part. You're going to find what fits. If you don't want to do that until you think it, you're going to stay as you are. It's always your call.

"Believe in yourself! Have trust in your ability! You cannot be effective and satisfied without a confident but fair belief in your strength."-Dr. Norman Vincent Peale They understand that you can develop self-confidence by how you carry yourself, look and act. But in the brain is the true arena of self-confidence. Confidence in yourself is all about what you feel, your behaviors, and what you believe is real. There's nothing else going to last long if you don't get your thought wrong. All two things function together; the physical and emotional, but the secret to real self-confidence is your mindset.

Have you ever been worried about what you think? But, that seems like a strange issue, the vast majority of people never really talk about what they feel. I bear pessimistic and frustrated feelings around and wonder why they're not satisfied. We spend their time worrying about everything that might go wrong in life and asking why they're scared and depressed. They're talking about how much work and effort it takes to succeed and asking how they can't accomplish their objectives. Ask yourself, "What do I think of most of the time?" The answer will most definitely shock you.

One of the distinctions between success-minded people and those trying to settle and begin their goals is how they feel, not what they do. Also, it has been the case that some individuals have read books and heard for achievement, but never seem to reach it. They're doing all the "wrong" things, but for them. it doesn't seem to perform as well as for others. That's because they're waiting for what they're doing to be the answer, and they're talking about what counts.

When advising individuals who want to reach out into something they have never experienced before, I've seen this. Some are going to discover their vision, prepare and pursue it with the feeling that they can't succeed, and they're going to do that. There are no suspicions, no concerns. Such men still excel in what they do, indeed I have always said.

Some are exploring and enthusiastic about their future. But their approach is, "I hope this works. Nothing happens to be the way I want it." These people will always fail. What's the reason? Because they have chosen to collapse before they even start. We have nothing to risk because nothing to win has been spent. We simply say, "I knew this was going to happen" if we lose. Not only did they know it was going to happen, they expected it to happen and made sure it would.

Self-confidence is thinking you're going to achieve what you're trying to do. It doesn't mean, "Yeah, this is a piece of cake" or it's smug and confident. You know a lot of effort is involved; it's not going to be easy or simple. Yet you know you're going to excel and you're going to stay with it until you do. It all comes down to what was once said by Henry Ford, "If you think you can do something or think you can't do something, you're right."

Any progress research should show that your mindset is the first and most important thing to get in order. If you're talking of disappointment, you can't achieve everything that needs to be done. Success comes by overflowing your head with what you want to do, how you can do it, and what you can learn to move closer to your target. As Earl Nightingale claimed, "Each of us is the total sum of his thinking." The thought is a deliberate act. You have to choose what your feelings are going to be and then work on holding them in place. The brain that can go in whatever direction it wishes will always run down to the bad. It is our instinct to consider the worse and cause our emotions to be dominated by terror. Successful people strive to maintain positive thoughts and concentrate on the task at hand. The human mind is a powerful force, and it will be effective only for those who strive to use it for the better and regulate their emotions to achieve their goals.

We must always remember that the Maker gives us power over one aspect out of all the things in the universe. He offered us no influence on space, climate, life, or others. You and your emotions are the only things that you have power over. Self-confidence allows us the courage to take charge of ourselves and become master of our emotions rather than master of our feelings.

"Faith on the outside starts by living with dignity on the inside."-Brian Tracy I had a young man going to me for training many years ago. Throughout his career and personal life, he had a challenge and felt as he described it, "stuck in a cave." We sat down to talk and the first thing he said to me was, "The one aspect I don't want to learn is that positive thinking nonsense." I told him that in that one statement he showed me why he's suffering so much, that he's going to keep failing with life and he's not going to change it. Believing that I shouldn't waste my time when there will be no improvement, I told him to seek another teacher.

Nothing is a kiss of death for failure more beautiful than a negative attitude. Negativity robs us of self-confidence and makes us believe we can't be successful. Anyone who hangs on to a negative attitude understands too well that they never seem to be going forward or attaining the level of success they desire. With what Zig Ziglar called "stinking thinking," you simply cannot win.

A positive attitude on an exponential scale builds and enhances self-confidence. You realize that there is to be progress if you feel good about yourself, your family, and the environment in which you work. You're getting along with others and that's a key to success. Because others like you want to support you to give you chances to avoid others with a less friendly disposition. If you have an open position and two individuals have applied for it. One is highly skilled and capable of doing the job. The other one is talented but wasn't as experienced as the first one. Nonetheless, the first voice is other people's pessimistic or sensitive. The second person has a positive attitude and is functioning well with all. Who are you going to choose? The second, of course every time.

Successful people with positive attitudes feel that they are doing the unthinkable. We realize that it can't be done because something hasn't been accomplished before. In reality, they find it fun and thrilling to compete. That's why we tend to find responses. I agree with American author Theodore Roethke when he said, "What we need is more individuals working in the unthinkable." Not only does a positive attitude make others feel comfortable and love being around you, it will make you feel better and like being around you. It's a case of positive people getting better, happy, and doing more. You tend to appreciate the blessing every day when you see it as a gift and use it for the better. Positive people are grateful for everything they have and the ability to make their dreams come true. This builds the confidence that these dreams need to follow, no matter how impossible they may be.

"The distinction between a successful person and a loser is often not that one has superior talents or strategies, but the confidence to gamble on one's thoughts, take a calculated risk — and act."— Andre Malraux Competent people love a good line. The English poet, Isaac D'Israeli put it this way, "Citations will retain the knowledge of the learned, and the memory of centuries." Quotations can be good builders of self-confidence. It's like having a pep talk from Benjamin Franklin, Abraham Lincoln, Napoleon Hill, and the world's many other greats. Here's an activity that will help build the day's self-confidence and anticipation. Collect three quotes of meaning every day. Things you're reading are talking to you and encouraging you. That's not hard to find, they're packed with social media. Do it for a week and see if the way you think or behaves doesn't make a difference.

Here's the catch for everything. Sure, a trap is always there. Statements don't make much difference, as with all the facts, if you don't believe them. Let's look at some quotes that are simple and common. Each in their way expresses a basic yet profound reality that can change your existence if introduced and believed.

"What the imagination may imagine or believe can be achieved."-Napoleon Hill "You are born to succeed and the roots of success are within you."-Zig Ziglar "Be assured that He who began a good work in you will carry it to completion."-St. Paul, I'm sure you've heard all these several times before and may even have them written down so that you can update them from time to time. So tell yourself this: "If you understood those terms, how would your life be different?" You see, many of us say all the right words and have learned and given great guidance, but not many believe it for reality.

The conviction that you can succeed in life is self-confidence. You're not trying to win. It's not that you're going to succeed if all goes right. It's not that if you get the support you want, you'll excel. It's the confidence you're going to succeed. You may not immediately know how or when however you know you're going to.

I'm sure you've heard or been posed the simple query, "What would you do if you realized you couldn't fail?" It's more than inspiring your imagination or encouraging your acts, it's a genuine and very important question. Your ability to answer this query will decide how your life will be fulfilled.

How would you behave if you realized you couldn't fail? What would you try to achieve if you realized you couldn't fail? What would you feel about the whole day when you realized you couldn't fail? How would you communicate with others if you knew you couldn't fail? When you KNOW you couldn't lose, what would your life be like?

Here's why this issue is so critical. When you think you can't fail to achieve that target, you'd be behaving and walking with confidence. You'd do what you might find unlikely and you realize it's not unthinkable now. It's like the former United States. Marine slogan: "We're trying to do the hard thing right now. It may take a while for the unthinkable." This is an important fact. Take a minute to get prepared for it. Breathe slowly and sit up straight. Say it then. "I can accept that it's the fact because I can't fail." Get it? Write it again, with certainty this time. Believe it, it's a reality. There's achievement every time for those who believe they can't succeed. Why? Because you're never going to stop trying because you believe you can't lose. You will always be learning and moving forward if you believe you can't fail. When you think you can't succeed, you're motivated every day because you realize if you're getting closer to your life goals. Preventing a speeding train with your bare hands is better than preventing a person who believes their ambitions will be accomplished.

This is where trust is a vital part of the mindset of successful people. I believe I was created for a purpose as a person of faith. God didn't have a quota to fill in and I'm not a physical cause. It was the purpose of God that at this moment I would be here to serve as part of His great plan for all life. So, if I was made for a reason by the Creator of the universe, do you not believe He has every intention of seeing that I serve that function? I know tha, because I trust that nothing can work against me if Christ is for me. Be a person and strive to do that. Know and believe that you can be confident as a successful person that you will fulfill your dream. What are a good person's characteristics? We are these: we try their best, they love God, they seek the unseen, and they transform their universe.

Confidence in oneself emerges from within. But some sites have reported that you are building with-out self-confidence. Examples of how to learn a skill, achieve a goal, dress well, or change your physical appearance. With these approaches, you will certainly improve your self-confidence, but you will not be able to address the source of the lack of self-confidence.

Because self-confidence comes from within, to access it, you need to get within. You are asked to search outside in many books to boost confidence in yourself. Moving outside can create a gap to gain self-confidence. A void you can't find out what's going on inside you. The causes of your lack of self-confidence will not be found. This does not construct your self-confidence on a solid foundation.

True confidence in oneself stems from conviction and attitude. In some places, you can be extremely skilled, but lack confidence in yourself. On the other side, have you found someone who in some field is not especially masterful but is filled with self-confidence?

It indicates that self-confidence may have nothing to do with achievements, skills, and presentation. What counts is your self-confidence.

Creating self-confidence

Creating self-confidence is directly proportional to how much confidence we have for ourselves and what we set out to do. We encounter multiple obstacles in life, starting with early childhood, and as we grow older, the difficulties get larger.

Whether we cope with them is a mystery, and as we reach adulthood, some choices can determine whether successful or unsuccessful we are. It is our self-confidence that will build our future in all areas of life and occupations.

If our self-confidence is high, our trust grows, and when our self-confidence fails, our trust eventually diminishes.

You only need to look at areas of success, such as athletics, wherein some situations the odds are stacked against the athlete, where they lose over and over again, but still have the self-confidence and energy to go on and have that mentality of' never say die.'

We refuse to give up and see defeat as another step on the road to prosperity. The same can be said about other groups of people with disabilities, but we seek inner strength and confidence in making near-impossible milestones.

In these two examples, building self-confidence is not an option, because they have it in abundance. self-confidence is so deep and steady that at all times esteem remains high.

We can also have the same self-belief by possessing the ambition, patience, and concentration to succeed. Without it, there will never be the aim of creating self-confidence and making it a reality.

Were you ready to begin to trust in yourself? What's your heart for? What are you going to do? Were you willing to make a difference in your life? These are concerns that you need to tell yourself to lift your self-confidence to new heights.

Put behind the past and make a new beginning. Believe you're able to accomplish anything you want. Decide what to do and don't give up until you do it. Let your faith grow and make it happen. It all starts around your head with that five inches!

Don't let you be overwhelmed by losses. We all have them, it's part of life, and it's essential how you treat them. See failure as a step closer to success. If Thomas Edison had given up, no light bulbs would have existed. He struggled to win!

Set your sights on the finish line and trust your goals will be fulfilled. With self-belief, there is something special that sounds like sorcery. You feel in control of everything you're doing. Without doubt or hesitation, you dare to take the next step in everything you do.

They don't seem to want to make a choice when self-belief is lacking, so anxiety takes over and chances are lost more often than not. This is due to a lack of self-confidence, which is due to a lack of self-confidence.

The brain will accept only one thought at a time, so hang on to that self-belief feeling, that anything is true, and let no negative thinking take its place.

Thought about what you want to do every day when you wake up in the morning. When you fail to beat yourself about it in your daily tasks, it's a learning curve and you need to step on.

Maybe when you go to bed at the end of each day, reflect on what you've accomplished for that day and be happy in the knowledge that you show the attributes of inner self-belief to even think this way.

You build confidence in yourself and others will always believe in you when you start to believe in yourself.

What can you do to increase your inner self-confidence?

Failure Is Not Defeat

Continue to look differently at failure. Do you become depressed if disappointment strikes you? When things don't turn out the way you want it, do you get desperate? For some point in our life, we all do it. This is because you perceive defeat as a loss.

I had a bad laboratory in 2008. I couldn't imagine after five years of training how I screwed up the lab. For me, a huge failure. Two days I stepped into my room. From that encounter, I gained, picked up myself, began training again.

Turn away from the "loss is failure" philosophy. We've been taught to believe a loss is college failure. Mind the outcome of the test we are afraid of getting. Today it has damaged our trust in ourselves.

But if you look at today's successful people, how many of them have struggled more than once? They're all there. Though they struggled many times, they kept coming back better and wiser.

It's not a failure. Loss is simply a warning that something doesn't work. With this new belief, your existence will no longer collapse, there will only be suggestions and lessons. None keeps you back in that situation, you may fly like an eagle. You develop self-confidence by simply shifting one conviction.

Live Life

Adventure is supposed to fill a life. You're able to see and do things differently with this attitude. When you begin to believe you're here to experience life, you'll gain confidence and bravery in doing something you've never done before or things you're always terrified of doing.

It's easy to start a conversation with a stranger if you feel it's about having a conversation with another human being-a new experience. It's a new experience for you, regardless of a great conversation or a bad one.

So the results are no longer very relevant. Because it's about life. With the experience-building process, you can growing self-confidence. You will learn that self-confidence builds confidence in yourself. But first, you are already in your Self-confidence. You do this by moving from experience-oriented results to experiential.

Removing The Perception Of Other

The lack of self-confidence most of the time comes from the uncertainty of how others view you. Strip away this anxiety, you have miles to improve your self-confidence.

Usually, the reason we don't do stuff we want to do is that we're afraid of others ' views. Many people are afraid to sing out loud as they know how others feel about them. I've been one of them.

The day I decided to remove that insecurity and dance, no matter how I want to, I understood that nobody is really worried about how I perform. Strangers are those who loved, so it doesn't matter anyway.

It has nothing to do with you, how others view you. It is not the fact which we perceive. It's their perception if others feel the singing is terrible. You're just yourself. You're not supposed to buy into their narrative.

The day you choose to trust in yourself as compared to how others view you, your self-confidence should grow.

The goal here is to develop inner self-confidence. There has always been self-confidence in you, it's always there. It should be more about rediscovering your self-confidence rather than telling establishing your self-confidence.

Practice the three forms described above, change your unsupportive beliefs. Look at the rise of self-confidence.

Why Creating Self-Confidence Is Also Vital for Self-Esteem

Self-Confidence is an inward feeling of complete self-confidence and self-confidence.

Successful people know we must first be confident of our ability to be successful. This ends with our body, and then this sensation is transferred into our brain.

It's the mindset of self-belief; what we have to say and what we can do. Therefore, it is no surprise that self-confidence is very necessary to be effective in any field of our lives.

It's just a state of mind. It is the attitude that will shape our attitude, and this attitude can be learned. We can learn to have self-confidence by learning to consciously cultivate these attitudes.

A sense of self-confidence is also interrelated with our self-worth thinking.

Is a personal assessment of one's worth and importance as an individual, to oneself vis-à-vis others. It is impossible to express the feeling of self-confidence without a fair degree of self-worth.

Having a high degree of self-esteem is a very important factor in developing healthy self-esteem and vice versa. We will greatly enhance our lives by understanding how to be positive and by improving the importance we place on ourselves.

There is an aspect of bravery in our journey to learning to be sure of our abilities. Courage will help us build our self-confidence in the face of our anxiety.

Lack of self-confidence is usually caused by an overwhelming sense of fear, particularly fear of the unknown. Such worries are closely linked to the fear of failure, humiliation, dismissal, contempt, and the likes that are typically baseless after the event(s) has finished.

When these unfounded concerns are not addressed and resolved, our capacity to function properly and successfully will be compromised and hampered.

We all have a certain degree of confidence in ourselves. The faith in ourselves will fluctuate up and down. In many different areas and periods of our life, this feeling will be reflected.

It relies on the day-to-day problems and the ability to tackle them. The faith may be expressed in some ways, but in others, it may be absent.

Their sense of self-confidence and high self-worth on their side, however, can be misunderstood as pride. Arrogant people are arrogant and self-confident.

To tell the truth, there is a lack of self-confidence among arrogant people. In compensate for their lack of self-belief, they use pride.

We will be humble enough if we are self-assured to accept that we are not always right. They will be ready and willing to accept the views of other citizens and will not be offended if our thoughts or beliefs are questioned.

Individuals with self-confidence can consider lively conversations and will tend to disagree. We must aim for a healthy and balanced sense of self-confidence.

It is possible to build a stable and positive self-confidence.

The outcome of our intentional action plan should be to boost our self-confidence. From the start, it is important to understand that the reason we don't trust in our own capacity is that we make the conscious choice not to do so.

I say, it's the self-affirmation of our own failure, which we can't do well! From the very start we will escape this psychological trap; for we will succeed what we believe!

This simple but immensely emotionally fulfilling act will boost our spirits and help us to be more confident in ourselves. As we begin to practice what we believe and begin to build self-confidence, we will be creating more successes in our lives.

These achievements will start to aggravate our confidence development. When our self-confidence is strengthened by the positive outcomes and achievements we achieve on an ongoing basis, our self-worth will also raise our value!

It's a method to learn how to build self-confidence. Challenges will not hamper those who are serious about improving their self-confidence but instead are inspired by it.

Like building our muscles, we build our self-confidence systematically and purposely. We will obtain a level of enhanced self-confidence with each minor achievement.

Each success leads to building self-confidence.

They will then know, without doubt, or apprehension, to depend on ourselves and our own decision.

Exercises and Strategies To Develop Self-Confidence

Think of these ideas as the foundation of increased self-confidence in every aspect of your life.

1. Start creating a journal.

Starting to begin with your journal or diary would be a great way to carry out a good self-analysis. Identify your self-confidence ideas. Write down any ideas that come to mind. Furthermore, try to think about what prevents you from moving to a place in your life that you want to achieve.

Create an inventory of points within your diary that allows you to be special. For instance, under the heading, "What Makes Me Different," you may build a stock. Identify interests as well as personal preferences that render you special.

Keep in mind that such methods don't work for everyone, and if it doesn't boost your self-confidence while carrying out the journal, check an alternative solution.

2. Recharge sometimes.

Prepare to have confidentiality for emotional, physical, and spiritual refreshment. Take the time off to relax in a peaceful location on your own.

3. Carry out a self-assessment.

Know how to objectively judge yourself. This encourages you to escape the current state of chaos arising from depending on the views of other citizens. Focusing on how you think and feel about your behavior, way of life, job, and so on externally can give you a better sense of personal consciousness. This can interrupt the habit of giving away your energy to others.

4. Recognize yourself and respect yourself.

The real awareness of your deficiencies goes along with the behavior of the self-assessment. As a consequence of this specific growth, don't let yourself be deterred.

Know how to embrace and respect yourself as a human for what you are. Everyone has special talents, qualities, and attributes of their own. For a good reason, we were all made differently. Always equate yourself with others.

Always be satisfied with your successes and show the originality of your own. You should learn to accept what you are and stay happy with it. Only then will you feel your skyrocket of self-confidence!

5. Instead of your real weak points, concentrate on your own strengths.

From within, self-confidence emerges. Reflect on your good points. Keep in mind that the past is over; you will change the future only. Identify 10 good points for you. Look through your newspaper and see all the good things for yourself.

Concentrate on your ability. These are the main reasons you love and trust in yourself. Give credit to yourself for any good thing you've read for yourself. Keep in mind that you are a unique person.

6. *Conquer challenges and fears.*

Many people feel vulnerable, imagining that they can never end up being good at anything they do. This kind of low self-esteem will only lead to a loss of self-confidence in anything you do in your lifetime.

If you haven't done something, you can't ever say you're going to fall short with it. Your manager suggests you watch over a team, for example, but you're worried that you're going to make a mess out of it. Certainly, this kind of dread will prevent a person from accepting this task. Nonetheless, you wouldn't think twice about faltering when you're a self-assured person and willingly accept the mission. Insufficient self-confidence may affect the development of your profession.

7. *Inspire*

Whether for a presentation, a job interview, or anything at all, find out that you can do it for yourself. Encourage yourself every day; and you will soon discover your self-confidence.

A helpful tool for motivating yourself is simply to keep a list of at least five tasks that you have done perfectly that day. Every particular exercise reaffirms a firm belief in doing what you set your mind to achieve.

8. Participate in self-talk of confidence.

Using constructive self-discussion as a good opportunity to displace harmful ideas that clutter the mind. Whenever you hear about pessimism, try to "hang" and swap them all with good ones.

For example, if your head is full of nasty thoughts, simply replace them all by talking of happy times. When you find that you are striving for perfection, remind yourself that you should strive to do your utmost. This tends to make you much more self-forgiving; at the same time, continue trying to improve.

One great way to get rid of pessimism is to read through and hear positive things. Learning and listening to resources that are positive and affirming would certainly improve your skills and ability and develop your self-confidence.

Read and listen to the uplifting stories about the wealthy. You can note that most of these people have experienced difficult circumstances; they have encountered many problems and challenges in everyday life, but these people have resolved all kinds of challenges and have evolved to be productive in their undertakings. Surely, this kind of approach will yield great returns later as these are positive knowledge tools in your head.

9. Picture your success in the long run.

Picture yourself often enjoying achievement! Feel the real pleasure, expectation, excitement, and success buzz. You have to picture yourself as a man or woman wealthy in self-esteem to become much more confident. Imagine that you are grappling with a difficult issue and then overcoming it with poise and confidence.

Use your 5 sensory faculties to build a vivid and true picture in your mind. Let's say you're going to have a recital of your piano and you're having trouble calming. Imagine yourself on the screen, taking the piano with confidence. Imagine playing with complete confidence and enjoyment. Picture folks clapping their hands and yelling, "Encore!" Take sight of achievement, scent, and flavor. Isn't it boosting?

10. Recognize the success of your own.

Give credit for anything you're going to do. Stress the whole cycle of achievement, such valiant and easy efforts performed, rather than focusing solely on performance as the end product.

Congratulate or reward yourself whenever you're doing something that makes you feel good. Take a break from a bar, a good health salon, or maybe a day off for the remainder of the day.

Cultivate these thoughts by recalling previous achievements. Write down the actual situations in your journal where you think the best. It may be an event or success where you experience joy together with a deep sense of accomplishment.

Bask in those memories and gain strength from them all as well. Say it plainly, "If I have been willing to do this in the past, I can do more today and in the future."

11. Identify Failure and re-frame.

If you can accept unfavorable facets of yourself, it is an indicator of a healthy mind. If you're constantly crying about the mistakes you made before, you're not going to get anywhere.

Note that it is not possible to correct prior mistakes or disappointments; what is done is done. There is no use crying over spilled milk, therefore. Recognize that there are mistakes. Realize that every mistake and error you create is a leap towards achievement. When you consider errors as a potential opportunity to learn, you reduce fear over the disappointment and increase trust in yourself.

12. Take risks.

Look at things that you haven't done before. Doing anything new will always be difficult. The simple practice of embracing these types of challenges will raise your self-confidence dramatically. The rise is regardless of whether or not you are effective.

Shying away from challenges prevents us from mastering additional skills, discourages us from assessing our limitations, and also causes uninteresting lifestyles within our comfort zones for people.

People with a high level of self-confidence are not scared to go out and do stuff. They may have little experience and capacity; but for these individuals, heading out and doing "it" is no challenge simply because they feel certain they will be effective. We are less afraid of making mistakes, as well as taking advantage of many more opportunities to succeed.

Quite definitely, self-confident people make a lot of mistakes relative to those who are not very self-confident, but because of their self-confidence, they are most likely to have much more enriching successes than average Joes.

13. Behave with confidence.

Your desire to achieve is mostly influenced by your self-image in almost any endeavor you take on. Those who value their self-worth become targets for success and happiness. Feel confident and be optimistic as well.

14. Go to the lectures.

Going to seminars with knowledgeable and encouraging speakers delivering guidance and help building self-confidence is great. You can get advice on speaking in public throughout the presentation simply by watching the movements of the speaker and how he expresses himself.

Such styles of techniques should allow you to improve your self-confidence in every phase of your life as well as to reduce it. Use these methods to find yourself an improvement.

How to Initiate the Process

It's no secret that self-confidence is very necessary for any area of life to achieve success. The thing about self-confidence is that it is very sensitive and inherently unstable in our personal experience. In other terms, you have a "snowball effect" in your self-confidence, and it can either snowball in a positive direction or snowball in a negative direction. Here's how it works: How the "Negative Snowball" works When you continue with low self-confidence (see below for further details on how this happens), you're less likely to face obstacles and try new things.

On the rare occasion, you're trying to achieve something, your low self-confidence could undermine your attempts and you're far less likely to succeed.

Your disappointment and loss of success enhance your low self-confidence.

Then it's back to step 1 and continues the cycle; reducing the opportunity to live a better life.

How the "Positive Snowball" works

If you have confidence in yourself, you're more likely to try anything, so you're trying more.

And you're very likely to succeed if you do something with trust in your ability.

It increasing your self-confidence as a product of your performance.

Go to stage 1 and repeat and repeat until the full potential is hit!

Wearing a groove in your brain At the risk of over-simplifying a phenomenally complex process, what happens in your brain is that through the vast array of neurons and synapses these snowball cycles "wear a groove." Neurologically, however, you are cutting through your mind a path of least resistance. You build a response for certain forms of the stimulus with enough encouragement.

For example, if a smoker attempts to quit smoking and loses- and causes a detrimental phase of a snowball to happen-he will lose confidence in his ability to quit. And eventually, he will develop a negative reflection on the idea of quitting. Once that occurs, if someone proposes leaving or somebody offers a new way of trying to leave, the idea would immediately be denied by his mind. The mere suggestion of leaving in his mind would cause an instinct that takes the well-worn path of least resistance; the road equating "trying to quit" with "failure."

But this also works the other way around. A positive phase of the snowball is going to wear a rhythm that produces a constructive outlook. We've always met these men. We are the ones who are eager to try anything and seem to be successful at all. And when they crash, they become undeterred on rare occasions. The motivational reaction they have developed in their mind helps them to learn from their mistakes and pair "failure" to "I'm going to do even better next time!"

Sadly, nearly everyone has been conditioned with stereotypes from infancy that make us believe that we are unable to achieve things we are innately qualified to do. Much of it is software that is self-imposed. When we struggle to do something completely the first time we try something, it's human nature to start thinking we can't do it.

We also obtain from other derogatory stimuli that can have a significant impact on our self-confidence. As a baby, we are repeatedly told "You can't do this" and "You'll never be able to do that." Unless we follow that conditioning-which, again, is only human nature-then our self-confidence will be diminished.

Take a moment to reflect on your own experience now. Think of the things you've been led to believe you can't accomplish, however you realize it's entirely possible mentally. It could be anything; an income level; academic performance; great athletic performance; loving achievement, etc. This won't take long to come up with a substantial collection if you're like most men.

Fortunately, when some people are told they can't do something, they refuse to accept the software and show they can. For example; the instructor of Beethoven said as a musician he was hopeless.

The educators of Thomas Edison said that he was too stupid to learn anything that was said by Leo Tolstoy, the writer of War & Peace, that he was not able to learn that Albert Einstein did not speak until he was four, that he was not taught until he was seven. He was named intellectually weak by his instructor.

One of the great opera singer's early mentors Enrico Caruso said he had no tone at all and was unable to perform.

There are many other reasons, but the argument is that at least one item has been abandoned by every one of us because we lost the confidence to try! And because of this cynicism, the planet has certainly been deprived of the great contributions of many talented people.

The good news is an inherently reversible negative self-confidence period! You will learn to remove existing negative reflexes of thinking and substitute them with constructive reflexes of mind. You will be able to recognize and dismiss disruptive programming by learning a few simple strategies until you encourage it to begin eroding your trust.

There are hundreds of strategies available to help you develop confidence and self-esteem.

These include:

- Positive Affirmations

- Guided Visualization

- Cognitive Imagery

- Goal-Oriented Training

- Breathing Strategies

- Subliminal Software

- Whole-Brain Practice

Here is one simple technique you should begin practicing now that will help you facilitate a virtuous cycle of increased self-confidence.

Use Positive Affirmations to Create Self-Confidence

Positive Affirmations are carefully worded positive words that you say to yourself and are intended to create new patterns of thought in your brain. It is a very powerful way to build self-confidence by using affirmations. It seems easy-and it may be a little awkward in the start-but note, what you're attempting to do is wear a new rhythm in your head. You are trying to create a new least-resistance direction and to create a positive image in your head. And by recalling positive thoughts, pictures, and emotions, the best way to create a fresh reflex is.

I have included a small handful of important points at the end of this book for you to continue using today. Repeat the statements to yourself (out loud or silently) is the way to use affirmations. If you repeat a statement, feel it, believe it, and know it! Bring in it a certain positive emotion. The most strong and long-lasting emotion-backed programming. Enable yourself to encounter the feelings of happiness, fulfillment, energy, and self-confidence as you do each claim. Making everybody a real part of your life.

Routinely use and hear your daily affirmations throughout the day. You'll eventually make a quantum leap when you do it. Finally, you will be far beyond the questions that go with wanting, expecting, daydreaming, and even believing. You're going to enter the information field.

Once you reach the information area, there is immediate absolute self-confidence. The uncertainty has vanished. You know that you can do that. You know it's going to happen, as certainly as if it had unfolded already. And it's probably happened in some way-for you! Your self-confidence is unshakable as you reach the information area and your untapped ability is released. You're unbeatable!

Another great way to use affirmations is when you look in a mirror and show them. Say it with emotion, and you will soon realize how strong your eyes are. It's said the ears are the soul's windows. Ralph Waldo Emerson wrote that we each have the exact sign of our rank in our faces. With our eyes, we send messages showing how we think about ourselves and how confident we are about ourselves. And that affects how we are reacted to others. The more self-confidence and self-esteem in our minds, the more likely we are to be held in high respect by other individuals. Some people have come up with a penetrating gaze that makes it look like they can look into your very soul. You will see this in your own eyes when you perform your affirmations in the mirror, and then others will sense the trust you are expressing.

Test Affirmations

- I now liberate myself from the artificial constraints
- I choose to be self-confident
- I now feel confident that I radiate self-confidence
- I resist cynicism at all levels of consciousness

- I love turning pessimistic into optimistic
- The more productive I become, the more comfortable I get
- I now know that as a positive person
- I breathe I feel positive and confident that I am smart
- I am competent.

Start Today

You can use many other important methods to develop your self-confidence and self-esteem. But that's going to get you going in the right direction.

The most important thing to remember is that to change the way you feel, consistency and positive emotions are essential. While it is possible to do this on your own, for the course and help they need to contribute to change, many people need a specified plan.

Most people find that listening to audio programs is the perfect way to deliver the continuity needed to develop fresh, balanced, positive thinking patterns. Including Positive Affirmations, the best audio services will include a variety of techniques including directed visualizations, cognitive mapping, goal-oriented relaxation, subliminal processing, brain-wide reading, and more.

So, use whatever resources you need to commit to building confidence in yourself. Whether it's an audio program or help from your friends, family, or therapist-it's too important for your self-confidence to let go of it. Be assured that your confidence can be strengthened and that it will change your life.

The Priceless Quality of A Great System of Self-Confidence

They all have some level of self-confidence. We simply won't be able to function in the future without it. We all need faith in ourselves and we really won't be able to do or do anything without it. And, what is true self-confidence? Self-confidence is your self-confidence or self-confidence. That faith can be expressed in many various areas of your life, and you may have confidence in some ways, or lose it in others.

Brian Tracy discusses the value of self-confidence in every area of your life in his groundbreaking self-confidence curriculum The Science of Self-Confidence. The ability to achieve your objectives depends heavily on your self-confidence. That way you're going to be right, whether you think you can or if you believe you can't. All you believe or feel sure of is what you're doing or what you're struggling to do.

In the stuff we're seeking to do, we all need this sense of certainty. Certainty makes us feel assured that we can handle a situation. We appear to pause without confidence as we don't know what might happen. We all need a sense of certainty as human beings. When you lose that sense of certainty, your lack of trust will hold you immobilized.

I have to confess that I was one of those people who believed deeply that you were born with faith. I say you've ever seen someone who's truly self-confident and self-confident. They seem so vibrant and in control; as if nothing can deter them. Is this something you were' given' or are you studying more? The truth is that we all want it either way, and you may not have enough of it ever. Only after engaging in a good self-confidence program did my self-confidence outlook begin to change-and happily so.

Confidence in oneself is nothing but a state of mind. It's a mindset that can be practiced and something. Talk about it - if you feel confident in yourself, is it just a thought, isn't it? It does not rely on anything outside of yourself but relies solely on the thought process and how you organize your thoughts and reactions in your mind.

You will grow to be optimistic by having to deliberately maintain certain habits. While building muscles, you build confidence in yourself in a systematic way before you begin to depend on yourself without delay. Creating trust in yourself is a loop that can either support you or further tear you down. The cycle of self-confidence is self-reinforcing-the more you act on your doubts, the more confidence you build, and the easier it is to do it with certainty, the more willing you are to do it... and the cycle is going on.

Investing in a good self-confidence plan would prove to be invaluable as it is not that easy to develop self-confidence. Self-confident people have this tendency in every area of life to' turn on' their self-confidence, even if they haven't achieved anything before and even if they're scared. It has become an exact science to build your self-confidence. They already know exactly how the most confident people are doing and what they are doing to build that sense of self-confidence. As some self-confidence programs might promise, this is not a quick fix or magic bullet strategy. It's an attribute you need to develop inside yourself. The view of yourself is what will change immediately, and that is the vital element in improving self-confidence.

Your ability to pursue and achieve your goals is directly related to your level of self-confidence and your ability to be effective.

Whatever you want to be, do or have in your life-you're going to need confidence in yourself. Without that internal confidence about yourself, to be truly successful, you simply will not have the required support from within. Trustworthy people radiate their confidence and in more than one sense they are appealing. The secret to switching yourself ON is self-confidence. You can get the most out of yourself and activate your ability to create and direct your own life only when you learn to trust and believe in yourself.

Hypnosis for self-confidence

Hypnosis for self-confidence is a great technique of self-esteem building and regaining a sense of self-worth.

Low self-esteem, as you probably know, causes you all kinds of vulnerabilities and worries. These are emotions that have begun in existence earlier and have continued to grow deeper and harder to manage. Sometimes, even if you try to maintain a confident attitude, recalling your many good qualities, too much is occurring in your head, dragging you down and not helping you to sustain your positive energy.

If you can identify with your attempts to conquer low self-esteem and feel frustrated, don't quit. Hypnosis for self-confidence may help you get out of this very negative mindset because it interacts with your brain at a deeper level where worries, phobias, and other things have been accumulated from an early age.

Hypnosis is an excellent way to fight a unique challenge internally. The principle of using hypnotherapy is still elusive to some men. Unfortunately, there seems to be a common myth that when you're hypnotized, you're putting yourself in a dangerous position because you're not supposed to be in control of your actions and somebody can take advantage of your frail state. In fact, as in relaxation, you are hyper-relaxed and therefore very suggestive, but still in command and consciousness.

Hypnosis was first used in the late 1800s by James Braid, a Scottish physician. The terms hypnosis and hypnotism mean "nervous system rest," which brings the person to a deep mental relaxed condition. It becomes better accessible and receptive to constructive feedback when the mind becomes calm and liberated from the incessant negative self-talking.

Hypnosis for self-confidence is about being orally directed to a point of cognitive calm so that the counselor and you (using your own recorded voice or a controlled self-hypnosis mp3 or CD) will function through encouraging visualizations or constructive feedback to help you to reach your self-confidence objectives. You will be able to see yourself in a different light in this current state of mind with no worries, no apprehension, no mistakes, and no need to consider others.

Through hypnosis in self-confidence, you and the psychologist (or an audio-driven self-hypnosis) will have the opportunity to focus on getting out your heart, ideal or beautiful, and a feeling of worthiness by creating new positive self-confidence and removing external noise.

You're going to be pleasantly surprised the next time you think about your skills.

What does self-confidence have to do with Forgiveness?

We must remind ourselves who we need to forgive when we lack self-confidence. Forgiveness allows us to break free from the fetters that hold us back. We're freed from the past from our jails.

You are tied to the person or event which harms you through an emotional bond if you hang onto a past hurt. The only way this connection can be broken is by redemption.

Forgiveness is a gift to use for our own higher good. By considering how a lot we had been hurt, we no longer outline our lives, however with the aid of how a great deal we've grown.

It doesn't say we're getting others off the hook scot-free if we forgive. This means we're going to let ourselves off the line. We should go forward with a confidence that is not compromised by what has occurred in our history.

For too long, holding onto a grudge only increases our sense of injustice and keeps us stuck. We see the one that affects us for what they were, although they may have gone on and who knows how to become a much more beautiful person than they were before.

With a new perspective, we will start rebuilding our lives. In reality, we will begin to accept what happened to us and see things from their point of view if we genuinely forgive someone. We have had to struggle inside to do what they've achieved. It can be extremely powerful when we realize this.

That means we can choose to accept any painful experience we face when we go through our lives. We won't hold on to us by sacrificing others in the system and we won't give up our strength. No one should ever be permitted to take away our strength.

We will restore our faith and self-esteem after we have forgiven others for past hurts. We can choose fresh, stronger values. This will allow you to move from staying to a point of self-power (or inner strength) that allows you to live the life that we were born to live.

There are two aspects to the cycle of reconciliation-to forgive us for what they have done or what we thought they have done to us and to forgive us for feeling negative about them and having them influence us.

Say yes to forgive and get out of the memory. Ultimately, energy is at the moment. You could make a life of yourself.

How High self-esteem and self-confidence may attract better things into your life

Lack of self-confidence and self-esteem may make it difficult to be effective in many ways. At work you can find it hard to speak up, you might feel awkward to ask for support, you might feel incapable of raises and pay increases. It can affect the amount of commitment you make when you believe you're not going to get anywhere; you can feel like' why bother.' In marriages, it can contribute to mentally and physically embracing and keeping up with abusive spouses. It can contribute to extreme feelings of insecurity that fan the fires of envy, anger, and a variety of negative words from other relationships. It can even stop you from starting a relationship for fear of getting hurt, or because you're feeling' not good enough.' In social groups sometimes it can be hard to feel like you're fitting in with your peers and it can make it hard to make new friends. It can stop you from doing as much as you want for fear of not being successful, not like how you look, and feel about yourself and not feel confident in many types of social circumstances.

Within the school environment, a lack of trust can have a direct effect on how well you are doing and also how well you are doing. It can lead to decreased concentration levels and a lack of interest. It can also encourage harassment, of course, because those kinds of people who get an ego boost by throwing others around, mentally or physically, will know you're not going to stand up for yourself.

But be told, you will surely do something about it!

Confidence isn't something you either have or don't have, it's something you can learn and develop when you handle it in the right way. Many people are confident in some areas of their lives, however not in others. From time to time a confident character might encounter a negative occasion and feature their confidence ' shaken' or' knocked.' This may lead them to be less at ease within the future in the same scenario. All this is perfectly normal. You can also improve and develop your self-esteem, and the two can be easily worked on together.

True self-confidence and self-esteem are not milestones instantly, it may take some time, but how much you want it; it will decide how far you get there.

What are the advantages of increased self-confidence and higher self-esteem?

Picture this way of your living. Waking up every day, feeling healthy and full of energy, looking forward to the day ahead, knowing that your day is going to be enjoyable for the most part. Don't get me wrong, we all have' ordinary' days, but being able to deal with them and not having them to turn through bad weeks and bad years is a tremendous benefit to reap from increased self-confidence and higher self-esteem.

Feeling relaxed, secure, and confident with your partner's partnership. Understanding that you are valued for who you are and how you are, without the need for endless public reassurance and the opportunity to provide your companion with the same in exchange. Comfortable speaking about all kinds of things, even the tough subjects which pop up from time to time, and can express yourself and your thoughts without necessarily having to be right, and causing yourself to be railroaded into anything that you don't want or comply to.

Completely calm and convenient to meet new potential partners and compliment your life. People are often drawn to those who are self-confident (not over-confident, which appears to sit amid arrogance), but sometimes when you lack confidence, you end up joining the' right' form of relationships because of the affection you get when you first encounter someone is an internal source of confidence which enhances you, but these partnerships often end up as hard as possible.

Having immense pleasure from having relationships with your friends and family that are more fun. Feeling respected and valued as an adult in your own right, and engaging confidently in all kinds of social events and activities with ease, allows it effortless to build a lively, enjoyable social life.

Being on the pinnacle of everything to your existence, being more focused, organized, able to address challenges as they surface, and being able to create a balanced work/life stability can all bring about you finding more time to do the things you want to do and feature more time with the people that care in your existence.

Getting a fantastic sense of self-worth and achievement from being more productive and efficient at work and being able to interact with people at all levels and from all walks of life comfortably. All of this can lead to greater success in your work life, or better yet, feel confident in your ability to go out and get the kind of job you'd love to do if you haven't done it already.

Feeling like life never' lets you down' and' stresses you out' because you can deal with challenges, struggles, and losses much more intensely. Understanding that your self-worth is not bound up with outside events, thoughts or perceptions gives you a great sense of control over your daily life.

Believing in yourself, your ability and judgment allow you to take calculated risks in your personal and professional life, embark on journeys of excitement and anticipation rather than fear and anxiety, and try to achieve everything you want from life, both internally and externally.

It's not about being the party's life and soul, the one with the most to tell, the greatest at all, the highest earner, or the most' things' holder. It's about feeling confident in yourself; safe in the knowledge that you don't need the support or consideration of anyone else to be satisfied. It's about being happy with who you are, what you're doing, and how you're behaving, realizing you're your best self at any given time and recognizing you're a work in progress, as we are all. It's a very convenient way to be.

Evidence has shown that positive self-confidence development and higher self-esteem by coaching can be significantly improved.

Contrary to alternative methods, the powerful way of coaching interacts with you as a person brings in major and lasting improvements in every area of your mental and physical commitment to trust.

Without doing the inside work, the outcomes are rarely going to be permanent.

Assertiveness is the ability to stand up for your rights without being hostile or defensive, the connection between assertiveness and self-confidence. Usually, people who are not assertive let go of their privileges and finally feel poor.

Not only does a lack of assertiveness result in anger buildup, but it also degrades self-confidence. There is a very strong connection between assertiveness and self-confidence to the degree that without being assertive, an individual cannot become truly confident.

I explained before that self-confidence is created as your subconscious mind examines your actions and starts to believe you, therefore assertiveness and self-confidence are closely related.

Of starters, if you've managed to do well enough times in a certain sport, your subconscious mind will start to believe you're good at it and you'll feel confident the next time you play the sport.

But what does this say to be assertive? In case your subconscious mind maintains to discover that your rights are being violated by others and also you in no way stand up for them, your self-confidence can lessen. On the other side, when you hold your subconscious mind behaving assertively, you will feel that you are capable and you will become more relaxed.

How to become assertive and confident To become assertive you need to:

- Stand up for your rights whenever they are abused

- Using positive body language (straight back, relaxed hands and no arms crossed)

- You need to use "I" expression to be sure, for instance, "I can't see why you'd like to take it off".

Why Self-confidence Is Vital in Sports

One aspect is important to a successful business person, author, athlete, manager of Hollywood, ruler, president, and many more, Self-confidence and you can have it too. For business success and personal relationships, self-confidence is as critical as it is for sports success.

If you're not sure yet asking for any successful sports coach, he'll tell you that athletes ' self-confidence makes the difference between winning and losing, between being great and being mediocre. You will prepare two teams of great players, great tactical plans, good physical fitness, for instance, and both teams are inspired to succeed because they will earn a financial reward. However, if the contributors, or a number of the players lack self-confidence in a single person and do not respect their potential, the team will lose fast.

So, motivation can help, but not a good motivator is a financial reward. Something else has to be there, which is why a team with a good relationship between its participants continues to perform better. We are more than driven by financial rewards, we want to compete and be known as a team. The best motivation is the one that comes from within, such as the need to accept it, the desire to make your family happy, your nation happy, or something else that comes from within.

So, in really critical sports self-confidence, often you need it as a group and in other sports individually, but either way, your success will be higher if you feel you can give 110 percent of yourself and not be scared. Have you seen a great sports competitor, but was very anxious and bad results at the time of the competition? This is a clear example of a lack of confidence in oneself. You need to relax, have faith in your ability, avoid negative thinking, and concentrate on your target.

The important thing is that you shouldn't be afraid to make mistakes, you're going to make mistakes, and that's all right. You know and go on learning from them, don't equate yourself to others. If somebody's doing better than you, that's all right, you're only concentrating on your target.

Self Confidence in Teenagers

There is usually a period where teenagers are lost in an ocean of emotions. There are uncertainty and depression, as making the transition from adolescence to adulthood can be hard. Guilt also happens when the body begins to change. There is constant pressure at college to adapt and to be socially acceptable as well. Sometimes all these issues take a toll on kids and they can easily lose their confidence. Several times they become incredibly vulnerable, powerless, and unable to challenge anyone. It concerns not only them but also their family and friends. They can use the following self-confidence strategies to deal with this very issue: understand teens: if adolescents tend to have self-confidence issues and are unable to cope with them on their own, they need to step in. You have to make them realize how good they are at this stage.

Compliment them, for instance, if they get good grades for their accomplishments. Sometimes, thank them for supporting you with household chores and working for a service club. Make an effort to let them know how helpful they were and how important it is for you. This is going to fill them with a sense of value.

Encourage sports: Sports are mentally and physically stimulating an individual. Encourage your baby to indulge in his / her choice of sport. You may register and spend time practicing with them in a sports club. If, for some reason, athletics do not fit, then choose some event that needs equal effort, such as a music lesson. This will give them something to focus on. It also teaches them patience and gives them a sense of success.

Join their decisions: the reality that your kids are growing up must be accepted and they will be adults as soon as possible. You ,therefore, need to train them to be decision-makers who are self-reliant and attentive. Many parents think their kids can't make the right choices, but how can you know if you don't give them a chance to do that? Their intellectual abilities could shock you. You feel capable if you share their choices, which in turn helps them to build confidence in themselves.

Recognize the warning signals: your baby will be an adult, but now he's not one. He's still that little fellow somewhere who doesn't understand how to interpret issues or treat them. He unintentionally sends out signals if he encounters a problem. Your job is to detect and discuss these signals with him. So he'll realize he's not alone and he can come to you to fix his issues anytime he likes.

Improvements of self-confidence

Improving self-confidence is almost one of our life goals. No one needs to hate who they are during their lives. We all have something special about us, no matter who we are. Finding out is up to us. Once we have done so, we can test that for sure from our database. We will seek ways to prove it to ourselves when we grow to be secure in who we are.

Get yourself to learn.

Bringing yourself to learn. This is a peculiar leap towards improving self-confidence. By ourselves, we spend our entire lives. We all know who they are, right? We may share our entire lives for ourselves, but a small portion of this earth's inhabitants only understand who they are. Get to learn by reading who you are. Write stuff that pops into your head and ask questions for yourself and address them in-depth.

You will also help to identify who you are by writing down what's in your heart. Writing down the activity of your day may reveal trends and help you recognize good and bad qualities and behaviors. In other terms, you place yourself in the field to see who you really are. Don't respect the negative qualities and behaviors anymore. Keep both characteristics, good and bad, on systems of equal value, and work on the things you see that you want to change and further enhance the things you see that you are good about yourself.

Find and further develop something that you are good at (usually what you wouldn't mind doing for free).

I realize we've just been thinking about that, but it's very, very, very important. Every single one of us has a gift. It is up to us to discover and develop what it is. That's embarrassing to say, for starters, but I'm great at exercise, I enjoy it. Something I was or can be good at with the use of physical energy. Growing up, it was useless. I wasn't in any athletics or education, and the only aspect that influenced me and had meaning was being professionally talented. I couldn't grow my self-confidence, of course. The only factor I was correct at the time was in no way remembered.

I started playing football as I grew older in my late teens. I was so great, I only played for a couple of months. I was playing girls and guys on the right side since they were little. Understanding that about myself brought me a boost on the road to self-confident

Get rid of your Negative People in your Life

Get rid of your life's negative people (or just spend less time with them). Regardless of how much you learn about yourself and how much you build your talents and what your success is, if you have people in your life who are cruel and put you down, it will be very difficult to improve your self-confidence. I can't say about that anymore. Only rid yourself of them. And if this is difficult for some reason, just try to spend less time with them. You want physically, emotionally, and mentally to defend yourself. Consider a tactful way to let them understand you're on a journey to find themselves, and part of the journey is trying to improve trust in yourself.

Engage in spending time treating yourself in a way that is not destructive, but beneficial.

It's a good way to do that. Exercising daily or at least three days a week has so many advantages. Try joining a team if you hate exercising, go dancing, or learn a new sport. Whatever you want to do, make sure you spend some energy enjoying yourself every day. Whether it's running, relaxation, drawing, car service, or just taking a long bubble bath. Create something every day about yourself. Start doing stuff you're going to fall in love with yourself.

Make goals you will achieve and remember them automatically.

I have many ambitions, long-term goals, short-term goals, and urgent priorities. I think the immediate targets are the ones that make me feel confident about myself. I have something I can be proud of myself every day. I achieved in solving everything.

Examples of what my immediate goals are here are:

- Get up earlier than anybody else.

- Go and workout In my workouts, try to push myself.

- If I want to quit, don't give up.

Self-confidence in Females

Recent studies have shown that people have difficulty with self-confidence that women are studying how to achieve low self-confidence. Such studies have also shown that girls usually have this problem with low self-esteem, particularly intelligent ones. Because of this, people tend to underestimate their skill and quality.

The question of low female self-confidence can be a viral disease, contributing to a multitude of different or related issues. Girls are easily persuaded and prone to criticism and tend to change their minds often. They set our specific targets and expectations. With children, this is not the case, as they often enjoy challenging tasks and have more self-confidence and programs.

A study at Michigan University revealed that girls need lots of support from others during their growing stage. Such experiments uncovered causes that led to this situation.

Girls get less encouragement for independence compared to boys. Most of the time they get parental protection. They get less social pressure in establishing their own identity compared to boys.

She becomes more restricted to her surroundings and thus has little possibility of discovery.

As a result, women don't get much chance to improve their ability to cope with their surroundings most of the time. Her inability to deal with the world has damaged her faith. This led her to rely on her basic survival in adults. Under these conditions, she may want to preserve her adult relationship by any means that influences her independence and self-confidence.

Under these conditions, people must understand that autonomy is the result of having confidence in their abilities, making decisions based on their ability, and accepting their judgment in the end. As we have seen, there are not enough resources for women to make these choices and increasing their skills. We finally conclude that whatever they do, they can't achieve. We cannot secretly suffer from a lack of confidence or low self-esteem without such strong beliefs.

People must pose some very basic questions in order to resolve this lack of self-confidence.

Once I make a decision, will I always have to take the opinion of others?

Do I need to care about what others are going to think when I make a certain judgment or behavior Do I need to take action to improve my lack of self-confidence?

When I decide as to how can I boost my self-confidence?

Once you have addressed all these questions critically and properly, you will push forward and take steps to improve your self-confidence. You can't expect results overnight, of course, and you'll need to take one step at a time. But the most important thing here is that you can assume responsibility for your life again.

Here are some of the key strategies for growing women's self-confidence Next thing is to do anything you're involved in and excited about. For example: if you want to be a fashion designer, take a class of designers, attend shows, create your collections, etc. You don't need to be mindful of wearing them. Show off your personality and start a trend.

Start the list of your employees to make sure that you do it.

These are some of the only things that women can do to boost their trust in themselves. It will completely change the course of her life until she regains her faith. And the most important thing is that the course of every life that she touches will also change completely.

Research showed that women are more likely to suffer from low self-confidence than men. It has a direct influence on the feeling, behavior, and thinking of women. A strong sense of self-confidence in friendships, jobs, social situations, and other personal achievements leads to progress.

Here are some tips to help improve women's self-confidence.

Figure out how others would like to view you and handle yourself in this direction. People assume that those who are trustworthy are trustworthy and will treat them accordingly. Evidence has shown that behaving with trust can lead to growing levels of self-confidence in the long term, even if a person does not feel comfortable at that moment.

Be honest about yourself and your limitations and skills. Some people are better at some things than others, but dwelling on what we are not so good at can be all too simple, rather than thinking of ourselves as a whole. People sometimes assess their performance by the things they feel should be good at, rather than their natural talents, and consider their lack of it. For example, the self-confidence of a woman might suffer because she feels she ought to be better at a certain type of sport, when in fact her strengths lie in more artistic pursuits, but because she focuses solely on her sporting abilities, she feels she is under-performing.

Response and success build confidence in oneself. Women are usually multi-taskers. This can be good in many respects as people are responsive to doing a range of things, but the negative side to multi-tasking is that it can contribute to resentment that they do not have the chance to pay full attention to one issue. Alternatively, be conscious of simplifying what you carry on when you work on projects or bring on a reasonable number.

Seek not to be affected by women's media portrayal. Today's media was blamed for many misleading women's photos, and this in effect is responsible for many women feeling uncomfortable in their looks and body shape. Try to appreciate the natural shape of you and your natural resources and reflect on what's great in them.

A good sense of self-esteem and trust will aid in many other areas of life and terms of success and accomplishment can be self-perpetuating. But start the process with small steps as with anything, seeking to focus on one thing at a time. Worthwhile changes are often not achieved immediately.

How to boost the self-confidence in children

When parents boost the confidence of a child, they send him/her a positive message that can follow them for the rest of their lives. In the later years, how parents handle their kids at an early age can decide their level of trust. Mothers who raise self-belief for their kids provide them with the knowledge they need to be effective in the world.

The self-confidence among children is largely based on how those who are essential to them perceive them. Families who relate to their children's needs are creating the framework and faith that creates their interest. Kids are going to grow up realizing that somebody truly cares about them in the universe.

Kids will meet some negative people trying to take away their self-worth, but parents must strive to raise the trust of their kids. Parents should keep moving and hugging their kids to remind them how special they are. Families should be receptive to their issues if children have problems at school or with friends and try to give them a positive solution to their dilemma. Mothers should not always agree with their children, but they should also listen to their concerns because mothers grow up need to continue showing the same kindness and love in their early years. Kids are particularly sensitive to how they are handled, and if parents stop expressing love and concern to their kids, it may harm that child's trust. When growing up, kids will face some struggles and adjustments, but if they have their parents ' support and love, the transition will be smoother and they will have faith in making the right decisions in life.

Parents sometimes have busy schedules and they don't have time for their kids. Such parents must understand that their growth could be adversely affected by any missed opportunity with their children. Families need to realize that it takes time for their kids to have fun with them and build a strong relationship that can never be destroyed. Only if parents spend more time with their kids can this occur. Children know if parents merely want to have fun with them, so don't play to children.

parents have to take time to take a look at which academic environment is vital to them while seeing children grow up. If the baby seems to enjoy playing numbers games, the parent may want to include the child in math events. Once the baby starts to improve their math skills and at the same time have fun, confidence should increase. Kids like being great at something (including adults). As the child develops an interest in other learning fields, the parents must pay attention to the interest by getting them into programs that promote their interest. The stronger they get, the more relaxed they become in those places.

Parents sometimes forget that, like other people, children are people with opinions and concerns. It is necessary to respect children as if they were young adults. The parent would listen carefully as they were an adult if children give their opinion about something. This gives the child the impression that they're genuinely thinking about what they're doing. This will make the child feel that what he does is important and think for his family. Trust is being developed again.

Also very important are the words that a parent uses when talking to their children. When talking to kids, parents should try to be encouraging and positive, and never use put down. One of the fastest ways kids can lose their confidence is to be constantly put down. Parents should always try to elevate their children. Parents should try to frame their words to be more positive, like: he's hyper, he's curious, another way of saying it might be. He is dumb, or you might say, he sure has an interesting personality. This little strategy in a child's life can make a big difference.

Children should always take the lead in picking up what their kids are bringing into their friendship circle. Peer pressure is so critical that parents get to know the kids who are interacting with their kids and what kind of friends they have. This may be controversial with their kids occasionally.

Another way to build children's trust is to get them to join a sports team, and if they develop to be good athletes their trust will improve automatically. Even if kids don't become superstars, they will learn valuable skills that will help them build trust emotionally, psychologically, and most of all. All kids enjoy being good at something, so parents need to be supportive if sports is their thing.

Ultimately, the parent who spends time with their kids, interacts with them, shows affection for them, inspires them, gets them into positive activities, listens to them and makes them feel important, helps to raise happy kids who will succeed in college. Parents working to be a good parent should raise children with trust.

As a child grows in understanding, his increasing self-confidence represents both his positive interactions with his world and his rising self-confidence.

Confidence in oneself is about trusting in one's skills.

It is the inward confidence that we can be self-confident and have trust in our own decisions and assessments.

By our experiences with others, this implicit conviction and self-confidence are generally reflected in us and our integrity is further applied.

Ideally, self-confidence is better established early in life and maintained as they grow with understanding.

Fast, optimistic, regular breastfeeding provides the baby with the template or model on which it shapes its sense of self-confidence.

How to develop self-confidence in your Child

Do not make comparisons

In the best of times, contrasts between children are odious. When he thinks he is being associated with a parent or relative, a kid can be easily compromised. A large component of self-confidence is self-acceptance.

Seek not to underestimate his/her capacity

Parents sometimes criticize their kids unknowingly even in basic practice. Only hear, "Let me do that for you here," can be enough to undermine the internal confidence of a child. Then, "Can you see someplace you do that?" Encourage social communication Encouraging regular contact with other children and their families is a great way to develop self-confidence in social situations. Try to share with others the child's confidence and ease.

Be reliable

A child with solid, comfortable boundaries has more chances of self-confidence as he is subject to fewer scenarios of anxiety.

Follow normal, constant, efficient habits that encourage confidence in daily life.

Daily, healthy access to new situations Introduce your baby to various playgrounds, walks, and unknown individuals. Encourage him to inquire. Participate in various sports, cultural projects, passions.

Explain, teach, talk, listen, and share your feelings, expectations, fears, and dreams. Help your child speak to you about his emotions instead of driving them down and back. Teach him to say "I feel sad, angry, happy, nice, and so on." Encourage, applaud, reflect, encourage, rejoice each day, tell your baby something amazing you learned that day about him.

"I also enjoyed that you helped your mom set the table, played with your daughter, read your novel, and so on." Allow him to work with your baking, washing, planting, and doing household chores. Remembering to enable and encourage their children to work alongside them is particularly important for parents.

Play a lot with your child

This sends your child a direct message that he is valued and loved.

Give your child responsibilities

In a position of responsibility, even very young children thrive. They can pick up, put away, clean, pack up. Write chore charts for your kids as they grow.

Upping the kids always feeds self-confidence with a hot, caring, family touch.

Encourage acts that involve confidence Teach them why-don't do it for them.

Conclusion

Life's essence is that it sometimes throws a curveball at us. Not all goes according to plan, and many facets of our psychology will start to be questioned. This can be valid in any number of life fields from our jobs, to our spiritual health, or the state of our partnerships with others. But our sense of self-worth and self-confidence is the common thread that binds them all.

When life resembles a rollercoaster, then the courage to know that the rollercoaster must come to an end is self-confidence, and that the heights on the ride are as disingenuous as the lows.

Understanding the reality doesn't help if you appear to be at the low end of the spectrum, of course! Nonetheless, it is important to focus on times in your own life and realize that it is normally only when things go wrong that most of us start doubting ourselves and worrying if we're ever going to see the sunlight again.

Besides seeing self-confidence as an amalgam of the rich tapestry of the experience of life, it can also be interpreted as a minute-by-minute evaluation of how we see ourselves.

It tends to come into play in topics such as body image, and there are usually more gender differences in this respect.

Men most likely often struggle with body image, and it would be a rare man who said they hadn't stared at pieces of their own body at times and wished them to be unique. But the fact remains that while people are harboring feelings on how they want to change themselves (please, six-pack abs!), there may be more concerns of self-confidence around women's body appearance.

There are likely strong biological reasons for this in all fairness besides the often trotted out, "press effect" because the fact remains that people (shallow creatures we are!) continue to be unduly influenced by how a woman looks (at least at first, we get deeper later!). And women certainly aren't oblivious to that reality, so there's always a desire for young women to look good to find more popularity with guys, and that eventually plays into the whole issue of self-confidence.

Looked at in the cold light of the day, it might be possible to say that if someone had perfect self-confidence that they would inhabit some kind of island, they would be happy to look at others, but not too worried about their view. Yet we know that in reality there is no such man, and therefore self-confidence is a problem for us all.

And then there is, of course, real "internet power" which places photos of ultra-skinny girls on women's minds, then making them question their beauty.

Self-confidence is an issue that is hard to pin down like clouds, but it's all around us.

Where helpful tips fail to achieve the aim of improving self-confidence, it may be seen as an indicator that you may need to seek professional assistance by counseling, life coaching, and hypnotherapy. Typically, these approaches are used to help improve self-confidence. A professional psychologist is qualified to discuss the low self-confidence's underlying causes. To help build, strengthen, and boost your self-confidence, there are techniques and approaches developed. And as the triggers are decided, for example, a licensed hypnotherapist can prescribe exercises and strategies that help restore your faith in your ability.

Book 2

Self Esteem: *Gain Confidence, free yourself from negative thoughts, and enjoy the benefits of Self-Esteem to change your life*

Introduction

Over the past several decades, Self Help has been held with high priority. Self-help for women has burgeoned into a major industry and a global movement in just a few short decades. Countries that used to promote traditional cultures where women were expected to submit to their husbands are now embracing new values and becoming part of equality globalization.

Women's issues were traditionally overlooked because the jobs were men guided. Also, publications and counseling industry and economy were driven exclusively by males. Today, things have changed and for specific women's issues, there is plenty of self-help available as well. Women often face issues of self-esteem, fertility, and even "the perfect image of the body," but they can now confront these concerns honestly and learn to grow and evolve just as men do. We all have problems to contend with as human beings and none of us are perfect. It is a great step that we can now jointly recognize this and learn to grow spiritually irrespective of our gender.

Some of the women's issues media and product advertisers are challenging today are objectification and marginalization. These are problems that personally affect women and often require help from a man who has already "been there." The Oprah Winfrey Show is one great program that has led the fight toward women's marginalization. Breaking away from many other self-help gurus, Oprah rejects much of the male-driven negative language and instead reflects on the strategies that people can use to conquer. The Oprah Winfrey Show frequently raises awareness of many other topics outside of women's self-help, rendering itself open to an even wider audience. This places the struggle for women's self-esteem and self-empowerment in a broader context of issues around the world rather than cutting it off from its connection to all issues facing humanity. Greater self-esteem for women means greater self-esteem for all and because of this reality, the Oprah Winfrey Show has been a great benefit to mankind.

Women's self-help books are widespread but some of the earlier works are particularly noteworthy for those who want to gain a basic understanding of the issues. Interestingly, when she wrote the famous work The Ego and Mechanisms of Defense, Anna Freud, Dr. Sigmund Freud's daughter contributed very deeply to the work of psychoanalysis. This is one of the classic psychoanalysis works that brought together many of the ideas of her father more succinctly and clearly, making them easier for all people to identify. Another great book on women's issues that is part of the classic works comes from Nancy Friday and is called My Mother Myself. Here, Nancy Friday explores the core issues that involve women in their mother's relationship and explores common reasons for women's self-esteem issues. She leads the reader to a deeper self-understanding so that she can more readily identify her issues and find a way forward in her life. Although the third book in terms of women's empowerment has mostly been left behind, Carol Gilligan's book In a Different Voice was a landmark project in terms of women's activism decades ago and is still being taught in many university courses today.

Wherever you choose to start, know that there is always a wellspring of information about women's self-help that can easily be obtained. In many areas, women have taken the lead in personal growth and caused men to stand up and take notice as they lead the way for us all to a better future.

Lack of Self-Esteem in women

Have you ever asked why the latter was the second-class citizen until recently between a man and a woman? Today, women around the world are fighting for equal pay, equal benefits, equal treatment, and equal responsibilities at work and home. Yet there are still countless women suffering from low self-esteem caused by pre-generational beliefs.

Society has taught, for example, it's woman's responsibility to serve her husband, to take care of the children, to take care of her elderly parents, to share the responsibility of bringing the dough in to help with the daily expenses, to keep everything in order-appointment with the dentist, and orders to pay Something must be right without that smile, isn't it? I bet, you're so many ladies in the same predicament. You feel exhausted and being able to get through this life is all you want.

"Wasn't I supposed to do these things? If I don't do this, who's going to do it?" This is a typical question you had to ask yourself. So, every day of your life you go around juggling everything and you feel tired instead of feeling good. You feel old and you've been spending. You're feeling rejected and disgusting. This is how it should be, you resigned to your destiny. You end up feeling depressed and you wonder whether you deserve a better thing in life. This is one of the low self-esteem symptoms.

Symptoms of low self-esteem

Depression among women. Because worrying is a big part of what you're doing, you're worried about so many things in life. You're worried about what other people will think about you if you don't. If you choose to do things your way, you're worried about what they might say. You're worried about raising your kids the "right" way. You feel depressed because of too much worrying.

Anxiety. There's a fear of talking, doing, and acting in a way that will cause you and others to feel humiliated. That's why you'd rather keep to yourself and avoid interactions with others just to eliminate the possibility of making a mistake. Nonetheless, of course, no one likes to make mistakes-people do make mistakes, and women will be at themselves up mentally and emotionally for longer than necessary due to these mistakes. There's always a fear over her head that makes her feel anxious.

Expectations and perfectionism are unreasonable. Too many demands and the need to be "complete" lead many ladies out there to feel frustrated and insecure about themselves and others. This leads to negative self-talk and a sense of failure. We've been made to believe all this time that a beautiful woman is the one with flawless skin, captivating eyes, a full set of teeth, long silky hair, and an attractive, fit body. It is attractive and ideal for women who are the epitome of success. So, we're fighting hard. We do all we can to be the "good" person, and if, given how impossible it is, we don't meet that goal, we berate ourselves. We're getting down.

Hypersensitivity. Open to what others are doing or doing. Any action by others, whether consciously and unconsciously, would have a bad effect on you-causing you to think badly.

Unhealthy Relationships. Women who are in and out of bad relationships feel unfit and do not deserve a healthy relationship. Women with low self-esteem are working harder to maintain a man. They will compensate and invest more in the relationship because of the feeling of inadequacy. They're going to go "the extra mile" just so their partner won't look anywhere else. When they believe that they are not sufficient, the existence of uncertainty, self-sabotage, nagging and needing to be told all the time is always there. Eventually, their partners feel guilty and want to go out.

Feeling insufficient. "I'm not good enough," "I can't," "I don't know how" are just some of the words that show inadequacy and disbelief about yourself. Even with other people boosting you, you're stopping doing great things because you "feel" and believe you're not capable. Constant negative self-talking. "I'm always a failure." "I'm never doing the right thing." "I'm stupid." "I'm stupid" "I'm ugly" "I'm stupid."

It's time to assess yourself. Do you have low self-esteem? Where and to whom is your value tied as a person? Is it linked to success, appearance, and friendships with you?

If your self-worth rests on your success, you will constantly find yourself doing more and more to make you feel respected and admired. If our self-esteem is based on beauty, it's time for you to face the ugly truth that external beauty doesn't last forever.

You will be disappointed that it will not last, however hard you try to preserve your appearance and youthfulness. If your self-esteem is tied to your relationship, you will continue to work hard to be a good wife and a caring mother to the point of sacrificing yourself in the process. You're still not satisfied at the end of all these. So the more you're going to work hard and get what you think you're worth.

Ask yourself this question: what are you expected to do to reach deep life satisfaction and happiness?

Everything boils down to your self-esteem. Is it so bad to live an authentic self-based life? Must you go out and "prove" that you're good enough to others? What if you strip out in your life the words "must," "should" and "doing" and do something not because you've got to? Can you say you can live a life based on your true self and not on other people's and society's standards?

We often see women allowing the very people who make up the important part of their lives to be mistreated and taken for granted. Everything because they have low self-esteem. They don't think they're worth more than gold. Their beauty is not the face and body that they see in the mirror, but under her very being-her very soul-can be found their beauty.

The first sign that something is wrong is the reluctance to do things and to have negative thoughts about oneself. Therefore, you need to consider evaluating your self-esteem when you continually put off things that you know you need to do, when you feel unworthy of love, or when you feel that it is more important for everyone around you.

The internet offers a lot of different tests for a wide range of people. You'll find tests for kids, women or men, and general tests for everyone. There are tests you need to pay for and free tests that are slightly different from each other. We send you a ranking and a short example of where your self-esteem can be strengthened if you take the free exams.

You will need to sign up and pay for tests for a more detailed evaluation of your self-esteem and ways to improve it. Such exercises will give you feedback on how to use positive thinking, optimistic words, and a positive attitude to boost your self-esteem. Such exercises can also provide you with feedback on how to build faith in yourself so that you can experience new scenarios and problems without apprehension.

A qualified assessment is more effective in some situations than using electronic screening. When you believe that someone you respect is seriously affected by low self-esteem, you should talk of asking someone or someone you admire to be properly educated.

The internet provides adults with a wide range of tests to help them evaluate their self-esteem. They ask questions like;

- If you meet new people or try something new, are you comfortable?

- Do most people trust you?

- Do you respect your colleagues at work?

- Most of the time, are you happy?

- Do you feel excited about new challenges?

- Do you think your views are worthwhile?

If the answer to these questions is correct, you won't have a problem with self-esteem more than probably. If there are no answers to some of these questions, you may want to learn more about self-esteem.

Occasionally, reading about self-esteem is beneficial and then exploring how reading has made you feel. You may think your self-esteem isn't as strong as it should be, and you may believe your self-confidence could be growing with some. You might also feel that a little work might be able to do your attitude to things.

You will know more about how self-esteem is generated through learning, and this in effect will help you understand the self-esteem rate. For instance; our self-esteem is greatly influenced as we grow up by our relationships with family and other people. If these partnerships are successful and we have been handled in a kind, respectful, and reasonable way, our self-esteem will be high. If these relationships were negative, however, and you were treated in an unkind and unfair manner, your self-esteem would be low.

Do not let your self-esteem be ruined by society!

There seems to be a' bubble' in Western society. It's like being trapped in this' bubble' in a dark room where we can't see where we're going. What we generally fail to realize in this' bubble' is that we allow ourselves to be guided by those people who are just as' in the dark' as we are. As a result of relying on other people's guidance, we train ourselves to ignore our guidance; our inner being. What this means is that we are unaware of our emotions, intuition, and inspiration and are sucked into the vortex of limitations and negativity that hinders us and prevents us from achieving our desired lives; this is the' bubble.'

Since most people are consumed in this' bubble' in Western societies, whether they are aware of it or not, most of them are constantly trying to fit into it. In other words, most of us are in a constant battle to meet the demands of a society that seems to live in the dark to avoid the judgment of others. We become so attached to external influences in our attempt to fit into the' bubble' that we lose touch with our inner world; our sense of self. And, why do we get stuck in the' bubble' and how do we get confined exactly?

First, let's talk about how we tend to get sucked into this limitation ' bubble.' An example of how we're trying so hard to' fit in' is the' celebrity-driven' society we've created; we've turned celebrities into' God-like people' we seem to worship.It's like we're always using the lives of those in the media spotlight (celebrities) to fill a void in our own lives. If we watch or read about the' juicy gossip' about celebrities ' lives, we should tell ourselves "Who cares?"; then, we should try to serve our own lives so that we don't need to know their ins and outs.

Part of the' fitting in' they do in response to this fascinated' celebrity' community in which we exist is that we influence their attitude and appearance, as demonstrated in society. For example, if celebrities show a certain type of dress, the audience can pick it up immediately. Consequently, this new fashion style displayed by celebrities becomes the latest fashion trend, simply because we tend to follow whatever style most people consider the latest trend to fit in.

Additional evidence of how external influences negatively affect us is that we find it increasingly difficult to accept and love our bodies. For example, in an attempt to create the' perfect' body, many women become so insecure that they resort to plastic surgery. There are many types of cosmetic surgery, such as surgery on the chin, cheek, and nose. Further cosmetic surgeries will be made available in the future, but this will only be because there is demand. So why are so many people unhappy with their bodies that they are willing to undergo such drastic procedures to change themselves?

As we watch television programs, advertisements, films, magazines, and newspapers, we tend to compare ourselves to the models and celebrities we see negatively; this is one of the main reasons that so many people suffer from low self-esteem. Their self-esteem deteriorates so much for many teenage girls and boys that they cannot see themselves in a good way. Serious issues of self-esteem can then lead to mental illnesses such as anxiety or eating disorders such as anorexia or bulimia.

They usually fail to notice the reality that by using make-up and skilled modeling or air-brushing, these individuals they want to' feel like' are often made to look' normal.' We should remember that if we constantly compare ourselves with the media's pictures of' perfection' then our self-confidence will suffer.

If we allow external influences to control us, as many of us do, then our self-esteem will be destroyed by society, hence the low self-esteem epidemic we have. What this means is that if we create insecurity and allow it to make us better then we will be constantly trying to meet society's demands just so that we can' fit in' with it. It's pitiful, to say the least, that we're trying so hard to fit into this' bubble' that society seems to live in. When we're trying to' fit in,' what we're doing is getting approval from others, and as we're doing this, we get even more to worry about, so we're judging ourselves even harder. As this cycle continues, the more we deteriorate our self-esteem and become more self-conscious.

So, those people who live in this' bubble' will constantly try to change themselves to fit the profile they think other people expect from them, so they will spend a lot of their time worrying about others ' opinions. People who are worried about what others think of them will rely on others ' approval to feel good about themselves; therefore, they are depriving themselves of true happiness. If we have to depend on others ' acceptance to feel good about ourselves then we have negative beliefs somewhere within ourselves, otherwise, we would feel good about ourselves irrespective of others ' opinions.

Therefore, the more we stay in the 'bubble,' the more pessimistic we establish attitudes, and the more constrained we are-if we don't trust in ourselves and our wishes, then we will struggle to achieve something. Many people caught up in this 'bubble,' who generally refer to it as 'truth,' would consider anyone with strong values, aspirations, and goals as getting their heads in the clouds. Some might also claim that those people who live with optimistic hopes and enthusiasm are those who reside in the 'bubble;' this is because positive expectations, ideals, optimism, and high ambitions are all beyond. The irony, however, is that these people are the ones who live in the 'bubble' without positive expectation and optimism; they live with such limitations that they believe they have no control over their own lives.

This is a short excerpt from my book:' Living in the Moment,' which explains how to avoid being drawn into the 'bubble.' It also provides the tools and principles to build or prevent you from losing your self-esteem.

In short, don't let anyone tell you your goals, dreams, and desires can't be achieved. Generally speaking, when someone can't see how your objective can materialize and fail to do it on their own, they're going to try to convince you why you can't do it either; they're simply contrasting your aim with their restricting values. You can achieve anything you want as long as you believe in yourself and what you are trying to accomplish; the key to happiness, fulfillment, and success is belief and positive expectation.

Sexualization of self-esteem & girls

Throughout the life of a person, self-esteem as well as trust is critical. They are sometimes indefinable elements to bring both happiness and success. Often individuals with LD are vulnerable to attacks on their self-worth feelings. Luckily, they will be able to build the kind of self-esteem in any given environment with the appropriate help or support to gain potential achievements.

Nowadays, the news (including Tv, films, video journal, Twitter, advertising, or even lyrics) show woman representations (meaning all people, females in a very sexual way) with exposed clothing, attractive body posture, and facial expressions. And why do you know? They are presented to imitate women or girls as models of womanhood.

Let's dig into women's sexualization and problems of psychological health. The APA (American Psychological Association) came up with a special task force in response to reports from psychologists, journalists, child support organizations, and parents to take a closer look at these issues. And the Task Force report concluded that such sexualization of women (especially young girls) is a wide-ranging and ever-increasing issue. It is also harmful to girls ' self-image. The same goes for their well-being.

Sexualization is the occurrence of the value of an individual derived solely from its sex appeal and behavior. However, this is to the exclusion of their other features. The person is therefore sexually objectified (i.e. considered or transformed into something for the sexual use of others).

That report said the sexualization instances can be found in virtually all kinds of media. Moreover, since both the creation and access to the media of the' new media' has turned out to be omnipresent, you can see more examples of this.

The study further claimed that sexualization has adverse effects on a wide range of realms such as behavioral and emotional health, mental or physical health, and sexual development. The analysis has indicated that women's sexualization has negative effects on the willingness of a woman to develop a healthy sexual self-image.

You should allow adolescent girls to solve their problems so that they can make good choices. You should also avoid telling them constantly what they should do. Instead, they should be persuaded to find solutions to their problems. And it helps to follow some discipline to teach the kids. Do not control in a way that intimidates and/or humiliates the children.

Building Self Esteem For Women: Explode Your Success

Being a girl is incredible and empowering, even though we may lack self-esteem. This ranges from past relationships to continually being put down, there are many reasons for it. We understand how much it hurts to have low self-worth and need help. It should not be difficult to build self-esteem for women; it will be fun and empowering.

It is possible to achieve self-esteem for women in 3 simple steps. First, we tend to outline who we tend to want to become, second, we tend to decide what we want to achieve, and finally, we tend to have to create an arrangement that will build up our self-worth and make it easier for us to achieve objectives.

Let's start to change our lives.

Step 1: Definition

Let's consider why building self-esteem is vital before we begin to build it. Self-esteem is a word thrown around a heap, but it means quite a few things. For a person of high self-worth, it could mean turning into a rich person, whereas for many women it could mean having the arrogance to travel for that job that you have always wanted.

The best way to define what self-worth means is to think about successful ladies embodying high self-esteem. When you think about this, all that matters may be that it suggests something to you.

Write down all the positive traits that this particular individual embodies once you have an individual in mind. There are growing responses to attributes such as self-confidence and commitment.

We tend to get an image of who we want to want to be; this is the source of high self-esteem for us.

We tend to want to appear at what we tend to want to achieve now.

Step 2: Dreams

With Deadlines Is there anything you've ever wanted to achieve, though you didn't think you could?

Is there anything you've been told you might not want to do?

If you answered yes to the questions above, you're in the majority of women. Write down everything and anything in your life you want to know. Remember, no boundaries exist. The only border that we tend to have are those that we tend to impose on ourselves!

If you want a high-level organization to become CEO, write it down. Write it down if you desire to run a marathon. Whether or not you think you're going to be willing or not to do any of this stuff is meaningless because we continue to tackle that next problem.

Keep in mind setting your dream a deadline. This makes it specific and that's what your brain loves! Will self-improvement imply more money for women?

Self-improvement is described as improving one's personality, skills, reputation, or character through one's actions, and prosperity is defined as a large amount of money, valuable possessions, properties, or other resources.

But is self-improvement leading to richness? As a Certified Public Accountant who has dealt in money and wealth, and a person who has been on a journey of self-improvement for many years, I noticed that this does not necessarily mean that I immediately have the level of wealth that I want.

Why is it?

Is it limiting convictions?

I've heard it said many times that the main culprit is to limit deep-seated beliefs about money and wealth in our subconscious minds, such as money was not spoken of at a home or a negative subject when it grew up.

Cash, money, or the rich is viewed as ungodly, filthy, and cruel.

Feelings of indignity and unworthiness because of low self-esteem.

They do not believe that they are smart or sufficiently educated.

There's never enough to believe.

Believing the Bible is saying that money is evil.

These limiting beliefs can be held by anyone, and there are many known techniques (i.e. EFT) to clear or eliminate them.

The Special Problem for many women, when it comes to building capital, there is a unique problem that can only be what stops them from prosperity. Let me explain it to you.

Although women now have the most freedom we've ever had in history, most of us haven't embraced financial freedom to build the life of our dreams. Why is it?

That way we are raised!

Traditionally, women are raised to automatically expect that others (i.e. marriage, inheritance) can take care of our economic well-being in every way.

For this reason, most women are not taught how to build their wealth or even think about learning it on their own.

But that way we don't stay!

However, more and more women are becoming the head of the household due, among other reasons, to widowhood, divorce, single parenting, job loss of the male head of house due to illness or layoff, and lack of child support from an ex.

Building wealth is vital not only to enjoy life now but later in life to avoid poverty.

Self-improvement may not necessarily lead to wealth, but it may lead you to uncover the things that keep you from consistently having, creating, building, and maintaining wealth.

So, if you're a woman on a journey of self-improvement, and despite your best efforts, your wealth doesn't improve, consider this inherent belief that you're going to be taken care of. Maybe it's just what holds you out of the riches you need.

Self-esteem set up for Success

Now we begin to understand who we want to be and what we need to know we must build a set-up for success. They are thinking about positive self-esteem affirmations. Creating women's self-esteem helps us to conquer all challenges to our life to pursue something we want.

"I can be 100 times more important than IQ" Way back in the 60's just before Woodstock, you've had this chart-topper called "Good Vibrations" by the Beach Boys. The song goes like "Taking good vibrations; it gives me excitement." Good vibrations are always closely linked to self-esteem. They mean a good attitude towards life that is optimistic.

Before I take the three steps to build a self-esteem reservoir, let's stop for a moment and look at the coin's flip side. We're living in a world with repeat spin where the Popeye mentality rules, "I yam how You Yam."Bombarded by a million images on television and the internet all geared at convincing you how you should feel? What you should wear and what you should do to get ahead? How to get a better boyfriend when leaving the existing one or how to get better sex? You're like Claire (on a Claire Day) or Maeve (on Just Friends) at the end of the day.

Be confident is the first step to regaining your self-esteem. But it's said more easily than done. You've got to work on it. Positive thinking doesn't ignore reality. Although bad things can happen to people who are positive and negative, there is a tendency for the gung-ho types to make the best out of a bad situation.

In his book, A Primer in Positive Psychology, Dr. Christopher Petersen says that there are demonstrable advantages in being optimistic and adds that it is linked to a positive mood as well as good morality, good health, effective problem-solving skills, and even stress-free. It is ruinous to be pessimistic. It leads to low self-esteem which, through high levels of anxiety, stress, depression, jealousy, relationship break-ups, and an inability to think positively, will manifest like some hydra-headed alien. Negative thinking means negative vibrations. Remember the theory of chaos and the flapping of the butterfly in South America and the Australian tsunami! Effortlessly, your negative vibrations will spread, causing people to shy away like a salted snail.

The second key is that emotional security can't be purchased at any price. It's from the inside. You are confronted by other people's sometimes toxic diatribe against the universe, other people like yourself, and if you are unwilling to deal with it, you may end up living in a state of suspended madness. Or better still, by "training to be self-sufficient with the insufficiency of stuff," you could quietly step back like some Jedi knight to cope with these "interruptions." To be content with your way of being. It doesn't say you're starting to look like a frump, or you're going to plant... But be good with yourself, and several notches go up in your self-esteem.

Be Strong and Trust in Your Dreams Rudyard Kipling's third secret is concealed inside the section of a poem: "Only the holder sees;/ Where the ringdove broods/ And the badger lies at ease/ Once upon a time there was a path through the forest." It brings you back to being confident about the environment around you and yourself. Remember that the road to building your self-esteem is not without minor potholes, but there will certainly be no kind white-haired gentleman reaching behind his neck, removing his backbone, and using it as a wide-sword against you. It's just in the movies. You need to determine what you want in life and then go for it, no matter what others say or do to dissuade you because it's not your life. I always say you've got one shot of life on earth, so do the best. Don't let anyone hinder your self-fulfillment and stop you from doing so. And most notably, never bow down to those around you and give up on your vision of self-fulfillment.

All you have to do is trust in yourself and your wishes.

If you're a woman and believe you're not good enough or at least you've had thoughts along those lines then you're not alone because thoughts or feelings of indignity are the most common of all the Western world's negative emotions. You might have assumed that you were special, you might have figured that you were all alone and that it is only you who are trapped in a life of misery while everyone else is happy and enjoying everything that life has to offer. I'm not afraid; you're no different from almost everybody else.

The killer of women's self-esteem "I'm not great enough" is just as common in men. There are subtle differences, but there are the same' feelings.' These feelings of indignity are the greatest saboteur of a happy life that exists and are inflicted on themselves. The "I'm not good enough" mentality can ruin every effort you try to better yourself. It will only encourage you to enter a condition you embrace, but once you go past your boundaries it will take you right back into line. Typical feelings are "I'm getting ahead of myself," "You're kidding yourself." "You're a joke, and besides that, you're also ugly."

"Grow up, take a grip, face it... You've got to settle for less. "Harsh words but they're thought of by women all over the world. The biggest adversary is the person looking at us in the mirror every morning and we're punishing ourselves' mercilessly' every day for the perceived shortcomings. We live in a fantasy land of' if only' where fulfillment can only be achieved in fame or fortune, and where cash (or better body stuff) is going to be found.

You can only increase self-esteem for women (and men) by being grateful for what is already being given to you. It's a job inside and can only be fixed from within. What you look like, whose arm you are on or what you own is a worthy pursuit, but if you're inward' loathing yourself,' then nothing will bring you happiness.

Look inside and hug each other. "If you don't love yourself first, how can anyone love you?" You are who you are and you can't be anyone else. Begin by acknowledging that and see all the special things that make you, you, about you.

Pay attention to what makes you special and be grateful that you have it. There's plenty to be happy for, but while you're gazing at what's bad instead of what's good for you, you won't see anything. Look for your curiosity, it's there and it's going to reveal itself... All you need to do is look and find it abundantly.

We're both facing problems at some point in our life. Unfortunately, it seems that most people don't know how to let them go, and even though the source of their problems may be long gone, they hang on to them.

Tap into Your Feminine Power By Putting Your Needs First.

Waves your self-esteem when you see females that seem to be flawless? Women and girls often receive media images that are brushed with air. Would you like to fall further into the hypothetical bed just by staring at those ideal models?

Or maybe you're ignoring some news correlation, and suffer low self-esteem from the images you picked up in your family environment. Did you want a girl from your parents? Have you been valued? You're an awkward teen? Are you a stressed-out mother who ends up putting herself and her needs? Are you a manager who allows her colleagues to dump on her their extra workload?

You can turn your self-esteem around whatever the cause, and whatever the situation you find yourself in. Just like any muscle in the body, in no time will the right coaching program strengthen your self-love, confidence, and trust.

Some self-esteem growth suggestions are:

1. Note all the negative messages you have about yourself, your body, your value, your potential, and limitations-and determine where they came from. Keep in mind that some messages may have been absorbed at an unconscious level, i.e. we may have picked up patterns of self-esteem from our moms or other females at home.

Go burn the list now and never look back.

2. Create a new chart-full of all the best traits, observations, talents, and comments. Love yourself !

Every day, read this list.

3. Build a list of your top goals and take everyday baby steps. Think of your career goals, finances, hobbies, spiritual development.

4. Choose to reflect every day on the positive aspects of yourself and others, and don't personally take any criticism. Your new positive outlook might upset those stuck in the dumps, so stay focused on your positive feelings and don't get attached to the trash of someone else.

5. First of all, put yourself!

Yeah, you've read it right.

Women are often conditioned to be the support person, whether it's for their husband, kids, or manager, or all of the above.

Drop the label' martyr' and first place your happiness and needs. Be aware of your body by feeding healthy food and taking care of the needs of your body. Choose to focus on healthy eating benefits rather than the pain and punishment associated with dieting yo-yo.

Be emotionally conscious by doing fun and fulfilling things for you. Do not agree to do something with which you are not 100% happy, or cancel your plans to accommodate others. In a relationship, compromise is good, but not at the expense of your happiness, and not if it is a familiar habit of giving in.

So, for the sake of goodness-sometimes deprive yourself! You're worth it.

By developing your connection with what you believe in, be spiritually aware. Take time to relax and recharge your batteries in nature. Nourish your soul with love, peace, and beauty.

It is not an act of selfishness to put your needs first, but rather healthy self-love and respect. She commands respect and appreciation when a woman puts her needs first. If you have old patterns of giving in, thinking about other people's needs, denying any fun and pleasure to yourself-did those feelings make you feel good? Have you felt resentful and disliked?

You only feed your spirit when you give yourself, but you fill the reservoirs of your love and love others as well.

Low self-esteem can have an impact on your productivity; lack of trust can have a harm your business and personal relationships, thus impeding your life success.

Strengthening your self-esteem and trust can help you realize and empowering you, moving your pursuit of life-long success. Read on to learn three ways to add to your self-esteem and confidence.

Confidence relates to a state of trust, either that a theory or observation is accurate or that, given the circumstances, a course of action chosen is the right or most successful.

Confidence in themselves, and lack of it, is what prevents people from working firmly on what they want to achieve. It's their greatest UN-motivator that little power of speech telling them they can't do something.

What can you do to gain trust?

You have to be aware of who you are and who you are. There's no point moving on from here until you're branding it in your heart and soul that you're made in fear and wonder. You are the workmanship of God created in Him's image.

1. Face Your Fear: Are you afraid of something? Face it in total. It's a great way to boost your faith to do something frightening to overcome fear. So go on, hop out of that plane (with, of course, a parachute), ride the vehicle, chat to a big crowd, request for a raise, or whatever scares you. Once it's over, you should feel amazing. Embrace II Timothy1:7 God didn't give us a spirit of fear.

2. Enjoy Yourself: The Bible tells us to enjoy each other as they respect each other. With most of our relationships, could this be the problem, we don't love ourselves?

This may take some practice, and it looks really funny, but try it, it works. Give yourself a big hug when you wake up. Do the same when it's sleep time.

A million times before you heard this saying: "How can you expect others to love you if you don't love yourself?" It's true. Practice two weeks of morning and evening hugs, maybe three weeks if you're the stubborn guy, and you'll see how well it works.

3. Eliminate excuses: It's influential to resist the urge, if only mentality, to practice the comparison. In short, exculpate why you might have, ought to have. It might sound like the following; if the only.

The above two words have caused the following sound familiar to shattered dreams, broken relationships, missed opportunities, etc. If only I had more money, if only I could dance, if only I had such and such an education, if only I was thinner, if only I could gain more weight, if only I had such and such an education.

What do you know? Life is short and dwelling on if only scenarios are too short. If you can adjust it or make it better... All you do is do it. If you don't recognize what is and welcome your life's moments. Live, live, live, and live! Don't come with the final statement to the last days of your life. I could have lived a life that was good and full. If that's all.

How to Evade Low Self-Esteem

Myth: On the other side of the fence, the grass is greener.

Don't fall for the hype of what you see on a person's outside because the inner workings of that person might be awful.

Low self-esteem is one of the biggest reasons why we're not the successful people we've all dreamed of being. A key player in self-destruction is low self-esteem. Low self-esteem is a combination of a lack of self-worth, care, and understanding of the individual.

Have you ever found that the happiest people are a person who takes care of himself by organizing their spiritual values, eating well, and arranging their life to be successful? It's not a matter of money or prestige making them content, it's because they value themselves. They understand their value because they know how much time and effort they put in themselves.

Here's an example, many women think a woman is stuck up or a diva who has an agenda for herself. Sadly, this is far from the facts more than probably. A woman who takes time to work on her spiritual and mental well-being and her physical appearance tends to be too busy to get overly involved in destructive acts such as running behind a man who doesn't care about her. As she cherishes who she is, this woman knows her value. She looks forward to this one chance to live life.

Your psychological system starts with low self-esteem. How are you feeling about yourself? Do you constantly compare yourself to someone else who wanted you to be or looked like them? The media also constantly displays unreasonable images that many people are trying to accomplish. Fast success stories, hyped stars and airbrushed bodies are brought before us as a target continually. Self-esteem and pride are negatively affected when we don't meet those targets.

How can we fight these negative feelings to avoid falling into a stupor of low self-esteem?

Some few things to consider here:

1. Do you know the value of yourself?

How much effort are you investing in changing yourself? You're headed for trouble if you constantly buy things thinking that will make the change in your self-esteem. It's all accumulating things. You must be the change you want to see.

2. Create your agenda.

Keeping active is going to do wonders for your self-esteem. Getting out trying new things and being adventurous creates character and you start learning how wonderful you are.

3. Say makeup phrases to yourself as you gaze through the mirror.

Daily reminders are great ways of building up your self-esteem. Look through your favorite features to consider something nice to say about the favorite features of your rent. Accepting the discrepancies between us is what makes us so desirable can help you gain further respect.

4. Speak and look to others for the better, no matter how pessimistic they may be.

If you can find a negative person's positive side, we can see your positive side. Positive energy to low self-esteem is Kryptonite.

While for low self-esteem there is no one fast solution, there are many steps we can take to stop it as much as possible. Build and commit to a vision for yourself. Give your spiritual and personal well-being special attention, and eat a healthy diet. Ultimately, in the optimistic, just talk and think. No one needs a negative person from being around. Life is hard enough to make things worse by a dreary negative person.

And stop thinking someone else's life is so much better than yours based on what you see from the outside.

Actionable Exercises to Build confidence and maintain self -esteem

A report showed that women were speaking at least once a day about negative thoughts regarding their bodies and themselves. Imagine, that's at least 364 different bad thoughts about yourself and your body. So why some women suffer from low self-esteem and low self-confidence is no big wonder.

Society is setting a very high standard for women. Women should look to be considered beautiful in a particular way. To be considered successful, women must meet a certain level of achievement. Women should be able to handle their family and career-simultaneously. With too many expectations and such high standards, it is no wonder that if one of these standards is not met, some women feel so bad. Practice any self-esteem activities if you want to prevent your faith from falling down the drain.

Here are some activities in self-esteem with which you can start.

1. First of all, positive thoughts! Did you wake up and get a bombardment of questions and worries? These negative thoughts have an impact on how you think about the day and how you feel. The best thing to do is try to reflect at first when you wake up about something good. If you can't do that, at least try to keep your mind quiet. Focus on a blank wall or window and for a few seconds try not to think of anything. Then when you did that and blocked all negative thoughts completely, say something positive about yourself, or your day, or anything.

2. Pep Talk in the Mirror Bathroom-You can't expect others to love you all the time and tell you the great things about all. It's your job. You're your cheerleader and there's nothing like a strong pep talk in front of the bathroom mirror if you want to continue your day brimming with confidence. Ask yourself what you want to know and what you need to learn. Encourage yourself and convince yourself that you can do it whatever it is.

Look at yourself and don't dwell on the "ugly" stuff you say, but focus on the good things. You've got lovely faces. You've got lovely lips. You've got a lovely grin. Reflect on what's great, not what you feel is evil.

3. Stay away from your "Free-enemy"-this may be tough as you see her as a mate. You have to remember, however, that if you want to protect your self-esteem, you need to make sure you're not surrounded by people who put you down just so they can feel good about themselves. A frenemy is not usually someone who criticizes you and takes you down. You have to remember that you also have true friends who are there for you and who, no matter what will tell you the truth. These are mates you can respect, but keep away from people who put you down and make you feel bad for yourself, even about small things.

If you have high self-esteem, how do you know?

Ever wondered why in life you're not achieving everything you want? You think something is lacking, but you don't understand what it is? Do you feel you could do more or do more, yet be afraid to take action? There are many explanations why you lose progress and don't get what you want in life. Have you ever felt it might be that without you knowing your self-esteem has sunk to rock bottom? That life events are having a toll is incredible. So if in the last couple of years you've experienced life challenges like divorce, bereavement. Illness, stressful work, negative people may have destroyed your self-esteem. It can be a long backward cycle with things chipping away from your positivity and slowly breaking you down. The fantastic thing about it is that you can easily overcome low self-esteem. I understand because I've done it. Awareness is the first move.

If you have low self-esteem, how do you know? What you think about yourself is always down to. Do you have low self-esteem? In most situations, do you lack confidence? Do you tell yourself constantly that you're useless, stupid, you can't do things? What is your negative self-talk? Are you afraid to make decisions? There are many reasons for low self-esteem and hopefully, once you have recognized what it is, there are many avenues to boost it again so you can conquer the low self-esteem and feel confident again.

Consider some possible causes of low self-esteem.

- Should you look into your appearance?

- Putting the needs of other citizens before your own?

- Do you place your principles at risk?

- Perhaps you don't know what's important to you?

Will people cross the lines frequently and for fear of upsetting them, will you say nothing? This is a certain sign of low self-esteem and self-worth.

The individuals around you also affect your view of yourself. How do you see your parents? Should they motivate you and put you down?

You are in the right place if you want to feel good about yourself and boost your trust so you can manage anything that occurs. My passion in life is to share the lessons I learned from my life's experiences so that you can avoid making the mistakes I made.

I have restored my confidence and faith in life to such a degree that I am now operating my own company and building a wonderful life to serve. It wasn't always like that, however. I hit rock bottom more than ten years ago after a second IVF attempt contributed to a life-threatening ectopic pregnancy. I slowly pulled myself back together with enormous support from my wonderful family and friends. It took, however, the toll on my marriage that finally ended in divorce. I felt a complete failure as a woman with no children of my own and no husband.

Have you ever witnessed life-changing events you didn't want? In a job you dislike, are you stressing out? Have you adjusted your whole life to what other people want? Were you surrounded by low self-worth people? Does your self-esteem suffer so much of a hammering that you don't know you have low self-esteem?

Realizing you have low self-esteem can be quite a revelation and can fully explain what's going on in your life about the results you don't get. When you realize that you can switch it! Consciousness is the key. It's almost like putting a label on something, helping you make sense of the situation, and allowing you to act.

Once you diagnose which areas cause the problem, you can make improvements, including how you feel about yourself.

Here's a questionnaire for self-assessment to get you started. It is always best, to be honest with yourself to get the most out of it with any questionnaire.

- Should you worry about your effect on others positively or negatively?

- Do you ever anticipate what others might think of you when you communicate?

- How does pressure show up for you?

- If you are anxious, do you control your stress levels?

- When are you feeling most confident about yourself?

- When are you feeling confident at least?

- Should you feel self-conscious at times?

- Would you feel comfortable with your appearance?

- Which do you know more about: your strengths or weaknesses?

- Do you feel strong? If so, when will it be?

- Are you conscious of your inner criticism?

- When are you feeling the best you can?

- Once you speak, plan yourself intellectually, physically, and emotionally?

- Do you focus when communicating with the other person or people?

The introduction of yourself to the world begins with how you think for yourself. Answering these questions will help you understand if and where changes need to be made.

The connection between Self-Esteem and Success /Achievement

Success for many different people can mean many things. It might mean having a happy home and being a mom who is caring and compassionate. As a missionary, it might be traveling the world without a penny to your name. Or it might imply being a corporate tycoon in Ireland's hills with skyscraper headquarters, a support home, and a palace.

No matter what success means for you, your self-esteem is fundamental to reaching where you want to go. Indeed, self-esteem determines if you are going to enjoy success or not.

The catalyst for action is self-esteem, including making decisions. It's your view about yourself and how you blend into the universe, as well as how you think other people perceive you. If you have lowered self-esteem in one or more areas of your life, it also implies you will have lost confidence in those fields.

Self-confidence is based on behavior guided by your capacity and self-esteem's beliefs. If you don't believe your self-esteem to be able to do an action, you won't take action. You can't build your trust muscle act. And confidence is built over time, taking little steps, then anonymous steps, until you feel completely confident in meeting a role or activity's expectations.

Let's say you're dreaming of being a mom staying at home and raising three kids. You want them to be directed, nurtured, trained, and cherished. But let's pretend you were a single child and never really had close contact with babies or children.

Pretend that you are invited to the party of a neighbor to mark the birthday of her two-year-old. You're coming and everywhere there are kids. Someone is telling you to carry her child and the kid is crying her head off instantly. You're trying to calm her down, but it's no use, and the mother comes back and snatches the child out of your hands as if you'd grab it or something. Then you're trying to help all the children eat the dessert at the table and a little boy spits his food on you. "I hate you," he snarls.

However, an adult with kids will know the baby was just freaking out because she didn't know you... you didn't smell right and she wanted her mother! Let's just claim the little boy spits on everybody and you're no different.

But there's no training you want. So how do you feel it might impact your self-esteem? You might be sad to abandon the crowd, now thinking all the kids hate you. In your mind, you would probably go over and over it. You'd be persuaded after a while that you're bad with children. Why can you go to the man who wants children tomorrow with your wedding? You're going to be a complete disappointment.

Regardless of the situation, by silencing the NEGATIVE self-talk and finding the reality, you will resolve low self-esteem.

Ask:

1. In this scenario. Would you hate all the kids? No. No. No. You have had two short encounters that can be described quickly.

2. You're going to be a terrible mother? There is no correlation between parenting experience and ability.

3. How are you changing the low self-esteem that your psyche has now gripped? Positive, reality-based self-talk.

a. Thought: I want a family and I want to be a wonderful mom.

b. Action: Ask your children's friends if you can hang out. Ask questions from them. Slowly and quietly address the kids like you'd treat a puppy you don't recognize. Or, allow them to come to you. Bring a small toy and just sit down and play with it on the floor. No child can resist joining you. Build trust in small steps.

c. Learn: To have a way with kids is often about patience, creativity and your ability to redirect them to positive activities when they go to negative ones. All you need is the positive experiences of people who can show you and direct you.

Negative self-discussion is detrimental to self-esteem. The only cure is optimistic and constructive self-talk, reinforcing acts that disprove what the pessimistic voice says.

87.9 percent of all people suffer from decreased self-esteem in one area of their lives or another, according to recent studies. You are not alone, so falls are not a negative thing to hide or cover in self-esteem; they are good opportunities to grow and thrive.

Women's self-esteem For Stress Reduction, Balance, and Autonomy

It has been found that self-esteem is the common denominator of many women's issues in working with women for decades. Females are more able to find equilibrium, manage stress, and assert their independence with better self-esteem.

Universally, women are considered inferior to men, and while our culture is changing, most women are suffering from impaired self-esteem, including successful women. Our relationships with others and our relationship with ourselves are influenced by self-esteem. Self-care, parenting, boundaries, and communication are affected. Self-esteem defines how we encourage others to relate to us, including our children, and how we accept and express our desires, thoughts, and feelings. It supports personal integrity, our ability to pursue goals, and is essential for effective parenting. A mother may praise her child and try to give her self-esteem, but if she is low, it will inevitably be revealed in her behavior, and children will learn most through emulation.

Balance is a women's ongoing struggle. As individuals, caregivers, earners and professionals, finding a balance between our male and female sides, spiritual and material, work and family personal needs and those of our employers, children, parents, and partners require self-esteem and autonomy, not to mention time, which is always too little. Instead of understanding how much they do, women are typically self-critical of not accomplishing enough at work as wives, homemakers, sisters, or in their private pursuits. They feel guilty if they don't meet the expectations of their own and others. The fact is that there is not enough time and energy to go around, but it makes all the difference in how we think about it and allocates our resources.

Women are used to working and taking care of children as they bake, wash, or talk on the phone. Working moms have increased pressure and making time for themselves is a bigger challenge for them. 55 percent of mothers (63 percent of college-educated moms) are working with infants, according to the latest census. Of mothers who are less than 45 years of age without infants, 72% are employed. After a stressful day practicing law, when I returned home to my children, I would park my car outside my house for ten minutes to meditate before going in. It helped me to concentrate on time and adapt to parenting. Self-esteem makes it possible for women to practice self-care and manage these conflicting expectations, reducing stress, and empowering them to be responsive with their loved ones and any task at hand.

To reduce stress and find a balance, setting boundaries is vital. The dilemma of feeling guilty plagues women when they say "no" or resentful when they don't. They are concerned about the loss of the relationship or the esteem of the person. Loss of relationships is women's greatest stressor, as is men's failure. It takes self-esteem to feel comfortable setting boundaries. They are more able to claim their autonomy when women value themselves. Autonomy is a feeling of independence and wholeness that helps us to feel independent when we are in a marriage and total when we are alone. Many women complain that when they are alone they do great, but they lose themselves as soon as they are in a relationship or the presence of their partner. Some abandon their hobbies, friends, careers, and pursuits of creativity. We have trouble transitioning from an enjoyable weekend to the workplace, and we can't articulate feelings to their friend or an authority figure regarding issues.

Attachment to women is paramount. Another explanation for the challenge of independence is that girls don't have to split to become adults from their parents. Femininity is characterized by proximity, according to Carol Gilligan, and female gender identification is undermined by separation. On the other side, when boys have to distinguish themselves from their mothers and bond with their parents to become adults, sexuality challenges their gender identity. *(In a Similar Voice: Women's Growth and Social Analysis, 1993, pp. 7-8).*

Codependency, the opposite of independence, is common among women. Many symptoms such as stress, addiction, domestic violence, and emotional abuse, communication problems, worry and anxiety, depression, guilt, and anger may be caused by a lack of autonomy and self-esteem. Untreated, women's health is deteriorating over time.

The self-Esteem of a Woman Leader-Self-Esteem Issues Faced by Women in Leadership

If you are a woman leader, others seek advice, wisdom, and action from you. Just being a leading woman doesn't mean that you sometimes don't face issues of self-esteem. Here are seven issues of self-esteem in leadership positions faced by many women.

1. There's a doubt. Doubting yourself as a manager is not uncommon. Doubt comes from thinking that you are not in control of the mission. Recalling that you don't have to understand everything is important. You just need to learn enough to find the information at any point you need to tackle the activities before you.

2. Projects that are not completed. It's counterproductive to your self-esteem to think like things rarely come to an end. Leadership means multitasking, but at the same time working on multiple projects can also mean having many loose ends. It is important to know when the conclusion of what you are expected to do with any plan has already been achieved. Sometimes you've done but you don't know it because you've offered someone else the final touches. You must know what it means for any task to be finished. Make a list of your projects to see what has been completed and what is not. Do what you can and pass on afterward.

3. Incomplete thoughts. It is expected that leaders will come up with ideas. Others are looking for you to tell them what to do and how to solve issues. You can think you're hopping from one

concept to another. You might probably use several of your proposals, but perhaps not the entire plan as you originally thought about it. Leadership can move quickly. Write down your thoughts. Use the portions that fit the issues at hand and save or let go of another portion of your good ideas. When you need new ideas, your creative mind will come up with new ideas.

4. Look like a fake. Has leadership come to you very quickly? You may have made a statement that was encouraging or that took the reins at the right time on an important issue, and the rest of the people voted you the ruler. If leadership quickly came to you, you might not feel up to the task or even feel you're a fake person. You don't have to stay forever in a leadership role. Complete the issue you've been given responsibility for and then move on. Build your leadership skills if you remain the leader so that you feel comfortable in the position.

5. What you need is a mentor. People in leadership often neglect the leadership resources and mentoring given to men. This can cause you to feel lonely and alone when you make decisions that affect other people's lives. Search for your mentors. It could start by reading another leader's biography and gleaning ideas for leadership. Look for your area's leaders and see if you can take her to lunch to discuss issues. To be the trainer, there are ways to approach someone, or you can seek an executive coach to help you privately.

6. Want Help. It can be a time-consuming task to be in a leadership role. Having support to do tasks and remove some of the load from your plate is important. It's terrible for your self-

esteem to be overworked and stressed out so take the leadership opportunity to do something about it. If you don't already have assistance, be proactive in selecting someone to work with you, even if they are in a volunteer position. The advantage to you is that certain jobs will help you. The value of receiving training for a future leadership position for the other guy.

7. Stressed out. Stressing yourself for long periods has affected your levels of self-esteem and trust. Leadership can be a position of stress. It is stressful to need to make a decision constantly, be in the spotlight, and have the right answers. You will need to take control of your life as a leader and consider ways to manage your time to leave sufficient space for self-care. If you don't feel about yourself, there's no one else. Step up the plate, know when to say no, and maintain high self-esteem in your health.

Being a leader means having to have strong self-esteem. Not all women in leadership need to be a strong leader in self-esteem. But you can help build your self-esteem by knowing some of the trouble areas. You're going to know how to make choices that will give you the help and mentoring you need to have good self-esteem for performance in leadership.

Women's weight loss-Most Overlooked Obstacles to self-esteem

Often women want to lose weight at some point in their lives regardless of their actual weight or size. For years and years, some of us have been seeking the aim with little or no progress at all. With a diet, exercise program, or supplement, we may have lost some weight and then put it all back on and then some more. And from then on, we start on this rollercoaster; try various diets, ingredients, exercise programs, and even some diet pills! some work and some don't, but we end up devoting a lot of time, effort, and even money to this pursuit. Eventually, we get to the point where the harder it gets, the more we try.Occasionally, even when we've let go of our body and weight obsessions and are more focused on our wellbeing, we're always trying to cut away our body's excess fat.

I want to explore some of the possible causes/reasons in this book as to why weight / fat loss seems to be quite challenging for many women. I also propose some simple specific actions that helped me to lose excess fat without restrictions, radical diets, or intense exercise routines.

The post is not intended to provide medical advice, please do discuss a health and nutrition plan with a qualified professional for any questions. The details and advice in this essay were focused on my structured Nutritional Science studies, numerous literature reviews on the subject, shared experiences with other people, and my journey resolving an eating disorder, unhealthy diet, and exercise, as well as gastrointestinal and hormonal issues.

Why sometimes our biggest weight loss challenge is our view of ourselves in the community, our confidence in appearance, the power of the press, and eventually the motivations why we want to lose weight will decide our success or failure in maintaining a healthy weight. Some common hidden reasons women want to lose weight are to be more attractive, fit in, fill emotional gaps, gain acceptance, trust, etc. Let me clarify, for several years I had low self-esteem and I assume that if I were slim, I would be more relaxed and welcomed socially. Even though I had lost a lot of weight, I still didn't feel good enough, I still didn't find my place in the world, and I still had low self-esteem. I gained some self-confidence, but it wasn't real and long-lasting, because it depended on my perception of being "skinny," it was kind of a borrowed trust, because when I put the weight on again, that trust went out of the door, leaving me right where I started.

On the other hand, I achieved much better results when I made health my priority, and first and foremost committed to healing; I was naturally more loyal to my goal. I set out on a journey of my body discovery, emotions, driving forces, etc. I discovered what I was hoping for and knew it wasn't going to give me what I needed to lose weight. I figured some other things had to be addressed first, and then there would be a weight loss. If the reasons are genuine, it's okay to want to lose weight; to have better health, to live longer, to have more quality of life, etc., understanding that when we're healthy, weight loss is easier. "What cures your body is slimming your body."

Weight-loss becomes a more nourishing and rewarding process when we become focused on the causes of why. You will have a better starting point for the next phase if you understand how.

Good digestion= Good detoxification= Better chances of fat loss
One way to assess how good your health is by looking at how good your digestion is. Good digestive function is a crucial

factor in ensuring that our body processes nutrients, absorbs what it needs, and excretes anything that does not serve us well normally and efficiently. If you have any kind of gastrointestinal disorder, however minor it may be, it is important to work first to restore normal digestive function. This should be a focus, and a diet must be formulated to restore normal gastrointestinal function before thinking about counting calories, fats, and carbohydrates. Sometimes even our exercise routine has to be adjusted to accommodate the energy levels from the intake of food when our digestion is compromised as the body may not get all the nutrition needed to support the exercise metabolism.

Stress often influences our metabolism in many respects, so when we try to fix our digestion it must be remembered, sometimes it is not the food we eat, but how and how we eat it.

If you're one of the lucky ones with a steel gut and immaculate digestion, there's one thing you have to worry about and you can start looking at the next move.

Restrictive feeding and pressure—— > elevated cortisol + decreased insulin + hormonal imbalance= more fat storage Restrictive diets with low calories or heavy activity are stressors for the skin. Nowadays, we have stress coming to us in every way, and we add more stress to our bodies by eating and exercising too much restrictively. Simply put, when we're stressed out, the last thing the body wants to do is burn fat, because the body needs to feel safe, especially in women, and if it detects any signs of hunger or danger, it's going to go into the fat-saving mode, and if the restriction is severe, it can even lower and shut down some of the body functions. Research has shown that the human body is very effective at storing fat, that's how the body was designed, and it's important to understand that so that we acknowledge it and function with it and within it instead of battling the body's existence.

The pressure is a biggie, and you've probably heard this everywhere, so I'd just like to list a few things to watch out for in this post that add a lot of pressure and stop weight loss.

Stress sabotages our efforts to lose weight through a variety of mechanisms in the body and the way the body has been designed to work.

Some common behaviors in women that signal hunger and therefore stress are constant diet, calorie counting, fasting, under-eating, going to bed hungry, over-training, the rapid loss of weight, etc. Men can usually afford their bodies a lot more abuse, but women can't afford it because we've been designed to carry children. Whether you get pregnant or not, the female body prepares to give birth to a child each month, and when hungry we place ourselves at serious risk. Our fertility, mental health, libido, skin, the health of the bone, hormones, thyroid, and sleep are all affected. We can lose the ability to burn fat as well.

The longer we starve ourselves with diets, the higher the potential for harm to our body, and the lower chances of sustained fat loss through training.

Stress also causes a decrease in the production of sex hormones that will impair muscle growth, cause the deposition of excess fat in certain areas, mood disorders, irregular and painful menstrual periods, etc. If the body is deprived of certain nutrients, it has to choose between temporarily shutting off certain processes or leeching what is needed from somewhere else in the body. This would indicate a potential catabolism/breakdown if from diet and training you are already in a catabolic condition. This puts a lot of stress on the body by asking it to provide a further breakdown to sustain itself in another area, which is just adding more stress to the system. This can manifest in muscle loss, fatigue, weakness, hair loss, thinning hair, reduced thyroid function, etc. Other sources of stress:

- Health problems require more energy and specific nutrients to enable healing. The body spends a lot of energy and resources trying to heal when we have a specific condition, especially chronic conditions such as colitis. Pain and infection are stressors for the body, they raise cortisol, signaling the body to store fat, particularly when we are pressing the body beyond its current coping capability. Before focusing on weight loss, we need to focus on providing the body with appropriate care, otherwise, we will promote further breakdown and overcompensation in the body.

- Doing too much, over-training, lack of sleep/rest I'm not sure when it became more culturally acceptable for women to be active, running like men in the industry. Jogging a full-time job, taking care of children and running a family, exercise like an athlete, dress like a fitness model, and lifting heavy weights to show strength. Don't mistake me, I'm the first to believe in women's strength and intelligence. We are the ones who can bear a child for a reason! But my question is, can all the demands I mentioned above be supported by our female biology and physiology?

I assume the response is focused on the health status of most people with highly demanding careers, professional performers, or women working full-time jobs, or more than one career, studying and working, plus running children about, sleeping short hours, and much more than many females do daily these days.

What I hear from the online women's health community recently is that many women suffer from the harmful effects of demanding lifestyles, excessive exercise, diet, and stress caused by doing more than the body can handle, and not having enough rest! In the increased incidence of amenorrhea (loss of your menstrual cycle), infertility, metabolic damage, hormonal imbalances, low energy, PMS, painful periods, low thyroid function, digestive problems, stubborn weight gain, and more, these effects show.

That said, I'm sure some women (although the minority) may be more resilient to stress than others, and there's a different level of activity for each of us that supports good health. It's about being honest with us and finding our threshold. How much can you do frankly when preserving excellent health? Because that's right! We're supposed to feel good and perform well. We can't and shouldn't drag on boosting caffeine.

Most women need to sleep for repair and detoxification at least 7-8 hours a day. Some of us need more, I'm one of them. Don't let go of your night! Sleep, and sometimes more than eating, should be a priority over-exercise.

It means different things for each of us when it comes to over-training, depending on our level of health, and even our genetics. I'm going to share with you that the phase I'm in on my healing journey; over-training is more than 30 minutes of light exercise a day! And if I push harder than that, I do my body more harm than good. One session of high-intensity interval training can leave me exhausted for a whole week, and with that type of exercise, I can notice my stress level and growing anxiety. It took me a while to realize it, and it was difficult to give up the pool, but I made a leap of faith, and eventually, I felt better cutting down.

Healthy Weight for Women

There's a lot of discussion about what's now considered a normal weight for women. Weight maps provide us with general guidelines, but a lot depends on our particular type of body. weights from a health perspective are considered normal are much higher than what the media shows as the norm.

Obesity has reached epidemic proportions in the meantime. This is an issue not because of the perception of it by society, but because it puts those who suffer from it at a much higher risk for a long list of health issues. High blood pressure, heart disease, diabetes, and cancer are some of the most notable.

So, we have celebrities and other famous people on the other side who are underweight, according to health standards. On the other hand, in our daily lives, we see more people who are seriously overweight. It's no wonder no one seems to be able to figure out what's normal!

The representations of women in the media tend to be highly misleading. The celebrities also follow a strict diet and exercise plans to remain at the weight that is appropriate to them by the business. They also have access to personal trainers, which can afford some of the rest of us.

Besides, they often undergo plastic surgery to get larger breasts, smaller noses, or more youthful looks. They also have a dedicated team when they're on a movie set or photoshoot to make sure every hair is in place and their makeup is perfect. All that attention to detail adds up to something that simply cannot be measured by the average woman, no matter how hard she tries.

For the people who follow them, these unrealistic expectations also lead to low self-esteem. That, in effect, may increase the chance for a woman or girl to develop eating disorders to achieve the perfect look. These can be a threat to one's health greater and more immediate than being overweight.

The Obesity Trend

Although it is considered unwanted by society as a whole to be overweight, an increasing number of its members are becoming obese. This is due to several factors, one of which is our busy lifestyles. We often simply don't have time three times a day to cook healthy meals, so instead, we choose fast food on the go.

Another reason cited is inactivity for the increase in obesity. This is particularly problematic for children as they spend more time playing video games and watching TV and less time participating in physical activity. But as their busy lives and often physically undemanding jobs lead to less movement, adults have also become less active.

Being "natural" is where we should aspire to be between these extremes. A good indicator of the healthiest weight for us is the Body Mass Index (BMI). It requires sex, height, the form of skin, and percentage of fat into consideration to determine what is natural for each adult.

But for some, even a healthy BMI can be cumbersome to achieve. The best thing to do is consistently eat and exercise a balanced, sensible diet. It will help us achieve our best personal weight and ensure the proper functioning of our bodies. And that's about as fine a "natural" description as one might imagine.

Steps to Build Self-Confidence

Each process of self-discovery starts with an honest assessment of where you are now, and I presented several questions in Part Two, the responses of which can act both as an index of your abilities and skills and as suggestions for strategies to boost your self-confidence.

Before I give you some steps to help build your self-confidence, I would like to point out two things. Second, the essential task of building self-confidence is that no essay or book can ever frankly do justice. A new set of skills are needed to build self-confidence. It takes time to build all skills... and persistence. Decide to give importance to building your self-confidence. Engage in it. Allow yourself to achieve this with time and consistent focus. Give yourself the support gift to keep you on track by getting a coach.

Second, we don't all begin in the same position because of our unique experiences as women. Some of you may already have a fair amount of self-confidence in reading this and want to finally blow over the barriers that prevent you from achieving the success you want. Some of you may have an acute lack of self-confidence and need more time and encouragement to reach a healthy level of self-confidence.

Here are suggestions to build your self-confidence and the secret to make it all come together:

Change yourself talk: Self-talk can range from dis empowerment to abuse. The first step of any process is to raise our awareness of what we say to ourselves. If you find yourself saying abusive words, stop right away. If you're using words like "I can't...," "I should have...," "Yes, but..." then change them to "I can or I'm on the way to...," "I'm going to... in the future," "Yes, I can do that..." Practice Daily Self Care: Tend to your daily physical, emotional and spiritual needs. Get enough rest and eat so that your health and vitality can be supported. You can find small ways to pamper yourself, even if you can't afford a lot.

Learn to take a compliment-Whenever someone gives you a compliment or acknowledgement, you just have to say two words "Thank you." Delete the clause and clarification which usually follows your thanks.

Take full responsibility in all aspects of your life we have been told to take responsibility for every thought we think, every feeling we have, every action we take , nd every result we get. Just doing this on your own incredibly strengthens your self-confidence.

Stop Explaining Yourself to Others: As girls, once we respond "no" to a query, we always feel compelled to answer. We always feel compelled to justify ourselves if somebody disagreed with what we think or do. Just because someone asks why you believe what you are doing or have done what you have done, this is no reason to explain yourself.

Stop Comparing Yourself to Others: One way you disempower yourself is to compare your achievements with others ' achievements. You are unique; there is no such thing as you. You are here in your voice to bring your unique message to the world. Revel in the fact that this cannot be achieved by anyone else and honor your individuality.

Surround yourself with encouragement and protection from those who don't have your best interests at heart-one of mutual support should be every close relationship in your life. If it is not, the amount of time you spend with that person must be considered seriously. The corollary is to express your ambitions, expectations, and thoughts with those who can help you.

There are wonderful tests out there to understand your personality style, strengths of character, and instincts. MBTI, Seligman Signature Strengths, and the Kolbe an Index are three tests that measure these facets of you.

Set goals for yourself but don't make them perfectionist, all-or-nothing goals— you can set goals for every aspect of your life... bodies, minds, and spirits... but keep them achievable and build on them incrementally.

Always put your best you forward: Always choose to look your best (and you don't need to spend a lot of money). Choose to always take the highway... speak from a place of high integrity (no gossip, no conversation behind another's back). Choose to be an outstanding reader. Choose to be good.

Now for the secret: From this moment on, behave as the self-confident person you want to be— whatever you do, wherever you go, whoever you encounter, live like and be the person you want to be, the self-confident man you expect to be. Over time, you're going to grow into and become this reality... after all, it's who you're already— you're just peeling off the layers to get to your self-confident self.

In your personal and professional life, training to develop self-confidence is important. Self-confidence is an integral part of having a positive attitude and an important tool of success is to have a trainer or teacher to help you work on your mentality.

Is Beauty or outward appearance self-esteem?

Beauty is a universal concept that is difficult to define but is understood by everyone. Body appearance appears to be appropriate standards in many cultures, although some of these norms vary from one society to another. When we are asked what is beautiful for us, we may have a hard time explaining. But, if we were to pick out a beautiful woman in a crowd, it would be easy and natural for men and women. As the saying goes, we'll know it when we see it when it comes to great beauty.

Nevertheless, not everybody admires elegance the same way. Beauty is a subjective experience. This includes the sensation of attraction and psychological well-being of the person. The saying is often here; "beauty is in the beholder's eye." Nevertheless, as culture places the general expectation on the attractiveness of females, beauty transforms into a popular perception and a standard female contrast.

So, what then is a "normal" beauty definition? My best guess is, it's the physical attributes that she exhibits if we were to talk about women. The woman can give the senses of the viewer intense pleasure or deep satisfaction. The positive feeling of pleasure or goodness of the admirer is usually derived from the body shape of the woman, the clothes she wears, or how attractive, among other things, her facial features are.

Beauty can also be about the character of the individual, however. It's about being caring and supporting people, weeping on a hand, honoring others, respecting yourself, showing love to both humans and animals, serving others, and, of course, loving yourself. This is defined by having the right dose of self-confidence and healthy self-esteem as inner beauty.

While this is usually not the first thing that comes to mind when we're talking about beauty, inner beauty plays just as important a role in how beautiful a person looks. Even more so than the elegance of the outside.

Inner beauty is not something that is said to feel better by unattractive people. Inner beauty can be as captivating as the outer appearance can be, if not more.

Inner beauty can be characterized as something perceived not by looks, but by the character of a person. It's a person's real beauty that goes far beyond just physical appearances.

It is the inward confidence of a person that they are desirable, rendering them more appealing to others. The light of confidence and visual beauty emerges from within her. Some of the most fanciful characters are not physically attractive, but they are desirable to every member of the opposite sex thanks to their radiant confidence and self-belief.

First experiences don't always rely on our visual and facial characteristics. We must believe it comes from within ourselves. That's where our real beauty lies. Originally, people can judge us when we start a conversation; as friendly and not-so-pleasant. As the conversation continues, people will begin to pick up the beautiful traits and attributes that emanate from us, and then people will begin to consider us more and more appealing and charming.

When we like, respect, and feel good about ourselves, we'd feel more confident about questioning and engaging with others. Outer beauty attracts glimpses when inner beauty lets one live. This is the secret of sound self-esteem.

Of course, we will first notice the physical appearance of a person. But when a woman has bright eyes that flicker, a smile that warms her heart, a radiant glow that surrounds her as she enters a room; she harnessed her inner beauty.

The best part of inner beauty is that, unlike our outward appearance, inner beauty with age does not wrinkle, gray, or decrease. It's only going to radiate more when we develop it.

Self-Esteem Plays a Huge Role in Personal Safety For Women

Women like being loved. Women like to win. Women like being motivated and creating a difference in the world. Women can raise a family, have a career, and make our own choices.

Nevertheless, few of us realize at the time a decision is made how much our choices are affected by our self-esteem. If you're taking a day off, there's a fair chance you're going to take that option you'd make on a day when you're feeling great with yourself.

For instance: I was talking about the partnership mistakes I made in the past. They all stemmed from my low self-esteem at the time after tracking them back to their roots. The good relationship (and I'm talking to mates, employers,and relatives as well as dates) choices I've taken seem to be focused on feeling confident.

Tracing back my good relationship decisions showed me I chose the right friends, letting go of the wrong friends, and wisely picking up my battles. These "confident day" decisions have had a dramatically different impact on my life than those made on an "off day." YOU are Most Important!

Although you probably have a bazillion things on your "To Do" list, I ask you to pay close attention to yourself before making decisions. It takes just a second. If you don't feel fantastic about yourself, think about your decision if you were, and then decide. It is similar to establishing and enforcing a clear head personal boundary.

You know that self-esteem is an inside job and we rarely do as much as we would love to think about ourselves as our loved ones think about us. The smallest off-hand comment could weaken our light if we feel vulnerable. It takes us a bit to rock when we feel strong. Sometimes, on the self-esteem roller coaster, a single day may seem like a trip. It may not seem fair, but you do not realize that you are alone.

Women have greater intuitive sensitivity, which in most situations is great and in others is detrimental. Women tend to take it more seriously than men do, and when there is always nothing there, women want to read between the lines. This is why we can be delicate in our self-esteem and why we need to take extra good care of ourselves to be there for our loved ones. This is how self-esteem plays such an enormous role in women's safety.

Ways to Help Females Overcome Lack of Confidence

Women are vulnerable to low self-esteem, according to research. Since women are said to belong to the lesser sex, they appear to be more distressed when they are struck by issues. As a consequence, as tough dilemmas come along, they seem to be more wounded, and this adds to very low self-confidence.

All of you girls out there, don't panic! Here's a post on self-help for women of all ages. If you want to change your life fast, then read these useful pieces of advice for a minute or two.

1) Receive a makeover. A lady feels good most of the time when she can sense a physical change. Call it sorcery, but a quick makeover such as a new haircut or a small change in clothing can do wonders for a woman who has trouble with her self-esteem. When a woman feels radiant with the outside shift that has happened to her, she immediately improves her self-confidence. Makeovers are women's self-help that any female can do without any difficulty. You don't need cash to have a new haircut and buy new clothes; only wear a new hair portion or use cosmetics you normally don't patronize or change your appearance subtly.

2) Surround yourself with very supportive people. Women must always have people behind them to support them in their worst

problems. A team like her girlfriends and her community that is very encouraging is enough to boost her expectations if she questions. Normally this support group encourages her to do something she knows she can't do well. In case your trust falls, this effective self-help for women should be kept in mind.

3) The media pressure should not be affected. Televisions, newspapers, posters; all these things show female models with good bodies that most men find sexy. Because of this view, many women, who are not as thin as these models, feel afraid of their bodies, preventing circumstances where they are going to face the audience. These reasons make these women in their respective jobs dysfunctional. Consider closely: many jobs require workers to address the audience or a group of people they don't even meet. When people are influenced by the world's wrong impression of appearance, they're going to think they're hideous, and as a result, they're not going to have confidence in the huge crowd. That's why ignoring beauty beliefs (as imposed by the media) is good self-help for women that should be considered good.

4) Be a cheering band of your own. Last but not least; you ought to be the first person to trust your abilities. Just in the case that everybody in the support group is busy fixing their own miserable life, you can still hear a voice cheering for you. When you believe you can do anything, you can do what you want absolutely, given how big your weight is or how upsetting your limitations are. This is the last self-help for women not to be excluded from the list of women.

Self Esteem in Teenage Girls

Self-confidence teenage girls can be a frustrating thing for many people, and in my experience, it's generally girls and women who have the most trouble with it so girls, this book is for you!

While some women's self-esteem activities may give the ideas of getting a makeover and new hairstyle, I'm going to try and get away because I found this is not building self-esteem, but a very temporary way to give you fake confidence and it's not helpful. I'm not averse to dressing up and looking nice (every woman loves to look great, of course) but it can't be the source of self-esteem and trust because it's too incoherent and circumstantial.

1) Follow the steps for happiness-as mentioned, the three phases provide the very straightforward keys to easy happiness and can be a good boost for self-esteem. These include regular exercise, regular mental exercise-that is, learning new things and challenging your mind, and frequent social interactions, of course. Make sure you do as often as you can each of these three things because these three steps alone can lead to very simple quality of happiness and trust.

2) Giving in to Social Stress — The massive social pressure placed on us in our society is a very feminine issue of self-esteem. When you glance at the tv, media, films, commercials,

newspapers, there's a very similar pattern that asks us to have a small butt or strong tits, or else we're unattractive. So fundamentally wrong is this whole social misunderstanding that I could write a whole book on it!

How a woman grows into her teenage years can sometimes be described as a tight rope walk with her self-esteem intact. Construction of self-esteem begins as a child and continues to build one step at a time on itself. If she finds herself missing her steps along the tight rope walk of self-esteem, there may be substantial falls and injury.

Keeping in mind the tight rope walk of self-esteem, how can a teenage girl or teenage daughter stay one step ahead of the other to avoid tumbling down to the ground? Is there anything that parents can do to help build self-esteem? I think the answer to these two questions is a resounding YES!

Indeed, if you're a teenage girl and you're reading this book, ask your mother or some other trusted adult to help you build self-esteem. If you're a teenage daughter's parent and you decide to read this book on your daughter's behalf in pursuit of knowledge to boost self-esteem, you've come to the right place.

Possibly the hardest step to restoring self-esteem to a healthy point. It requires total self-honesty. It is necessary to remove the disguise of deceit and false self-representation and the victim must be able to see himself as transparent and pure.

There might be some of the masks in the context of rage. Anger is a tool of protection that can be used to defend against others from seeing what is occurring inside an individual. The mask of anger is put on when the individual feels in some way threatened. The image of bravery is seen to those on the other side of the mask while, in reality, anxiety remains on the inside of the rage. There is also the uncertainty that is generated from the detection of inadequacies. The vulnerability and perceived weakness sit under the "anger mask."

Another mask might be the "class clown" mask. This mask also does a pretty good job of sending the message that a person is always laughing around. Joking around and not being professional keeps others from knowing what's going on inside is not at all amusing. It's much better to laugh at the jokes than to laugh at the person behind the class clown's mask. The mask wearer tells jokes to keep everyone laughing at those rather than her as a person to avoid being perceived as a "joke."

The "Pollyanna mask" is also available. Such masks trap everyone on the other hand in a constant desire to be as good as she is always so nice and kind as she is. Pollyanna never makes mistakes and it always looks like everything is going right with her. She is often the sickest of all of us in all reality. She is far from being flawless behind her mask and holding the character too good keeps her from developing real relationships. No one knows who the perfect Pollyanna-miss is, not even herself.

The "over-realizer," "workaholic," "cleanaholic," "committeeaholic," "schoolclubaholic," etc. masks are all very close. These are the people who engage in things over and over because the busier they are with their time, the less time they have to spend on their own. These mask wearers hide behind their business to keep others focused on their hard work and activity involvement rather than on the deficiencies within themselves. We can try to prove to everyone that they are deserving and that they can be someone people consider as significant or intelligent. We also force themselves into a state of emotional collapse in their efforts to erase the wrongs in their history. It's difficult to wear the shell of "everyone can count on me" and to be all things for everyone.

Girls and women put on a mask called the "beauty mask." This mask disguises the many flaws lying under the brand clothes of the make-up and name. Ultimately, no amount of eyeliner and mascara can hide what the eyes say. They say, "I want you to believe I'm beautiful on the outside because if you saw what I looked like below, you wouldn't think I was beautiful at all." Hiding behind the fabulous outfits, fancy beads, earrings, and make-up "beauty mask" is a shallow shield against the truth that cries out "I want to love myself, but I don't!" Help your teenage daughter to discover and name the mask she may wear to improve self-esteem. When you look close enough, you may even notice that you're wearing and having a similar mask in the past. The road to building self-esteem can be a journey that you can take together. As I said before, the first step is the hardest because it calls for honesty and the mask to be removed.

The great smiles of teenage girls are not fooled by techniques to improve self-esteem for teenage girls experts on facial expressions. It's obvious when a girl is really happy inside because she's got a "Duchienne smile." The involuntary muscles around her eyes are wrinkled with this smile. And there's no lie in those muscles.

On the other hand, only a smiling mouth is revealed by fake, superficial smiles, there is no twinkle and no wrinkle. Looking at many of the images of today's magazines where the girls sometimes show with depressed eyes fake smiles. BUT this is not noticeable by teen girls. We concentrate on the perfect figure, eyes, hair, and smooth picture that has been airbrushed. Instead, we want to imitate the MYTH of fulfillment, alas.

Dr. Linda Miles has been struggling with such problems for over thirty years as a psychotherapist. She has also addressed this subject on national radio and television numerous times. He has a desire to support "de-program the misconceptions" in our queen system of attractiveness for girls and women.

She purchased herself as a student at Leon High in Tallahassee, Florida, with create identities. Faye Dunnaway talks about her experience at the same school in her memoir, where the worth was dependent on your looks and money. Interestingly, both Faye Dunnaway and Dr. Miles became "famous" and won competitions of attractiveness, yet they both understood that joy was being faked.

Dr. Miles dedicates her work to her 12-year-old granddaughter, Merritt, in hopes of helping her to keep smiling from the inside out, because teenage girls with Duchienne smiles grew up to have more fulfilling lives, better jobs, happier families, and more successful marriages, according to long-term research-based only on yearbook pictures.

1. Live passionately and not for passion: Our best protection has been written by Mother Theresa is a happy heart. Research shows, surprisingly, that teenage girls laugh more at children than at each other. Too many women are purchasing the "Cinderella fairytale" we need to be content with the right Prince.

2. Wake up without make-up: Girls need help asking questions and finding answers-Who am I? So why should I be here? Once they explore their gifts and talents and learn to share them with the community, they want help and understanding. Although puberty pressures drag them to peer-to-peer, they want help learning how to be their leader against their internal beliefs.

Recently a 17-year-old girl was arrested for armed robbery and murder in North Carolina because she helped her boyfriend steal a convenience store. For women, abuse is increasing as they are conditioned by peers and representations of the press. To help them wake up from feeling worthless, they can provide the resources and guidance; a condition that inhibits purposeful leadership and honesty.

3. Stop the worthless dance: Girls decide that they are worthless for many reasons, some of the theme games of comparison, childhood traumas such as sexual abuse, cultural beauty queen trance, or neglect. Many young women who Dr. Miles worked with decided that when their fathers left the family, their mothers were overly critical, they had a more

beautiful sister, and so on. When each girl first decided that she was worthless and worked on healing that lie, it's important to retrace. They need to see how they made this decision and why they made it real and developed false selves.

4. What good do you make with your brain? The adolescent brain is undergoing huge changes when knowledge it does not need is pruned and other associations are enhanced. The mind does not develop entirely until we abandon adolescents with too much speed in our twenties and not enough braking!

A Duke neuroscientist once discussed with Dr. Miles that he still thought of himself as small, even though he was a tall man because he was so short in middle school. Girls who liked themselves often develop a false shell against the middle school assault on the developing brain in elementary school. They need assistance in focusing their brains on their purpose and dreams. Dr. Miles employs other methods including journaling, self-hypnosis, and assumptions to do that.

5. Do not despise, visualize: Dr. Miles visualizes the ideal life for young women. Using a meditation practice to calm and communicate with the inner self and reinforce what every girl wants, she guides the girl on creating neural pathways for high self-esteem. Negative thoughts fill the unconscious mind. Most girls have few examples of trustworthy women living with a higher purpose. Once reported, a prominent neuroscientist, "Made good in brain training."

6. Sweet inspiration: Since the mind is not fully mature until the age of 23, teenagers are attracted to high levels of stimuli,

but lack the experience to manage life situations. We need classes such as Relationships 101 or Life 101! Instead, we're spending more time teaching our kids how to drive a car than having healthy relationships and lives!

Maya Angelo should be required to read as a role model who addresses her mistakes and how she evolved. She has a wonderful story about being fired at the age of 16 and how "fired" was explained by her mother was just a word and she needed to get back there.

7. Practice the present: Dr. Miles has girls wondering at the moment what's real. She remembers hours of waste wishes she had a better day of hair! The truth is that, if she chopped it off during Home Economics, her hair would not improve.

I should be thin, have straight hair, green eyes, blah, blah, blah, blah, and blah. Women want help in dealing with what, and what, and what if. Dr. Miles writes about her near-death experience at age 52 in her book, The New Marriage, Transcending the Happily Ever After Myth. She found peace and acceptance of herself as she realized how much she had loved was the only thing that mattered in her life.

8. Love the spiritual and it will be difficult to despise the earthly: young girls need to develop a spiritual practice to focus on the forces that are greater than themselves. It is possible to do readings, prayers, meditation alone , or to share.

The bottom line and the best advice I can give you is that knowing that true self-esteem and self-confidence comes from within and is not eye candy that will disappear once we all reach a certain age. The trick is to realize that looks are not all.

Self Esteem for Immigrant Women Who Wants to Achieve Their Goals

Are you an immigrant woman who once had dreams and goals for a brighter future? Did you lose self-esteem and confidence in your ability to create the life you want?

Here is how your self-esteem can be restored and your goal achieved:

1. Pride yourself on who you are!

The fact you've moved to a new country doesn't make you a human. You don't have to feel invisible and worthless. You're someone! Living in a new country doesn't change the fact that you're a strong, brave, smart woman with the guts to move into a new country and start a fresh one. You are the woman who now has the opportunity to create a better life and the desires of her hearts. Don't look at yourself., be happy, and confident. Who you are and what you represent, stand tall, love, and value? Don't let your brave spirit die and suppress your speech. You, too, must make a significant contribution to the world.

2. Stop playing small and play a bigger game.

There's more to you than your ears touch. You have so much talent and you are waiting for so many chances. No more time is needed to withdraw from existence and settle for less than you deserve. Write about how your life's going to work. Stop applying for jobs you're overqualified for. Stop wasting your resources, mention meeting your ambitions, and yet do nothing to change the situation. Elevate the play to what you expect. Remember always who you are, a brave woman!

3. Have a lifetime plan.

It's very important to have a plan for your life when you move to a new country. The saying goes, "If you don't have a vision for yourself, you're going to be part of someone else's." The problem is... do you have a life plan? If you're not... what are you working on? Do you know what you want your life to do? What's the plan for your life? Why are you important? How are you going to achieve this? How are you committed? Start living in line with your strategy.

4. Act on your dreams and goals.

You can still achieve them if you have dreams and goals and turn them into reality. Starting in a different country doesn't mean the dream's end. If you don't enable challenges, personal insecurity, and a victim mentality to deprive you of the joy of achieving your goals, you can still accomplish what you want. Take control of your life as no one is going to do it for you. Believe in yourself, develop and become unstoppable a positive "I can do it" attitude. Immigrants who overcame obstacles and achieved great things are so many inspiring stories. You can also become the story!

5. Take control of your path and pave it.

Be willing to live your career actively. Don't let the views of people and others decide who you are and determine the course of your life. Identify what you want to do and then intend to do it. If possible, go back to school, join organizations, and network with liberal people to help you achieve your goals. Take control of yourself, expect great things, and be open to challenges and rewards. You can do it and believe it better!

6. Be assertive. Speak up on your own.

Take control of your life and speak for yourself. You don't need the acceptance stamp from anyone, so don't worry. Create lines and let people know when they don't like what they say or do. Wherever you come from, you are a wonderful person with rights, and no one has the right to violate them. Be assertive and know how to honestly and openly express your feelings and opinions. Find your voice and begin by just learning to say NO.

Raising Girls with a Positive Self-Esteem

Nowadays, women have made a place in different fields of expertise that were once dominated by men. Throughout terms of rights, men and women are now treated equally. But little do we know that a lot of people also suffer from low self-esteem given this justice.

Low self-esteem for women begins at the age of nine when they face many internal and external pressures. Here are some observations that will help you in your self-esteem to understand the effect of these pressures.

Eating disorders and depression are the most common mental problems that affect girls.

The majority of graders from 5th to 12th are not happy with their body shape.

Graders 5th through 12th want to lose weight because of the pictures they see in magazines and websites.

Women suffer as early as the age of 10.

Anxiety among girls is more prevalent more than 15-year-old boys.

Girls ' health is at risk due to poor eating habits, anxiety, and unwanted pregnancy.

Girls between the ages of 10 and 12 are already introduced to topics of puberty such as dating and gender. At an early age, they also like dressing up and talking like teens.

The above findings typically lead to low self-esteem, as both pre-teens and adults tend to focus more on their appearance and physical attributes than on their general self-esteem. They tend to think it's smart to be sexy.

Self-esteem is now related to physical attributes and what others say of them, rather than how positive they are about what they can do and how they feel for themselves. Often recognized as sexualization is this prevalent problem. It occurs when the interest of an individual is reliant on sexual appeal, having the absence of other characteristics. This commonly affects girls in a variety of domains:

- Cognitive and emotional health sexualization weakens a person's trust with his / her own body resulting in shame and anxiety self-image problem.

- Mental and physical health Eating disorders, anxiety, and low self-esteem are commonly associated with the sexualization of women.

- Research on sexual development indicates that sexualization has a detrimental effect on the development of the healthy sexual self-image of women.

Remember that parents have an important role to play in helping their daughters develop healthy self-esteem amid the sexualization challenge. Here are some tips on how to raise girls with healthy self-esteem and body image:-Be vigilant about your daughter and yourself, especially when it comes to appearance and weight.

Through the assumptions. Support your mother patch the sink and get your brother to set the table for dinner. Let them choose what fits their purpose and not just what expert girls should be.

Let her talk to your daughter.

Let them struggle and begin again instead of encouraging them all the way.

Together with them, using different media (TV, films, the Web, etc.) to explore the pictures of the women they see.

Girls within their communities may begin to develop their self-worth. As such, a family needs to be ready to help them achieve their full potential and get rid of their negative feelings to grow into women with strong self-esteem and a healthy body image.

How Can Women's Self Defense Help Self Esteem

Are you shy or afraid to try new things because you're afraid of uncomfortable settings or anxious about them? You don't have to be. As a woman and a human being, you have every right to be free of fear and anxiety in any situation. The self-defense of women can bring out a personality lion that you have deep within you. Self-defense lessons for women will give you the confidence to overcome the doubts that have long plagued you. You will be able to enjoy the stuff that the anxiety has stopped you from doing in a long time with these doubts being defeated. After taking this type of training, your self-esteem will rise and you will be a more competent and confident woman.

It's important to your self-esteem. If you're not feeling good about yourself, you won't feel good about what you're doing and how you're doing it. The self-defense of women lets, you put in or bring back your self-esteem into your existence. Due to your safety insecurity, the lack of self-esteem and avoidance of new things can cause you to live a sheltered life that can prevent you from enjoying life to the full. You're not ready to take a self-defense course for women now?

Whether some women are married or single, they live a life of physical and emotional abuse. Those kill the will of the person to stand up for herself and she is living a life full of fear and despair. The woman's self-esteem is very small as she thinks she has to live up to that overbearing husband or boyfriend's standards. This fear keeps her from making new friends or experimenting with new experiences. The self-defense course of a woman will teach if she is abused to stand up for herself or defend herself. The self-esteem will grow so much that most people can finally find the gumption to leave the relationship before therapy and remediation are completed or to fully leave the relationship.

You're missing the best part of life if you're afraid of being attacked and go out of your way to avoid potentially dangerous situations. Women have avoided going on a holiday to an exotic land because they fear dangerous situations and personal security. They're losing out on a wonderful experience because they have low self-esteem and they don't have the confidence to take the risk and go on the trip. These women are left with a life full of opportunities that are disappointed and missed. The self-defense of women will give that woman the self-esteem to believe in herself and the horns will take her life.

Healthy self-esteem and financial self-confidence

Healthy self-esteem helps you to financially prosper and not just paycheck work to survive. How? By offering you the courage to know, gain, and succeed in your emotional self.

Here are three ways to improve both your financial self-confidence and your healthy self-esteem: 1. Take the next level of your financial self-confidence-read, learn, and grow.

Have you recently read any good books on financial self-development? Healthy self-esteem allows you to feel more confident about your ability to make money and be more confident about those everyday decisions. The more confident you are about your ability to earn, control and grow your money, the more confident you will be about your ability to build a prosperous future.

I found that reading or listening to a self-development book or CD daily is a healthy habit and powerful self-esteem booster. One day at a time, financial self-confidence is built and one new "aha" is built at a time. Here are a few powerful and possibly life-changing suggestions: Women and Money, Suze Orman The Automatic Millionaire, David Bach Prince Charming Isn't Coming, Barbara Stanny Rich Dad, Poor Dad, Robert Kiyosaki My suggestion is to get up early or grab time every day (or at least three or four days a week) to learn new self-confidence building skills.

Here's a quote from Jim Rohn that I like in particular: "Formal education will make you a living; self-education will make you a fortune." Networking with others to boost your self-esteem in financial matters.

Positive people are producing positive results. If you want to make more money and become more self-confident about your finances, then network with people who make money and already have healthy financial self-confidence.

How about joining a cash flow or investment club. Another suggestion is to select networking functions where you will meet like-minded people who are financially successful. Ask questions, listen to what others are doing, and then make wise choices and decisions using your judgment. Know, learn, and determine what's going to work better for you.

Your most important tool for financial success is healthy self-esteem.

Your self-esteem is stronger, your financial decisions are smarter. You will only be as confident in yourself as you can be in your healthy self-esteem. It is just as important to consistently nurture, foster, and build healthy self-esteem as building your financial wealth.

Financial self-confidence is about learning, growing, and believing that things in life are worthy and worthy of the goods. It's about gaining financial knowledge from the practical side. It's about believing that you deserve to be financially self-sufficient and happy from the emotional side.

Relationship between self-esteem and eating disorders

Anyone working with women with eating disorder recognizes that self-esteem is intricately linked, but it is not entirely well-defined how the two are related. Inevitably, all analysis about eating disorders or self-esteem leads to the question of the chicken and the egg which came first: poor self-esteem which rendered a person more vulnerable to eating disorder and eating disorder which caused damage to the self-esteem of an adult? While there is no simple answer to this question, there is substantial research that has investigated the relationship between eating disorders and self-esteem and provides interesting insights.

Ghaderi (2001) stated in a review of the literature that low self-esteem, along with other causes, not only puts women at higher risk of developing an eating disorder but also helps to perpetuate an eating disorder. Numerous reports support the claim that low self-esteem is often present before the initiation of an eating disorder and that low self-esteem is an essential risk factor for bulimia or anorexia even in young girls of school age (Ghaderi, 2001).

According to Robson (1989, as in Ghaderi, 2001), self-esteem is "a sense of contentment and self-acceptance that results from an individual's assessment of their worth, attractiveness, skill, and ability to fulfill their aspirations." Given this definition, it is clear that self-esteem is multifaceted. Similarly, the nature and continuation of eating disorders are complicated, involving variables such as family environment, cultural environment, food history, genetic predisposition, trauma history, age and cognitive problems, duration of an eating disorder, immediate influences such as support system, emotional factors, and religious factors, of which self-esteem is only one aspect. Self-esteem, though, tends to be a primary risk factor that can contribute to the development of other eating disorder risk factors. For instance, three independent research studies showed that perfectionist tendencies and body dissatisfaction predict the development of bulimia only among women with low self-esteem, while women with higher self-esteem did not have these risk factors and therefore did not develop bulimia (Vohs, Voelz, Pettit, Bardone, Katz, Abramson, Heatherton, & Joiner, 2001; Vohs, Bardone, Joiner, Abramson, & Joiner, 2001).

When addressing eating disorders and self-esteem, personality development is a focus area. Attention has been paid to the partnership between parent and child and how perfectionist demands of parents operate to restrict the growth of independence of the infant, thereby creating an environment in which the baby becomes based on parental standards rather than on personal needs and desires (Stein, 1996). Bruch (1982) argued that as children try to meet unrealistic parental demands, they often develop a sense of being "nothing." As these children grow into adolescence, they may turn into an eating disorder as a means of self-defining and self-control (Stein, 1996).

Self-esteem interventions

While self-esteem is a major risk factor for eating disorders, one research team found body dissatisfaction to be the strongest single predictor of an symptoms of eating disorder (Button, Sonug Barke, Davies, & Thompson, 1996). Therefore, by treating body disappointment, counselors are doing well to help improve self-esteem, which is a major determinant of one's body image. For example, one study found that having teens understand what is good regarding their bodies and physical appearances while that their sense of personal ability contributes to less internalization of thinness-idealizing socio-cultural norms (Phelps, Dempsey, Sapia, & Nelson, 1999). This resulted in significantly less body dissatisfaction, which in turn resulted in less adolescent eating disorder behavior (Phelps et al., 1999). Improving self-esteem for people with an eating disorder is a challenging task. Pessimistic feelings and values are often deeply embedded and therefore impossible to give up. These help to maintain low self-esteem and eating disorder until suicidal thoughts are formed.

To start challenging the deeply held negative beliefs, a vital treatment for people experiencing anorexia, bulimia, and compulsive eating. For example, most women with eating disorderS equal weight, dress size or shape to their worth. The earlier a person can let go of those negative self-assessments and substitute them with more positive solutions, the faster she can be on the path to recovery. This may involve answering concerns such as, "What do you want for your career, your future, your loved ones?" Answering these questions may be daunting and could lead to significant changes in the occupational responsibilities, recreational activities, and relationships of an adult (Ghaderi, 2001). Therapists may help women recognize and draw on positive self-definition channels. Eating disorder works to restrict the capacity of an adult, but people can be encouraged to try new positions by counseling and undertake behaviors where they can gain trust.

Too often, people with eating disorders are the exception to society. They believe others deserve happiness, love, and joy, but they deserve sorrow, disappointment, and punishment themselves. One of the first obstacles that counselors will bring to the eating disorder is to start challenging such false beliefs. Therapists may start to figure out how the patient has become the anomaly, and then begin to explore where these false beliefs come from, be they previous violence, unpleasant social relationships, adolescent bullying, or other traumatic encounters. Teaching the consumer that she is worthy of love and approval, and that there are no criteria for her value, can be necessary to improve self-esteem.

It is important to remember that, at least initially, people dealing with anorexia, bulimia, and compulsive eating are likely to reject certain forms of treatment along with the psychologist. Negative mindset challenges don't fit in with what many of these women think is true of themselves. Therapists, however, can help clients recognize their value with persistence, patience, and ongoing acceptance and can help create hope- one of the most critical components of overcoming anorexia, bulimia, or compulsive eating.

It is also essential to address perfectionist tendencies to address self-esteem among women with an eating disorder. Such women typically find their value-based on their accomplishments, whether through qualifications, professional achievements, or other practices. Nevertheless, inevitably as these women achieve goals, their standards become less achievable, creating a cycle in which they can never reach the point of acceptance or value. One of the therapy tasks is to separate the value of the individual from the strivings of perfection.

The eating disorder becomes their identity for most women with anorexia, bulimia, or compulsive eating. These women often desire to become perfect in terms of perfectionist tendencies-striving to exercise longer, eat less, and do more than they are healthy. Many women claim that they are "good" at the eating disorder and it becomes all-consuming. The identity of a woman based on an eating disorder prevents her from trying new activities, especially since there is a risk that she may not do them "perfectly." From these women's perspective, doing the disorder perfectly is safer than risking failure in other areas.

Therapists are doing well to explicitly make this pattern in therapy. Such people may continue to face their fears by taking small steps and receiving support from counselors and other supports by addressing the underlying fear of failure and unmasking the illness for what it is. Initially, such small steps can be linked to disorder behavior. Of starters, such individuals may be encouraged to start replacing eating disorder behaviors with healthier alternatives, such as calling a friend and exercising when the desire to self-harm arises. As these people excel in pursuing healthier alternatives to the illness, their self-esteem is strengthened and they may be encouraged to take much greater risks such as engaging with family, strengthening friendships, and trying new behaviors.

Most women with eating disorders compared with others, especially other women, along with perfectionism. When these people compete with others, they never seem to measure up-in their eyes anybody else is ever more competent, younger, or desirable. These comparisons serve to further destroy self-esteem, perpetuating through a disorder the deleterious cycle of compensating for negative feelings. Comparisons weaken friendships as well as damaging self-esteem and lead to further alienation from others. Therapy must therefore focus partly on the comparisons that these women make and how these comparisons serve to harm self and relationships. Therapists should encourage women to choose a new way of being about themselves and the others-a way that is focused on kindness and respect rather than hurtful similarities. Since these women recognize that there are no self-worth gradations, they can hopefully begin to let go of needless comparisons.

When conducting an eating disorder therapy group, counselors must be particularly aware of similarities. Sadly, group therapy can be a breeding ground for group members to contrast. Apart from the impact on one's self-esteem, members of the group that direct animosity towards those members they think are not measuring up to. Group leaders do well to call out attempts to compete within the team, or participants may want to set a standard within the community not to compare. Identifying and labeling group comparisons can help these women recognize harmful behavior, and then women as a group can choose new paths.

Command has long been recognized as a key issue for eating disorders individuals. As predicted, if their lives feel overwhelming and dominated by others, individuals pursue a sense of control.

This is achieved in the form of body management for many women seeking a sense of control over their lives. While women may feel more control in their lives in the beginning, this is fleeting and inevitably leads to feeling out of control. Also, people with eating disorders use regulation as a proxy for self-esteem, thinking that "When I regulate myself and my situations then I will be reasonable." This protection is, of course, misleading and does not provide genuine self-esteem or confidence feelings. Therapists have to educate their patients that the influence provided by an eating disorder is misleading and is not a replacement for self-esteem.

Because people with eating disorders are finding power, isolation is often used as a way to hide from their discomfort. Avoidance of truth undermines their ability to live congruently, leading to a cycle of low self-esteem and eating disorder. Such people foster feelings of inadequacy and self-restraint by ignoring what they know is best for them. Eating disorders depend on denial, and counselors need to render authenticity as a central therapy problem. An honestly-based therapeutic relationship allows the client to begin to be honest about behaviors, fears, and past experiences. Clients begin to break the cycle of low self-esteem by being completely honest in session. However, through genuinely recognizing concerns, consumers can begin to understand and overcome them, and they can continue to excel in the very places that once were most terrifying. These kinds of triumphs instill hope, reinforce self-esteem, and encourage people to choose healthier alternatives to eating disorders.

In contrast to direct self-esteem strategies, eating disorder prevention programs facilitate the critical evaluation of existing socio-cultural norms, help articulate personal values, and improve tolerance through group discussions, problem-solving exercises, and collaborative education (Phelps et al., 1999). Another such participant-oriented curriculum has proven effective in increasing participants' self-esteem and boosting their body image (Ghaderi, 2001).

Although eating disorders and low self-esteem remain difficult to separate, the need to resolve self-esteem issues in therapy has been established through studies along with clinical knowledge. Additionally, strategies focused on self-esteem, particularly how it impacts body image be effective and should be part of extensive eating disorder treatment for girls. As a psychologist, it can be overwhelming to help clients boost self-esteem. Recognizing, furthermore, that every approach which contradicts false beliefs and negative thoughts, each gesture of care and compassion, each discovery of solutions to perfectionism and contrasts, each genuine relationship based on honesty can help women with eating disorders find the courage to accept something different for themselves and bring them, as the client puts it.

The Connection Between Self-Esteem and Attackers

Attackers, whether verbal, mental, emotional, or physical, have low self-esteem. Attackers look for people who are weaker than themselves to attack so they are sure to "win" outdoor body language self-esteem shows Attackers are experts in reading body language. If your self-esteem is lacking, Attackers can tell Tips for Safe Self-Esteem The favorite topic of everybody is themselves. It usually has to do with how they affect us when we talk about others. It's often about getting the attention that goes back to us and our self-esteem. Complaining about someone usually means we want something, looks, attention, trust, career; the focus is us again.

Once we know that we are on the right track wherever we are at the time to learn what we need to learn and that everyone is of equal value, we do some wonderful things: We relax We feel motivated We affirm our right to protect and defend ourselves We have a deep desire to help everyone see their worth. Surround yourself with friends who understand you and support your self-esteem rather than attack. If you're feeling bad for yourself, get them out of your ASAP life. Staying positive and impossible can be challenging if someone is disempowering (bullying) you in your life.

If you don't have any great, positive people right now in your life, be your own best company and attract them. They're worth waiting for!

Weight Issues, Body-Image Issues, And Self-Esteem Issues

On ABC's "The View" Recently, the cast spent some time speaking about weight issues and attitudes in this culture— and other cultures— throughout the years and around the globe. The media-propagated images are at issue, which makes women feel fat even when they are perfectly healthy. Whoopi Goldberg also listed a recent study which found that most women prefer to have cancer rather than thin! Women would make a huge favor of themselves by thinking seriously about the way they are taught to feel. They're programmed to hate themselves, their minds, and their lives; and it's that hatred that makes things worse.

People have shifted back and forth on the issue of weight over the years. Thin is in some philosophy; while overweight is where it is in other communities. But that's not always the case. In times of abundance, when people don't have to fight for survival, being thin is a sign of health and success— plenty of time to play or go to the gym— while being fat is a sign that you're eating well in times of lack. In this age of television, movie stars, and supermodels, the average person receives misinformation and faulty body image programming-making people feel inferior, worthless, fat, and even ugly.

When two-thirds of a population is overweight and women would rather have cancer than carry a few extra pounds, there's something terribly wrong with how we think of ourselves as a culture and we're being "programmed" to think this way through the entertainment, food, medical, fitness, and diet industries. By 2010, another study predicts that more than half of all-American kids will be overweight! What do you think the kids do "bad" to ruin their health? That's right; they listen to the television programming of their parents!

Ultimately, the cast made very good comments about the issues of weight and body confidence which affect people with overweight, especially women. The critical point in this whole issue, however, was missed as one of the cast members told how she intended to change her negative thoughts and negative self-talk. It is indeed one of the most valuable things a person can do; but the statement was made saying, "I believe my emotions are not influencing my body..." Saying assertion is the absolute opposite of accuracy; the thoughts form and shape your body just as they shape and shape your acts and existence. In reality, the only factor influencing what your body does is your emotions.

Consider Mohandas Gandhi's words: "Our thoughts become our words as they become our beliefs; our beliefs become our actions as they become our customs; our customs become our values as our values become our destiny." This is no different from Jesus saying, "As a man thinks, so it is done to him." And, not only does this teaching appear in the Old Testament, but it appears to me that this teaching is not the same. For example, Buddha is said to have put it this way: "Man is formed and molded by his thoughts." This is basic human wisdom; and it is perfectly in keeping with the latest advances in medical research. The direction between the thought-and-thing and the mind-and-body can now be easily identified through scientists.

Our thoughts create electrical and chemical signals that were not there before that thought and are different for different thoughts. These signals direct cellular expression or behavior- literally shaping our bodies thought-by-thought as they move us into and out of different conditions and situations that shape our physical form at the same time. For starters, your emotions can motivate and encourage you to exercise — changing your physical form's structure, speech, and capabilities. You can easily say the weights were responsible, but you can also see plainly that it was the thought processes and motivation which brought you to the weights and the impulses which prompted your arms and hands to grasp and push the weights.

It's the thought that counts, conscious or unconscious. You don't need another ineffective diet plan, system, or medication if you're trying to lose weight; you need a new mind frame. Change your mind about how you look; and you'll soon see a change in how you look. But the shift in thinking will occur before the body discovers any permanent changes. The emotions create either a reaction to anxiety or a reaction to relaxation; when you try to change the body and your body image, you need to visualize your ideal body while being good to yourself and looking in the mirror. Words are powerful and imaginative, and words are simply vibrational feelings. If you don't have to say anything nice, don't say anything-especially to yourself!

Why Counseling Could Help Women Achieve More Positive Self-Confidence

Our confidence in ourselves influences our emotional emotions, shifts why we view life,and can influence our actions towards others. Many women recognize that low self-esteem limits their potential, prevents them from doing the things they enjoy, and causes problems in important areas of their lives.

One way to look at low self-esteem is that it is a form of prejudice against us.

Most of us like to think we're not prejudicing others. We may not, however, realize that we hold on to a persistently critical' inner picture' of ourselves, a picture that is so distorted that it is, in fact, a form of prejudice; an insidious prejudice that we harbor against ourselves.

Also, most of us can see plainly if beneficial or positive behavior is detrimental to someone else. Many of us would jump in to protect an individual who we felt was unfairly treated... at least we could consider unfair treatment. However, sometimes our ability to distinguish between fair and unfair attitudes does not work as it should when it comes to understanding how we treat ourselves. When it comes from somewhere inside us, we don't defend ourselves against persistent, unfair criticism!

Signs of low self-esteem in women: low self-confidence can be seen in some or all of these situations: feeling unconfident in social situations that are passed over for work promotion, not sticking to projects or studies that do not try new hobbies, interests or sports, creating frequent problems in close relationships that accept an uncomfortable home-life that does not take care of health expenditure, Several girls, though, have told us about some of the less obvious signs of low self-esteem: feeling pessimistic about other people sometimes (or exaggeratedly). Groucho Marx's comment about:' Who'd like to join a club that allowed me to join?(or something like that!) makes a valid point unwittingly; some people automatically think less of anyone who shows that they like them. Some of the less obvious signs of low self-esteem can be a constant distrust for honest people, unreasonably high demands, fault-finding, micro-management, establishing' limits' for how much people care for and being unable to forgive.

Some even less obvious signs of low self-esteem:

This is usually more obvious and easier to spot in men, but women can also try to' puff up' to make themselves feel bigger due to the underlying unease about their real value as a person and the uncertainty about how important they are to others. Needing to be' wrong' all the time, showing off with the new designer labels, or gossiping or bitching about other women may result from an inherent low sense of intrinsic value' in ourselves' or from inflated anxiety for our importance in other people's eyes.

The behavior caused by a low self-image can also vary considerably from individual to individual.

For example, some women say that having a poor self-image or low self-confidence causes them to take unconsidered risks (such as drinking too much in public places) while others say they avoid the necessary risks to such an extent that they don't even want to try anything new (such as meeting new people or going after a better job). This can lead to frustration and loneliness.

Too often, some women apologize, while others blame others too much. Some women are neglecting their appearance, others are spending their entire time and money on beauty treatments and clothing. Of course, all these habits can be caused by different things, but a low self-image can be the cause of unhelpful and self-sabotaging behavior that is widely divergent.

Low self-confidence can affect close relationships. Often women find themselves overly centered on their husbands, perhaps by compulsively picking up disagreements, monitoring their location, voicing constant excessive envy of a trustworthy partner, being over-solicited, or being' clingy.' Housework and job activities can also display imbalanced patterns resulting from deep insecurity. Some women over-focus on making the perfect home or neglect their homes because they feel they deserve to have an uncomfortable environment. Some women are pushing themselves to work punishing schedules or allowing people to treat them badly at work (e.g. by haggling promotion that never materializes). Low self-esteem can create vicious cycle-our negative belief about ourselves and our lives can become a' self-fulfilling prophecy.' It can result in social isolation or even feeling caught in an abusive relationship. Women can look at a life that only reflects an impoverished, unattractive, and distorted self-image. It adds to their low self-esteem. When things get worse, stopping the' vicious cycle' can be important. This is where it can aid in peaking to the correct kind of psychologist and psychotherapist.

Expert counseling and psychotherapy can help women (who want to) learn how to surmount their own low opinion and live a fuller life. Counseling may help people overcome their unhelpful assumptions about themselves and improve their self-limiting unconfident behavior.

We can do something about transforming biased critical views into something more positive and optimistic for ourselves. We can develop more inspiring and realistic beliefs about our abilities and the potential that our lives might hold for us. Relationships can have more opportunities to develop and stay strong, and a better chance for careers, social lives, and interests to take off.

Women's low self-esteem research has a small yet strong past.

Over the last twenty to twenty-five years, clinicians, psychotherapists, social workers, and psychologists (many of them women) have researched the debilitating impact of' persistent internal critique' and how it can become such a strong destructive force. They looked at how low self-esteem arises from both early experiences and recent events. We have discussed that low self-esteem can be sustained by establishing compensatory (often dysfunctional)' laws' for how we should think and act. We looked at how it can give rise to hypotheses about what others will think of us, and how it can lead to distorted interpretations of what the behavior of other people towards us' really' means. This body of work has helped professional practitioners to develop useful guidelines to help women overcome low self-confidence. There are now a variety of approaches and methods that people can use to encourage their' inner critic' to back them up and build what some therapists term' healthy self-esteem.'

Some practitioners have been working intensively with a wide range of women on this issue. It is now easier to see some of the trends that have arisen in the lives of women as a result of this in-depth study. Counselors have learned a lot about how to set themselves up to improve the inner picture of women.

Something else significant has also been discovered by professional therapists. Some therapeutic techniques do not help women with low self-esteem, and may even aggravate a low self-image.

It's not as straightforward as' positive thinking,' although sometimes that strategy benefits. In reality,' positive-thinking' strategies may be counter-productive for some individuals. A balanced approach, with achievable goals that develop gradually into a more fulfilling life experience, is usually more effective and more likely to be sustained over time. A sensitive practitioner will have learned something about this over time from any therapeutic background. A balanced approach to self-esteem is reinforced by three primary psychological techniques: behavioral counseling, Pellin Contribution-Training, and Gestalt therapy. Some practitioners combine two or three of these approaches, especially if they've trained in the 'Integrative Technique,' which offers several complementary therapeutic models.

Skilled mentors will help clients build 'Healthy Self-Esteem' and learn new skills in life.

Coaches may help women establish positive and optimistic attitudes about themselves and their lives by dealing with low self-esteem. It is important to support women when they form new ideas and actions, as this can be a period of experimenting. Practitioners should inspire their customers to try new and different ways to do things. Learning life skills like Assertiveness and Non-Violent Communication can be very helpful, allowing women to express themselves constructively. Effective counseling can encourage clients to experiment with new beliefs and skills, first with 'baby steps' and then in significant areas of their lives in larger ways. (In many respects 'Healthy Self Esteem' is more of a verb than a noun; our self-esteem is better by knowing how to do things differently and by assessing the results.) Experienced therapists will 'tune in' to the particular reasons that will help every person discover the most successful (or safest) ways to overcome her low self-esteem. This can make women more capable of building lives that reflect a truer picture of themselves, their talents, and their desires.

How each of us first developed low self-esteem, how we learned to overcome it through the development of healthy self-esteem, and who helped us along the way can be a fascinating story, and varies greatly from woman to woman.

Self-esteem Mesotherapy

Mesotherapy helps many women to feel good about their bodies through self-esteem mesotherapy. The average woman must be happy and feel better about herself to live a productive life. Unfortunately, with their bodies, many women equate their self-worth. They aren't happy in life if they aren't happy with their bodies. Of women to be comfortable and have high self-esteem, they need to feel and look their best.

Cellulite is, shockingly, one of the many disorders that afflicted the bodies of women. It's those little unsightly orange dot patterns that make it unattractive even to the slimmest body. It's a skin condition mostly associated with women who are obese or pregnant, but slim women also get this condition. There was no way to get rid of cellulite successfully until the last few years, that is until mesotherapy was found.

Mesotherapy is a medical treatment that can treat cellulite effectively and restore a woman's beautiful body and self-esteem. With just a few injections to dissolve fat pockets in the right places, the average woman can feel good about showing off her body again. She doesn't have to keep wearing bulky and light clothes to conceal the areas riddled by cellulite. She won't have to worry about shielding her body from her boyfriend or husband unless she completes her mesotherapy sessions before completion. She's going to be the sweet guy she was meant to be. No longer to hide and hate her body.

The lack of self-esteem could affect a woman's way of going through her life's daily activities. Either she can continue to stress her ugly cellulite, or she can look for a doctor who is certified in mesotherapy and has started treatment.

Strategies for Career Women Looking to Develop Self-Confidence at Workplace

As a career woman, your self-esteem and self-confidence may be your ticket to the effective reality line, and your ticket to sit in the sidecar to none. No matter how stellar your training, formal education, or tactical skills maybe, you won't instill it in others if you don't have high self-confidence. And to ascend the path of corporate so business success includes gaining the confidence of others.

This is good news! You can develop self-confidence in any field of your preference. It may take some time, patience, practice, and awareness, but every day people build trust. We don't even know that we're doing it most days. Building trust is like muscle building. You start slowly, take little steps, push yourself just a little further each time until you reach your final destination with the skill to accomplish a specific task.

If you lack confidence in your job, the first thing you might want to consider is to write down where you feel confident about the tasks you are performing and where you are not. Once you've identified the areas you're missing, ask yourself what it would take for you to feel confident and write down in those areas. Need more training? Need more exercise? Is it in your set of skills? If you can look at what you need to do, then you can formulate a plan to begin to acquire the skills, tasks, or practice you think you need.

It will become apparent to you when you do this exercise that there are steps you can take. Not everything is lost and you don't have to endure it, tolerate it, or be embarrassed by it. Such awareness alone will help to boost your self-esteem and trust. Because instead of feeling inept about yourself and your skills, you will realize that once you have your new and different tools, you can improve your performance.

Now break down how to get the new skills and tools you need. Split them into phases of the kid so that the larger goal doesn't seem daunting. Then put in place a plan for every step. Every time you take a step, you build confidence in your muscle.

While you're working to build long-term, lasting confidence in your skills here's just a few fast things you can do to improve your attitude, mentality, and inner feelings of trust.

Ways to improve self-confidence and get the job done: give yourself make-up. Just take advantage of yourself. This is not to make anyone else impress, but to make you feel better and better. Studies show that when you feel good about how you look, it encourages you to see in a strong, optimistic way.

Take the extra time to prepare yourself. Give yourself plenty of time to prepare if you're working on a project or a presentation, longer than you normally need. Understanding the content, you're sharing or the specifics of a task you're working on will improve your self-esteem, trust, and awareness instantly. This will be shown with the staff and managers in your discussions.

Concentrate on your progress. Make a list of all you've accomplished in the past 90 days at work... and the past year. Make notes next to each of the things you feel very lucky to do. Remember any positive comments or appreciations the colleagues or managers have given to you about these accomplishments. Remember any events that you thought were not adequate. Think about what you can do next time, learn, or change to get a better or more positive response. It's good to have areas for improvement! It allows you to keep growing and excelling.

Remember, your belief in the level at which you can perform a particular task with the ultimate ability is confidence. So, start yourself raising the bar... just a little at a time. Take a course to help you become a professional in a new job-specific to your work. Ask if you can be served as a professional mentor by someone in senior management. Ask if someone who needs your skills can be a professional mentor. All of these actions will help you feel better, show off your skills, and gain new skills.

Life satisfaction begins with the mastering of self-esteem and confidence. You can have your family, your job, and your dreams.

Why people may encounter problems in a relationship caused by low self-esteem

If you have poor relationships with self-esteem, it can be very hard. People with low self-esteem have relationships that are usually shorter and less satisfying than people with high self-esteem. You need to increase your self-esteem to improve your current relationship and future relationships.

You have to listen to yourself as you focus on your self-esteem. If you're in a relationship right now, listening to yourself is important to figure out what you want, why you feel the way you're doing, what your needs are, and what your fears are. Most people with low self-esteem simply believe that their emotions are due to the actions of their mate. You must boost your self-esteem enough to be free to choose your emotions, opinions, and reactions. An emotion that you may have for your wife may be due to fear or a desire that is not met. For example, when you feel jealous if your husband is speaking to other girls, it might be because you're afraid to lose him/her. When listening carefully to your thoughts, lift your self-esteem, and self-awareness. If you perceive a relationship problem, is the problem within or within your partner? We will have less control over you and your friends as long as you recognize your desires, worries, and latent motives.

People with low self-esteem are often unable to support their friends. Specifically, they find it hard to trust that they love their partners. Low self-esteem people also want their mates to stop loving or leave them. If you have this kind of suspicion, you need to develop your self-esteem so you can feel you're worth loving. Once you know you're worthy of the love of the other person, you won't be afraid that he will leave you.

Exercise your partner's faith and practice self-confidence. Relationships become so much better if you know that you love your partner.

Because people with low self-esteem often expect their partners to dump them, they focus on their negative traits of personality. Understanding that their mates are not flawless makes it easier to break up prospects. It is very difficult to be left by someone great, but it is not that bad to be left by someone with lots of negative characteristics. Though, when you continually dwell on its negative qualities, it's not enjoyable for your friend. Your partner will have less and less enjoyment of the relationship with you and may eventually break up with you. You need to respect the positive qualities of your companion to build a good partnership. Boost your self-esteem and help your friend boost your self-esteem by sharing good points. You will feel good about yourself when you receive and when you give each other's compliments.

It can cause you to place more value in someone else's life than in your own life by suffering from low self-esteem. Low self-esteem is all about how you see yourself, and nothing about how you see the other person. If a woman doesn't like what she sees in the mirror, she'll probably look at someone else to validate it. This empowers her to take control of the existence of another human and to try to fix another person in some way. There's another man she can see below herself. So she's never really had the chance to focus on her inadequacies because she's too busy focusing on the man she's empowering. Instead of holding the person accountable for what she knows is wrong, she has become attached to the enabled and started making excuses for the bad behavior displayed.

While the sense of worthlessness is part of a low self-esteem definition, the result of low self-esteem may lead to potentially destructive behavior. The inability to say no presents the enabler with a major problem. I was sitting in a prison full of women with low self-esteem and the inability to say no. Some of the women have been enablers and some have been allowed. Generally, the people who were enablers had a drug dealer husband or pimp that they helped daily and made excuses for him, perpetuating bad behavior. The empowered women are typically the victims of a controlling mother, husband, or member of the family who made excuses for their continued bad behavior.

I often wondered why these women were going to spend so much time in one-sided relationships that they would give up their freedom. But without being in a one-sided relationship, I did the same thing. I soon realized it was because women were traditionally socialized and conditioned in some cases to behave in self-destructive ways that benefit men at the expense of women. My proof lies in women's lives whom I held in prison.

Ultimately, if you have low self-esteem, chat about it with your husband so he can help you. Talk about your worries and fears, and tell your partner how best he can help you overcome them. Speak about your dreams and expectations as well. Make the relationship what you want it to be.

Challenging your internal criticism

The "chatterbox" inside your head, which sometimes does its best to undermine your self-confidence and diminish your self-esteem needs to be eliminated. It's a good idea to ignore that chatterbox when it's clear she doesn't have your best interests at heart or when it is prejudiced against you and doesn't look at the facts about your particular situation.

I'm going to cut the chatterbox a little slack today. And for the rest of this post, I'm going to show good faith by referring to her more politely as your "inner critic."

Establishing a good relationship with your inner critic can bring tremendous benefit, and we will explore how to do this in a way that will help you make better choices and create peace and harmony within your mind.

One of my pet hates is the notion that "there is equal respect for all opinions." I'm not going to get off on a rant about this, I'm just going to say I'd rather listen to an informed opinion than any uninformed opinion on any topic.

If you hear someone's opinion on a subject, he or she is completely unaware of, I suggest you seriously consider rejecting it because it's going to be worth less than an informed view.

Nevertheless, indifference is not the only aspect that can disqualify an opinion's usefulness. There is another inappropriate motivation. If you're talking to someone who knows something, but chooses to use that knowledge to manipulate you into making bad decisions, you'd be well advised to be alert and on guard. And on the basis that it has no integrity, you should permit yourself to discount that informed opinion.

That brings me back again to your inner critic. Since she's with you every waking moment of the day, we know she's not completely ignorant of you, is she? But what about her motivation: is she "for" or "with" you working? Is she helping you make sound decisions, or is she weakening you and decreasing your trust?

Seek not to mute the inner critic. Let's dispel the common notion that the best way to deal with an overly harsh inner critic is to ignore her completely. Even if she transformed into the "chatterbox" we spoke about, it would only be possible to suppress her entirely if you were ready to abandon all your internal judgment and actions.

For several reasons, this is not a good idea: if you're a psychopath, you can't do it anyway. Normal people are constantly judging things whether or not they admit it. It is part of the mechanism of your life and is hard-wired into your mind. (Oh, and I should point out that you're not a psychopath or you'd stopped reading this book a long time ago!) It's dangerous to stop listening to someone who has the potential to offer an informed view because it's likely that not everything they've got to say will be worthless for you.

Stopping listening to your inner critic can be unethical because she is sometimes quite well-tuned into your morality and denying what your conscience tells you is a big step along a dangerous road.

Just think what it might be like when you decided to work as a team with your inner critic, realizing you're on the same hand, sharing the same ambitions, and having a strong degree of trust between you: wouldn't that be something?

It can be a good thing to criticize!

Just, I had to listen to my inner critic, and she had a few blunt things to tell me as I transformed my car back into a lamp post while picking up my children from class. Candidly, she pointed out that paying attention to the existence of large, immovable objects in my vicinity is a good idea rather than anything else that might be competing for my attention at the time. My inner critic contributed to my considerable sense of embarrassment about my incompetence, and that's all right because I think it's good for me to feel embarrassed about what I've done. My lingering discomfort will help me to be more cautious as I drive away from school from now on, as will the £ 300 bill for repair!

While I'm in a confessional mood, I'm going to share another case of bad judgment-rather more extreme. I left all my mates in a bar in my early twenties to go off in the middle of London with a complete guy because I thought he looked pretty good and I felt adventurous. At the time, my friends were furious, but my right to make my own decisions was respected. My inner critic was definitely on their side, telling me repeatedly that I was stupid (on my account) and selfish (causing so much worry and concern for them). The fact that I'm here to tell this story today after finally arriving home safely has everything to do with good luck and nothing to do with good judgment on my part. I subsequently felt ridiculous. After all, I was so frivolous, guilty of the anguish that I caused my friends, and immature and foolish because I refused to listen to my inner critic when she tried to act in my best interests as I made my decisions.

It made me shudder to tell that story. But I hope it helps illustrate my point that your inner critic is extremely valuable- as long as she's on your side.

Does your inner reviewer work well with you?

To find out, spend about ten minutes writing down all the self-criticisms in the few days you can remember saying to yourself. Then take a look at those self-criticisms to see if they are legitimate. Is it fair? Was it useful? Have they motivated you to change for the better? Or were they nothing more than negative, cruel, and demotivating?

The inner critic must be one of the best friends and be at one with your best interests. If she's too zealous, rarely shuts up, or chips away from your heart, then either: a) Push her through some intense, solid practice Let her rise to the mark and do her job properly. Catch her make put-down remarks, broad sweeping statements, or a chain of negative or inaccurate comments to retrain your inner critic and then challenge her to be more focused, accurate, positive, encouraging, and helpful.

For example: if your inner critic says: "Oh, you're never going to fall in love. You're just so fussy and not attractive enough," challenge her with questions like: can you not think of any couples who are clearly in love but not both drop-dead beautiful?

Is it fair to say that I am not sufficiently attractive? Sufficient for what, exactly?

Okay, I know it's never easy for anyone to find someone in love with. Can you think of certain things that I can do better to increase my chances of success?

Is it so bad to be fooled? After all, it's important to find someone after a while that won't just fade away.

Through daily challenge the inner critic, you will be able to retrain her to offer you positive feedback and suggestions instead of self-sabotaging ones.

Swap a better one for her!

Think of your inner critic as having your personality. If that personality is rude, filthy, unfriendly, inhuman, disrespectful, prejudiced towards you, arbitrary in its judgments, out of reach, intolerable, irritating, violent, damaging, then it is time to cast it out of your mind and substitute it with a personality capable of sharing your life! For instance, I've known women who have lived with an inner critic for years saying horrible things like: "You're just a big, fat, ugly lump of lard. I hate you. You're pathetic. No wonder nobody loves you. I wish you could get your act together and stop looking so miserable." Well, if your inner critic is as harsh as anything, then it's time to find a better motivated inner critic in yourself!

Reinventing the inner critic

Here's what to do; begin by visualizing the inner critic inside you at the moment. Focus on giving her personality and characteristics. Give her a monstrous and unsympathetic face if she acts monstrously towards you and imagines the contorting face as she delivers her negative speeches. Get ready to banish this inner critic out of your mind because you're going to replace her-slowly but surely-with someone with more beautiful features.

Each time she rears her nasty head over the next month, I want you to drive her back emotionally. Let's picture her fighting back, but she doesn't get you out. Force her from an imaginary door before shutting her down. Do this as often as necessary until she receives in your mind the message that she is NO LONGER WELCOME.

I want you to submit yourself to the new inner opponent who is going to move into your mind at the same time. She's dry, reasonable, rational, realistic, just, optimistic, solution-oriented, honest, compassionate, considerate, strong, intelligent, assertive, brave, calm, laughing, and she's a great friend. Imagine dressing her up, laughing, looking at her best. And make sure she looks just like you!

You will have persuaded your old horrid inner critic to move out and leave you alone by the time your month's ending. Spend a few weeks putting your energy into connecting with your new, more positive inner critic. Focus on strengthening your bond with her, building confidence in what she's got to tell you.

Choose two or three of the features I mentioned two paragraphs back each day to help you do this. Maybe something like "warm and accessible." As you begin to bring your new inner critic to life in your mind, focus on these characteristics. Make your own words to focus on if you prefer them to my suggestions.

For example, you might imagine yourself to be positive, smiling, and a great friend on Day One. On the second day, the picture is brave, relaxed, and concerned for yourself. You can put the terms together and encourage the creativity to take your fresh, fantastic inner critic to life as the days go by.

Continue to visualize your inner critic in the way described above after a week, but then, before you finish, ask her an important question relevant to the situation that you both share: "What do you think I can do to make tomorrow better than today?" This will invite your new inner critic to help you do well and feel better about yourself.

Just think how much better life would feel if you simply stopped wasting your time listening to an overly harsh inner critic and instead spent it building up your self-esteem in areas where it is weak, enabling you to think positively and build good judgment, believe in yourself, feel worthy, act wisely and succeed in things that matter most to you.

Low self-esteem is not a constant affliction, your inner critic can be your friend, and from this point on you can overcome it and grow.

Conclusion

Low self-esteem and lack of confidence emerge from feeling down on your current situation in a variety of ways, thinking about what you sound like, or just not feeling good enough. Regardless of the cause, low self-esteem may play havoc with the quality of life of a woman. Women with low self-esteem appear to be more lethargic, less inspired, and in turn not satisfied. People tend to judge themselves by their flaws rather than by their virtues. They see the achievements of other people as their lack of accomplishment.

While low self-esteem is an issue that affects both genders, it is more common among women. Issues of self-esteem can often lead to depression if not tested. Depression is twice as common in women as in men, and one of the root causes is the issue of self-esteem. Self-esteem issues can emerge from work stress, home pressure, struggles with body image, or just a general lack of self-esteem. Problems with self-esteem frequently begin in adolescence, when young girls sometimes feel compelled with compete to their peers.

A lot of people don't have good self-esteem. This is tragic because a strong motivator can be self-esteem. If a person has good self-esteem, he or she will have enough confidence to try something out of their comfort zone and make their dreams come true. Unfortunately, so many times before, most people with low self-esteem have been knocked down that they simply no longer want to get hurt. Even if it can hurt, it's necessary to increase your self-esteem so that you can lead a fuller life. So, how long will it take for your self-esteem to increase?

The answer to this question depends on the person. A few things depend on the amount of time it takes you to increase your self-esteem. Willingness is one of the main factors. If you are willing to increase your self-esteem, in a much shorter period you will be able to do so. When you increasing your self-esteem because someone else needs you to do it, it will be more complicated to do it and it will take longer. It's important to remember that if you want to do it, you should only boost your self-esteem.

Another factor that will determine how long your self-esteem will take is your past. If in the past your self-esteem has been severely damaged, forgiving yourself and moving on will take you a lot longer. For most people, the most difficult part of the process is to forgive themselves for allowing other people to damage their confidence. Once you forgive yourself, the reconstruction can begin to take place.

Age is a factor not heard of by other men. The explanation age can play a role in how long a person wants to improve their self-esteem is because older people know they don't have as much time left to live. Because of this, older people normally speed up the process because with higher self-esteem they want to spend as much of their life as possible. Younger people realize they have more time to live, so they can focus on the root of the issue.

Sex may play a role to improve a person's self-esteem in how much time it takes. Most of the time women spent on the healing process is more likely than men. Since they typically improve their self-esteem, this may be beneficial to women. To people rushing the topic, difficulties might emerge in the future as the source of the question was not solved.

The individual's personality type will have a major influence on how long it takes for the individual to increase their self-esteem. Individuals with active personalities tend to increase their self-esteem more easily than those with sensitive personalities.

If you want to solve your problem of self-esteem once and for all, it is crucial not to rush the process. Even if you want to heal and forget what happened in your past, flushing it out of your system first is very important. Typically, it requires going back in-depth through the incidents and finding out what went wrong. You could think about it after you remembered the experience. Many people either don't think about their past or don't find out why their self-esteem was so low. If at any time during the healing process, you feel this is happening to you, it is best to start over.

Since you now understand that the amount of time it takes to raise the self-esteem of an individual depends on many different factors, remember to take your time and first do it correctly. It's better to take a year to boost your self-esteem correctly than to do it in a month, but in the wrong way. When you first successfully raise your self-esteem, you can feel much better. Those who first attempt to rush the process and end up losing seem to suffer another hit in the level of self-esteem that could end up being detrimental. You'll feel so much better about yourself once you've increased your self-esteem. It all looks so much easier and enjoyable in life. In trying to increase your self-esteem, you are certainly making the right choice. You will achieve your target in no time if you put in enough work and take your time.

Women's self-help books are widespread but some of the earlier works are particularly noteworthy for those who want to gain a basic understanding of the issues. Interestingly, when she wrote the famous work The Ego and Mechanisms of Defense, Anna Freud, Dr. Sigmund Freud's daughter contributed very deeply to the work of psychoanalysis. This is one of the classic psychoanalysis works that brought together many of the ideas of her father more succinctly and clearly, making them easier for all people to identify. Another great book on women's issues that is part of the classic works comes from Nancy Friday and is called My Mother Myself. Here, Nancy Friday explores the core issues that involve women in their mother's relationship and explores common reasons for women's self-esteem issues. She leads the reader to a deeper self-understanding so that she can more readily identify her issues and find a way forward in her life. Although the third book in terms of women's empowerment has mostly been left behind, Carol Gilligan's book In a Different Voice was a landmark project in terms of women's activism decades ago and is still being taught in many university courses today.

There several women's events designed to help improve low self-esteem. Fitness activities are a great way to get away from life's stressors and boost confidence in yourself. All-female exercise clubs can help ease some of the self-awareness that many women feel when they attend a gym. Disciplines like yoga are focused on finding balance and healing, and less on creating a perfect body template or doing many repetitions. Find a new hobby or something you can do regularly that is not contractual. In social situations, many women with issues of self-esteem are uncomfortable, so the simple task of joining a group can often make a big difference.

People may have low self-esteem in many harmful ways, but you don't have to deal with it. Letting your existence consume such negative feelings will only stop you from being the person you are truly capable of being. Don't get too stressed out of yourself. Always find time to relax and get away from life's hectic pace. The more you are mentally at peace, the better equipped you are to face life head-on, which means that whatever you do, you are even more likely to succeed. Learning to understand and appreciate who you are is the most important thing.

Book 3

Self Love: *Find your inner love, increase your Self-Esteem and Confidence, and practice Self-Care*

Introduction

What do you think about the word love?

Should you think about the people you worry most about and about the things you care about? Does it bring happiness and goodness to a woman's emotions? Does it make a woman smile from the inside as she thinks of the word love because loving makes her feel happy? If we talk about the word love, most of us speak of positive emotions. When we encourage ourselves to love someone or something, it can trigger excitement and happiness feelings that are only experienced when love is part of it. The love of energy is strong. So why when we add the word "me" to the front of the word "heart" to build the phrase "self-love," we tend to pause and doubt whether self-love is good. Could thoughts about the term self-love create a negative feeling inside?

Let me bring a question to you. Do you respect yourself? If you said yes, how can you give yourself love? What are you doing to show your self-love? If you answered no, why don't you? You choose to respect yourself or not. It's up to you, if you respect yourself, you value yourself. You're doing it on your own.

Self-love, like the word love, is powerful. Though, you can't even find a consistent definition if you look it up in dictionaries. I remember as I looked up. Many dictionaries have a very positive spin, and some have a more negative description. For example, one dictionary had only the negative definition of self-love as being conceited and vain; whereas another dictionary described it as having unconditional love for your happiness. It's no wonder that we all have different views of the word self-love. How can a word of love, a word that creates such positive feelings and emotions be immediately questionable by adding the word self to its forehead?

Is it because we often perceive someone who has too much self-love as being egotistic or conceited? Is there a confusion between self-centeredness and self-love? Think of someone you know you're talking about with little regard for others or someone who's always talking about how big they are. Do you think they show you their self-love for themselves? I don't think so; it's often the exact opposite of what happens to that person inside. They often try to fill up with the approval and love of others because they have very little self-love.

To maximize our satisfaction, self-love is something that I believe is important. I love the idea that self-love in terms of our happiness is the love of "self." We allow self-esteem when we have self-love. I conclude that self-love is self-respect, accountability for your behavior, tolerance, and unconditionality. If we make a mistake, self-love is forgiving. Self-love is to realize that we have made a mistake and to learn from our mistakes by taking action. Self-love is good and nice. Self-love is not always simple. It often takes work inside to help create more acceptance and love for yourself, but if you do the job, you are likely to live a happier life and who doesn't want to be happy?

I don't suggest that you be pregnant, vain, or let your ego run wild, but I suggest that you take a look at yourself and decide that you're worth loving. I recommend that you agree that you need to think nice things about yourself so that you can relax and feel that you are good enough. You simply have more love to give to others when you embrace yourself and value yourself, and you can gain more love from others. Allow the energy of love to envelop you and decide that more than you did yesterday, you will take one step towards loving yourself.

How can you ask? You that decide to accept and love your body and, as a result, start feeding it healthy and more nourishing foods so that it can be its strongest. You might want to forgive yourself for a past mistake you made and take note of the experience you learned so that you don't do it again instead of beating yourself internally. You can want to do something you love doing because you've always been placing yourself last and depriving yourself for so long. Do you put the last ones you love on your list? Practice some self-love and move up on your "to-do" chart, perhaps not.

There's only one of you, and you're the only one who can want to appreciate you a little bit more. When you want to pursue more self-love, see as your satisfaction improves, and more will come your way of care, pleasure, goodness, and compassion. Loving is something important, and so is self-love. Grant you a little love and let it shine!

Self-Love: A very crucial issue for women

There is a wholeness that calls all men. We are born with its music ringing in our ears, and yet we come to know it because of its absence. For most men, when the gap within us becomes so high that it cannot be filled outward, the time comes in adulthood. And running from fears is a struggle we can't keep fighting. It's the awakening. The point wherein our tracks we stop dead and decide the fight is over. This recognition gives rise to some form of serenity. We see that "happily ever after" is never a place in the world around us that can be sought. It's just a condition that gets from within. We're following it like it's a drug. We chase it out of necessity because it is so deep and vacuous that it becomes a sort of living torture within us. We are addicted to a substance that we can never locate at all moments when the solution is with us. What are you thinking about this wholeness? Happiness is this wholeness. The wholeness is self-love.

The trump card is self-love. It's the center that all grows in. It's the end of our trip here. And it's the only action. Happiness changes everything in the same manner as it is itself. What this implies is that when a person assumes the practice of self-love, they devote themselves to re-surfacing and peeling back all that is unhealed and unloving within them. Without moving through the processes of awareness, truth, equanimity, forgiveness, self-reliance, trust, responsibility, gratitude, realization, compassion, unity, freedom, letting go, joy boundless love, you cannot complete this journey to self-love. It is the spiritual journey through which we realized all other journeys.

Most of us were trained to grow up implicitly that self-love was vain and pregnant. We were told that people who associated modesty with prostration were immoral in self-deprecation. This is why we have to know for ourselves what self-love is and what self-love is not. Individuals who are historically viewed as "selfish and conceited" do not value themselves, but are individuals who do not understand solidarity and who sense such a deep loss in their own lives that they feel the need to snatch it from others and conceal it. We shield themselves with self-defeating vanity for their insecurities. On the opposite, to such a degree that there is excess, people who show themselves affection are meeting their own needs. And they don't feel deficient in that quantity. There's nothing they need from us. Alternatively, they pour out their affection to others. We are truthful with their weaknesses and strengths, realizing we have no impact on all the meaning and seeking the stable platform of modesty in that transparency.

Self-love is the self's search for the highest good. Expressing self-love means recognizing one's own unwavering and deserving value that cannot be introduced or excluded, simply hidden or emphasized, and then pursuing actions and thoughts that resonate with the highest self-good.

It is the condition of completion or unification of selves. It is the state and focus of pure self-esteem. Such emphasis contributes to honesty, self-confidence, self-respect, self-admiration, and a deep sense of inner peace and enjoyment. Perhaps it is most important to note that self-love is the condition of total non-resistance to the self at a Vibrational stage. And so, if you want to start loving yourself, you may need to look first for the ways you resist yourself and resist where you are. Look for ways you can recognize that you don't show love to yourself, and start forming an idea of what new choices you might create from that perception. People who love each other choose the least resistance course. It's not virtuous to choose the hard way... It's self-penalty. Look for what you want yourself to appreciate. In this very moment (which is the truth of where you are), what do you value for yourself? Look in the mirror and bear in mind that you're never going to be what you think is "perfect." The only way to be safe is to stop attempting to contend inside your mind with the picture of success. Love what's about you right now. Find a way to decide that's not just where you should be, but that's enough. You're sufficient.

Most of us are so deeply in the mentality of self-hatred at the outset of this cycle that we can't even get a glimpse of life. And so instead of battling to reach the point of view, we should constantly ask ourselves all day long and particularly when there is a decision to make... "What would someone else do right now if they were standing in my shoes?"

The path to self-love begins by loving yourself for who you are. This suggests that you have to be brave enough to tell the ultimate truth, which is that in our lives, we are strong creatures capable of creating happiness and prosperity or pain and suffering. We're not supposed to be offenders. We have the resources to choose from, and this control is both our greatest duty and the greatest opportunity. Talking truth to ourselves, in particular, can be a daunting task because it implies we have to accept that we did not live by our happiness, wishes, and beliefs. Honoring ourselves and who we are implies we have to be able to remove our interest in the views of others about us because no one understands what makes us happy but us. And if we dedicate ourselves to living in harmony with our reality, we sometimes have to be willing to take risks to change course and go in a completely different direction. If we don't want to take this risk, we can't hope to be content.

Self-love means to honor our feelings and to respond to them. Feelings (like a compass) are in place to tell us whether we are in the path of our true self (and what we want) or in the opposite direction at any time. That's why you believe it is the most important thing to remember in general. If you're brave enough to make your number one priority feel good, all other conditions in your life will just fit in. Self-love involves recognizing that you are constantly evolving into a more powerful and loving being and just where you are. In comparison to where you were, where you are is perfect. The desire for self-improvement arises from a place of self-love from the search for the highest good for yourself, not because you don't believe you're nice enough or need to change because you're unlovable if you're not.

People who love themselves don't think in terms of what's correct for values. Preferably, they only hold beliefs that are useful and beneficial to them. We let go of what doesn't represent them anymore. Reach for a self-understanding. Get to grasp why you choose your life's limits and realize what you're afraid of. Life experiences also tell us that being powerless is the way to attract attention and love. Look at attempts to get acceptance, attention, and love from your own (as well as from other peoples). Tell yourself what I've been told to be lovable? Why have I been told to be responsible for my life? Learning these patterns is not our fault, but we can change them. We don't have to allow these fears to keep us away from what we want. They don't have to have power over us. Loving yourself means not allowing fear to operate your life for you anymore.

To love oneself always implies to forgive oneself. Forgiveness is much like letting an inmate free just to find out that you have been the convict all the time. Quite often in life, when we do not immediately harmonize things that cause us to suffer, they become wounds of the mental wounds that we carry with us every day in our consciousness and sub-consciousness. The suffering becomes like shackles that we're so used to dealing with that we don't even know we should switch them off. Of reality, forgiving has nothing other than us to do with anyone else. Although to a party that receives it can feel very good, forgiveness is always about us. Whether it's someone else we forgive or we forgive ourselves, reconciliation is always one-sided. To forgive them-or ourselves, we don't need the other person present. The recovery takes place entirely inside ourselves. Forgive yourself for making mistakes, mistakes have no impact on worth, and unlike popular belief, forgiving is not poor.

Many of us have a false, self-limiting core belief that we promote or excuse guilt because we accept ourselves and are therefore out of reach of our acts. This is frightening for most of us as we think we're going to hurt other people if we're out of reach of our acts. This is something we accept when we took the false idea that something is inherently wrong with us and that we are necessarily "evil" somewhere in our early lives. So, withholding forgiveness from one's self can become a form of self-control that becomes virtuous and "good" as punishment we are taught. In this sense, it becomes like self-abuse to deny acceptance from one's self. For this purpose, to forgive one's self, one must seek evidence of one's intrinsic goodness and build faith.

We just know what love is on this planet. As a cerebral concept, we may not know it, but we all know it inherently. The reason we know that is because we are at our most basic level. We are not separate from the source energy in our physical bodies. Alternatively, we become reflections of the root energy, and the same vibrational counterpart of desire is the source energy. Loving is therefore not something that we can ever avoid. It's a constant, and it's our choice whether we can resist it or allow it to happen in this lifetime. The universe is made up of love. And as such, your birthright is devotion. If we just wake up to receive it, like flowers opening up to the sun, it becomes possible to do everything. You're going to create your life the way you want it. And you're going to be able to say "I love myself" and mean it.

The Art of Self Love

Many of us are to some extent dissatisfied with ourselves, however, unhappiness that turns to self-loathing for some that affect every aspect of life. The desire to change ourselves and life are constrained by self-loathing. It encourages us to settle for less than we earn, contributing to bad choices and bad relationships. Some of us may not even realize that we are in the self-loathing mode, but if we are frank with ourselves, we can see that our lives are a direct reflection of what we believe we deserve. We will begin to understand the decisions we have created and why by re-evaluating the way we live our lives and the ones we choose to love.

Visual is the first step in self-love. Look in the mirror and see how you are. See and appreciate the individuality of each function. See your supposed imperfections as a perfect image of what you were intended to be precise.

The second step is to mention the ten most positive qualities; compassion, humility, and so on. Look at every positive condition and situation where the values were expressed. Visualize the gifts you gave to others and know they are important and you are important.

The third step is to compose yourself with a short letter and continue with your admiration of you. Read openly, not filter your feelings. Put the letter in a place where you can read it when you need a reminder.

The fourth step is to take control of your life's contaminants; whether it's your home environment, your work environment, or your life's citizens. Look at the things or situations that hinder you from having complete self-love. Anything or anyone that consistently produces bad feelings removes your self-love, which in essence is the very thing that can bring you happiness.

We settle for less than we merit without total self-love. We underestimate our interest without total self-love, and in exchange, we seek validation from others, and when we don't get it, we think we're worthless.

We welcome positive elements into our lives by total self-love and reject those that are not good. We tell ourselves and the world through total self-love that we deserve the best and refuse to settle for anything less.

The myth about self-love

It seems I learn more and more about self-love wherever I stop. Everyone is talking about how we don't love each other (meaning we're talking negatively and doing crappy things for ourselves) and that's the cause of all our problems. I think that's the biggest misunderstanding out there and that's why. I realize I've been doing and doing some crappy things to those I truly enjoy a lot of times. For coming home from a bad day at work and then breaking in and yelling at someone I love-I didn't feel so caring at that moment. But just because I said these bad things and did them, it doesn't mean I don't enjoy them. That's what I think is true of us too-just because we're thinking about ourselves and doing crappy things doesn't imply, we don't value ourselves.

The question is that throughout our days, we don't feel a lot of affection. And the explanation for this is that we do not choose to think and believe things that make us feel good. Our emotions are forming our perceptions and influence our attitudes and behaviors. So if we feel bad/unhappy at any given moment because of what we think and believe-then, of course, we'll do and do crappy things about ourselves (and others)-it's unavoidable.

Loving is who we are, and from where we come. When we didn't have respect for ourselves, we can't love anything else. I've had a lot of customers come to me upset and depressed because they're getting the message that they don't have to value themselves and that something has to be wrong with them all the time.

This is where I disagree as I think it's a joke to them-they just enjoy themselves and there's nothing wrong with them. The missing goal in our lives is to know how to feel loved more often. And this doesn't mean it has to be loving thoughts about ourselves (although this will happen naturally as soon as you begin to feel more loving). Think back to a time when you fell in love with someone (you feel joyful, giddy, happy, loving). I believe I don't personally promise that during that period you lovingly handled and spoke to yourself. Why? Because your actions and behaviors can only be compassionate when you feel love irrespective of the feeling that triggers it.

And I think we need to stop trying to figure out how to treat each other because we're already doing it pointless. We have to agree that in our life, we want to have more happiness and then begin to focus on things that fill us with joy. As a daily practice, you begin to notice and recall the things you love all day long (by saying it loudly). Start with little things like that great piece of chocolate, that steaming cup of hot cocoa, the sun shining on your face, the rubbish of your cat in your lap, the smell of wood-burning in a fireplace, and so on. So draw on it every day to see how often you should concentrate on feeling love-because at the end of the day, it's just the feeling that we like.

It is self-love in action that women are beautiful creatures of selflessness. We're offering compassion, consideration, courage, and understanding. We share our lives, we try community groups, and we often put other people's needs above our own. The problem with such acts of noble kindness is that we sometimes find ourselves in an undesirable situation. Setting boundaries and standing up for what we want and what we believe can be difficult.

What borders are there towards self-love for a woman?

There may be physical, psychological, or behavioral boundaries. There are clear physical boundaries: these are related to touch. Receiving an embrace from a close friend is soothing, but it is wrong for a stranger to contact us. When someone we don't recognize approaches our room too closely, we should step away. The limits we place on ourselves and others are psychological boundaries. This is about sharing personal information and investigating our psychological problems. Behavioral limits are the behaviors where we clash with others. Our ethnic, political, or social contexts may influence the formation of boundaries. These considerations will bring implications to our boundary understanding. Understanding our boundaries is very important because trust is related to the violation/respect of boundaries. The issue of trust is of paramount importance in a relationship (romantic or otherwise).

What is the boundary's purpose?

Boundaries are not fields of force or ways of preventing people from ever knowing the true "you." We are the "between rooms." We all need distance from each other to each other. It allows for relaxed behavior and health emotions.

Such emotions of safety and security arise from knowing that it is an act of self-love to establish healthy boundaries. And we express ourselves and protect our interests and needs to survive as an empowered woman.

How Do Boundaries Relate to Self-Love?

We also heard the saying: "You must first learn to love yourself to be true love." It makes a great deal of sense. Sometimes, though, it is taken out of context. Self-love act is a GREAT practice involving knowing why we are doing the things we are doing. You need to identify the target to set the boundaries and make them insurmountable (protect yourself and motivate yourself). You should embrace love when you meet it, appreciate it and acknowledge it. And you're going to fight tooth and nail to protect that when you enjoy it.

It is necessary to establish boundaries to build a strong sense of self. To sense incongruence, we use our inner wisdom and draw on our inner power to act. Then, in a new way, we approach life: a loving way. We see the reality, the shadow, and the sun. And we can choose a life of grace and love by knowing all the truth. After all, that's the life we both want.

Affirmations of Self Love

When you feel a little happier about yourself, to begin with, do you think your affirmations might have a simpler "band" of them? They could just do it. Self-love is something most people say they like, but when it may seem impossible, there are moments. Work with these ideas to bring the truth of your inner beauty back into balance.

#1: Get caught in the illusion that you're "supposed" to be fine, despite something that no one does. I don't, you don't, it's not the role models. Dream of it. When you learned all of it yourself, wouldn't you have a lot of motivation to seek out the best in others? I do, I say, by encouraging them to support you. So it's completely impractical, even at a social level. Look for these indications you feel bad about not knowing things: * Out of fear that it will make you sound stupid, you hesitate to ask a request.

You're hesitating to start a new project because you think you're going to find a phrase or two that you haven't yet figured out.

You just have to step in and convince everyone when you think you know more— so they can see you're not as naive as they assumed you were.

As a consequence, you hold back your life from this false belief in your expected success. You stick to the familiar, endlessly procrastinating on new projects, so you don't run into situations that you don't know how to deal with. You are stealing from others; Family, relatives, coworkers,etc. Out of the chance to share one's best gifts. Test these claims to support natural thinking.

I feel good when others share their knowledge and caring talents with me.

I enjoy watching new projects develop— progressing effortlessly through every little obstacle.

I forgive myself, just as I forgive anyone, for committing mistakes in life.

#2: You don't think you're allowed to have what you want.

At some point in our life, most of us consider limits. It might sound unfair. Yet as an empowered adult, the only real governor of what you are "allowed" to create as your world of dreams is the set of obstacles that you conceive. Who knew that you were so strong? When you see yourself in the following situations, this might be you:

- You see someone else having great success in an environment where you feel challenged. The internal reaction is, "Oh, that's cool for them, but I don't think I can."

- Your perspective in life is that it's a spectator sport. You are watching, but you are not joining.

You take stock of your current life and find some of the most important items you want are absent— home, work, friendship, etc. As a result of believing that satisfying your greatest wishes is a non-limited endeavor, you are setting yourself up for constant disappointment. You can find yourself in a set-up system to build what you believe you can get rather than what you want. Think about it. Expand all that effort to pursue something that you don't even want! Events don't go well, no wonder! Instead, try this: * It's safe to imagine the life I want.

Dreaming of the things I love is fun!

I will make it if I can visualize it.

#3: You behave or function as a survivor.

This can be a little difficult to hear, as most people don't want to talk about themselves as offenders. Then we do it again, occasionally. After all, if "to me" was doing all this material, then it's not my fault if things went wrong.

Here's the position of power. They always inspire yourself to make something more to your taste as they remember yourself as part of the innovative team that brought you to the point where you are now. If these conditions in life sound vaguely familiar, you may be on the verge of accepting existence in a whole new way!

You find yourself saying or thinking, "I haven't had a choice. I've been coerced into it."

You're spending a lot of time battling for the freedom to be who you are or to be handled as you want to be treated.

As an excuse to "guilt" others to support you, you invoke ill health or misfortune.

If some of you believe you're weak, you're still going to be at odds with the inner truth of your birthright —personal power. This tension will lead to poverty and ill health. It also leaves you extremely vulnerable to being manipulated. Consider affirmations like this to get you going and accept your artistic wisdom:

I'm a wonderful life maker! I am the source of love, unity, and wisdom.

I am surrounded by love and harmony. I am surrounded by Allah.

I float softly on my life's imaginative stream, treating each bounce and swell as a chance to learn and flourish.

Self-Love Principles

IS Sound familiar to any of these scenarios? You feel like angry dragons are coming to you, exhausted from carrying the world's weight on your shoulders, dragging around an imaginary ball and chain that's locked around your ankles, and if that's not enough, you're hyper-vigilant about having to constantly dodge bullets aimed at your head and chest! These are all distortions that we can experience when our Self-Love tank level is empty, and our Self-Hatred level is overwhelmed.

Their self-love degree influences every aspect of our life-our relationships, our jobs, how much money we earn, how peaceful and happy we look, and how people see us.

Here's a quick self-love assessment: do you think it's your job to define your value and lovability, and the job of no one else? Or do you think your self-worth is based on how people feel about you?

You can be compassionate with yourself when you make a mistake and learn from the situation, or are you beating yourself up?

Do you feel guilty about taking care of yourself or do you regularly do something for yourself?

Instead of seeing yourself through all the false beliefs and delusions, your self-love will improve as you continue to see who you are. They need to take responsibility as people and realize who we are. If we can embrace this obligation, we realize that we are linked to our wise and caring Adult-Self. There is a deep reservoir in the very essence of who we are in our ability to love, experience joy and compassion, and express our true-self with an abundance of creativity and self-love.

Here are 3 Self-Love Principles to help guide you into your beautiful essence today: not handing over to others who you are-this must be done with your wise and loving adult self. Others can see you only when they have an open heart.

Your Authentic Self's worth remains unchanged, unchanging, and nothing can alter that, including nothing that you can take away from you. Your Authentic Self is your True-Self, the one you truly reflect from a natural state of love on your precious heart.

When you hinge your Self-Worth on your performance or how others think of you, based on those events, your Self-Worth will fluctuate.

Many of the things people are struggling with —depression, anxiety, and relationship issues are signs of their True Self disconnection — their Authentic Self. Be kind to yourself when you begin to adapt these Self-Love values to your everyday life. Believe in yourself when you open your heart to the magnificence of who you are and let yourself be amazed when you step into your true state of happiness.

Self-love: Why have you destroyed it?

If you have to wonder what self-love is, you probably won't have it anymore. Yet, most specifically, you will question yourself: why have you missed it?

You were undoubtedly deprived of the constant injection of affection that would have nurtured and extended your own, due to some two decades of abuse, depression, and/or dysfunctionality. However, you were forced to swallow what it was not, originally claiming that its denial was due to your shortcomings and weaknesses, and if you had just followed the exacting standards of your father, then the floodgates would certainly have opened up.

Most possibly they never did, because you never did-that is, meet such exacting standards, sometimes compelled to embrace and manage parental put-downs, abasements, and defamations that had no association with your actions or achievements, yet that you still had to rationalize. After all, they were the adults, and they certainly knew more about the ways of the world than you were, leaving you little choice but to "learn" from your "misdeeds" and accept your "punishments," so that you would be properly "disciplined" to never repeat your "transgressions." Even if, later in life, you came to realize that what "filled your tank" was missing was lacking.

You were forced to look at yourself the way you were seen by your parents. You've got what they've sown. If they were growers, then until you developed into them, they cultivated their seeds of adolescent misery, poverty, and unresolved violence.

Abuse and alcoholism have broken your self-love, causing you to feel diminished and dehumanized, and you have attributed their treatment to the belief that you were exactly what they meant you were. They removed you from it instead of adding to and growing your passion.

If you want to see Him in anything, you have to search in it for love. In the case of your parent, you could notice it in them, particularly when they mistreated the way they did.

Unknowingly, using the images of your parents as reflections that represent what you thought they saw in you, you saw what they had in them, which may have been furious and despised at times until this warped vision as your own.

Self-love is worth it. Abuse is a cause of unworthiness. This converts what you are and have been made to be the opposite- in other terms, transformed into something you are not. If in yourself, you can't detect and communicate with affection, you can't extend it to others. This feeling must, after all, originate within before it can radiate without it, thus explaining why you rarely received it.

"How can an adult child who has been trained from the earliest years to give up true inner love?" questions the textbook Adult Children of Alcoholics (World Service Organization, 2006, p. 434). "We have an answer based on the experience of ACA: love is there, and God is given. Love has always been there. We need power from within to reawaken this love." Yes, but...

That ability relies to a significant degree on how much redemption you have achieved, as the overwhelming need for survival has turned the soul into the God-opposite version of what it was intended to be and before and until you can reconcile with it, the "strength to reawake" will initially be little more than a flicker. And without enough trust to allow you to affirm the equally important human connection, you may find it very difficult to reach that level of love.

Yes, the success of the recovery program, the length of which depends based on the individual undergoing it and the amount of effort one brings into it, would soon show that there are two specific phases to it— the physical one, during which you are only primarily concerned with survival tactics, and the spiritual one, during which you re-experience that all-important love you are ultimate.

Part of your struggle is the frustrating paradox that you are, at least, in essence, the reflection of the Higher Power that is created in you, but, shortly after your earthly first breath, you were converted and whittled down by the parental offenses and degradations that recreated you and that you believed you deserved. As a consequence, you could only see life from the level of the need to survive.

Without input, cure, or even knowledge of the actions that ignited your radical undo, you were unknowingly converted into what you were naturally to what was-that is, what you were not.

In the ultimate irony of insult-to-injury, the very parents who were supposedly there to defend you produced the damage from which you then needed protection and then ignored their disadvantage, forcing you to pick up your bits, sometimes contributing to a lengthy road filled with self-help training, counseling, counseling support groups, and twelve-step services.

Your inevitable and irresolvable answer to this problem was to kill your most self-loving portion of you. Looking for internal security by leaving and establishing the inner refuge of the infant, you substituted it with the fake or pseudo-self that is stripped of the natural, the real, and true property of God-reflective (translated as love-reflective), causing you to pull the plug on its light and plunge you into darkness.

As an individual, the false self is a cheap imitation of the real thing, but a required break that helps you to navigate the universe with perceived security as an unrecovered adult child, a word that, by the way, you may have never used until this point. Love is real, not a concept, and from this synthetic portrayal of what you eventually came to believe was the real you, self-love cannot exist or flow.

Yes, what follows from this self-replacement is the vital inner voice — the perpetually-playing, loop-lapping, self-looking,-abasing, and even-abandoning tapes that might coincidentally sound like parental voice-over and that you felt might have been substituted by their affection if you were only good enough to warrant it.

The false self is the ultimate sacrifice for civilization and, as an addition, the most basic need of the animal kingdom: shelter. Through a physical form, health enhances security and protection will precede everything else. Nothing else, like and especially love, can follow without it.

The painful and abrupt arrival at-if not a collision with— your bottom is the equivalent of your self-love search, the point where every conceivable method has failed to arrest your dwindling spiral and the only direction left is up or back to the Higher Power that created you. Hitherto outside control or contact, he is waiting for your willingness to strengthen the bond that depends on the success of the system. It will almost certainly involve periods of tenuous, broken, restored, and again partly reconnected alignments, as the cycle is nothing but smooth and continuous.

In this situation, relations do not necessarily involve height but emotional and spiritual healing. You will extend yourself to Christ as the hearts rise-literally.

By contrast, when you re-sink into the rapid sand of despair and depression, you cannot forge that connection or even feel its presence. The attachment material is not strong, but light, as you compare yours with his, which was the same before your existence.

There are also physical properties of connections. The neural ones between neurons or brain cells that reflect self-criticism and low self-esteem are most definitely as dense as cords, while those with positive self-feelings are likely to be as weak as threads because of the childhood putdown bombardment. Only a concerted effort, combined with frequent affirmations, to modify your self-image will initiate this re-wiring and create new neuro-pathways.

Integral to this re-climbing to the self-love that is the confidence that your Father has granted you.

During your greatest time of parental betrayal and harm, seemingly absent, it's hard to trust the eternal parent who seemed to be serving as a "bystander" during all of it.

The fact that you could not trust the earthly parents who inflicted you with the damage of your life and the negative attributes you associated with them, you quickly reassigned to your eternal one, is to exacerbate this dynamic.

Depending on your degree of pain and loss, you may sometimes also assume that both mortal and heavenly parents have compromised to render your death harder for purposes of vengeance, past-life penance, martyrdom, or causes outside your conceptualization.

There are many intermediate steps on your path back to self-love. First and foremost is your intrinsically known surrender to the Creator.

Second, you have to plow through the thick layers, often impenetrable, that divide you from him. Abuse-bred defenses require considerable work to infiltrate so that you can connect him with who he is and not the carbon copy of your parents you came to believe he is. Questioned as to the concept of "reality,"

Christ once said, "That which never varies." Integral to and the core of God is love and that is a fact.

Additional steps involve recognizing what your inner child required to be created; knowing why you've embraced the survival strategies you've done; separating the removed yet subconsciously interpreted features of your parental perpetrators from present-day others that could unintentionally cause you, causing awkward, nervous, or out-and-out frightened feelings; and realizing that most of your child's emotions are unpleasant.

Self-love is a slow re-climb of the mountain that kicked you off from abuse and alcoholism, requiring you to survive at its base. Nevertheless, the success of the process can be calculated with increases in height, such as those on the self-acceptance and other plateaus, supported by the instrument of confidence.

According to the Adult Children of Alcoholics textbook (p. 436), "Self-love is an important spiritual element of the ACA system." "Self-love helps the adult child to fill the esteem or nurturing that we have not earned as infants. In embracing oneself, we stop the negative self-talk... self-love gives us a new pair of glasses... Unhealthy behavior is no longer 'usual' for us." Self-love, sadly, is granted to the eternal-parent, but sometimes taken by the earthly-parent, and the detoured path from your roots to your destination may be a ride from your goal. But where else would you finally go but back to your inherent self and the affection it was born with?

Importance of Self-Love for women

When the words "love yourself" or "self-love" is used, there may be ambiguity about what is intended. This is because we think in terms of what we are comfortable with, based love when we hear the word "kiss." When we seek to value ourselves, we will take a similar approach to the one used independent affection, utilizing ourselves as the focus of our devotion. When we fled into others, we can try to escape into ourselves. We may become self-absorbed and self-indulgent, giving priority to our own needs. It's still the motive to escape. We deny unhappiness and condemn ourselves in this way.

Self-love has nothing to do with being the target of your interest for yourself. Self-love is described a feeling of inner peace, a relationship with Christ. It's not the act of "making" an item because you might be incredibly satisfied with it, whether that entity is someone else or something else or you. Self-love is a state of awareness, a form of perceiving, a mindset that contributes to an integrated perception of the world and, in effect, a realization of your relationship with God.

With the natural need to give and receive affection, all human beings are formed. We are formed in love that forms the basis of our divine spiritual selves and our physically embodied existence. Even the many obstacles we face in our early lives do not erase our divine heart from loving, because it is the core of who we are.

The solution to this process of trouble is self-love growth. Self-love is not a practice, but the reconstruction of our inherent divine center— GOD— which is esteem. From this location, affection flows freely into the body, mind, emotional energies, and spirit through our Divine Creator. Loving is conveyed as a natural flow to others outwardly and oneself.

This begins with self-acceptance to show self-love. They're the same. When you quit hating yourself, you start to love yourself, especially at the level of feeling. You will experience real shifts in awareness as you practice self-acceptance of your emotions as they are now. To find satisfaction, you no longer try to juggle individuals or things in the outside universe. You find fulfillment from within, just by acknowledging the emotions as they are right now, without acting out.

Do not underestimate the importance of recognition of yourself. It can put an end to the emotional pain you encounter or contribute to your ideal spiritual experience. You will hit the peak of inner awareness, beginning with the routine. You become whole by welcoming all your feelings; life becomes holistic. You are feeling peace. In the outside environment, you no longer compulsively try solidarity, whether with another individual or with an accomplishment. You embrace yourself, and you enjoy yourself.

We should start by finding a quiet inner place to meditate and reflect inside our spirit. Sometimes having a little bit of inner calm may seem impossible; especially when things are rough. Do you already know how much better you feel when you take time to find that quiet place inside? How many of us are taking the time to find that quiet place when we're stressed out? If we take the time to find that quiet inner place, this is the path to the inner peace and acceptance of ourselves that we all so desperately desire. For our inner and outer self, this means finding harmony.

Most of us as women are regularly attacked by magazines and newspapers, commercials, family members, colleagues, and even acquaintances with negative messages from our outward selves and our bodies. We are shown computer-manipulated photos of the "complete" body — a body that for the vast majority of us is not normal and can only be achieved by self-abuse and hunger.

They still forget that women come in tons of different shapes and sizes, and the media just don't represent this diversity. When we don't see ourselves reflected, it's hard to feel good about ourselves. What we feel about our bodies affects how we feel for ourselves. So we need to embrace our bodies and find ways of loving our bodies— and ourselves.

There is no doubt in my mind that the quality of love is the #1 quality that God wants our souls and personalities to be worked upon. Many unbelievers, atheists, and agnostics can see the power of love and how it can transform people and a change life when approached and carried out properly.

Hollywood has made tons of films just about the power of love— especially the special love that can happen in a romantic relationship between a man and a woman. Upon watching a very well-made film about the power of love, even strong grown men can be brought to tears.

The nature of love is truly universal-as it transcends cultures, countries, and ideologies literally. Love is this world's universal language, and people from all walks of existence are seeing it for what it is and realizing the strength in it. Surrounding yourself in affection brings your life positive energy and loving yourself is loving God.

The Power of Self-Love

I'm enjoying myself and praising myself."-Walt Whitman It's called self-love, self-confidence, self-acceptance, self-respect, self-esteem, self-esteem, feeling good for yourself-it's all the same and amazing. The opposite-doubting yourself, disliking yourself, feeling ashamed, believing that you're not good enough - that everything feels terrible.

As a coach, I find that self-love is one of the major issues that my clients are struggling with. Ah, for other purposes, they could call me. We may want to lose weight or have more wealth or have more fulfilling relationships, but it often points out that the real issue is a lack of self-love. It's easy to improve relationships. After all, you value yourself because you can give affection, and you can let someone respect you. You avoid using food to compress the pressure of low self-esteem because you respect yourself and it's easy to manage your weight. The pulse is strong when you enjoy yourself, so you draw wealth and everything else you desire, of course.

You've been raised to respect yourself and recognize your worth. You may have tried to become who they wanted you to be because of pressure from parents, teachers, and peers, so they'd love you, and you didn't love yourself. This is usually followed by the absurd conclusion that you're not good enough, which contributes to waste your whole life trying to prove your value and attempting to get others to accept you.

There is no replacement for self-love. You will be always frustrated in life if you don't respect yourself. You're not even going to see opportunities right before you. It's going to affect the partnerships. Even if someone else loves you, you can't feel it. Only to the degree that you respect yourself would you encourage someone else to love you. And it is equally true that only to the extent that you love and accept yourself, you can love and accept another person.

Everyone and everything in your environment reflects or lack your self-love. The good news is that you don't have to constantly "FIX" the outside universe because everything comes from you. Once you "FIX" your inner world and the strongest place to start is by wanting to value yourself more, everything improves. When you choose self-love, your well-being will strengthen, you will have more strength and optimism, your partnerships will become more positive, you will enjoy greater happiness, and there will be wonderful rewards wherever you go. You empower the World to entertain you and inspire you when you value yourself.

And how do you choose to respect yourself and want more? Start by seeing yourself that you are a different person. Start by doing yourself nice things like:

Get someone to clean your house.

Take the perfect vacation you've anticipated.

Give yourself a day of pure pleasure-often!

Buy a special present for yourself — simply because you are YOU!

Make a list of your positive characteristics and read your list every day.

Each time anyone praises you, believe it! Keep a list of these references as evidence of how awesome you are and return to them when you need a reference.

Look in the mirror of the bathroom every morning and whisper to yourself: "I love you. You are truly and eternally amazing and deserving of all good things." Yes, if you believe this with sincerity any time you look in a mirror, your life will improve immensely!

Eventually, make a statement: "I remove my restricting conviction that I'm not good enough and substitute it with the happiness of genuine self-love." It's amazing how quickly you will get what you want when you esteem yourself, treat yourself right, and realize that you're good enough. You will bring in what you want with the Power of Self-Love because you realize you deserve it. As you bask in the Self-Love Magic, you will find that you can be and do and have what you want!

Narcissism and self-love

How often people equate self-love with narcissism is fascinating to me because, in many respects, they are both opposites.

A woman recently asked a question about this issue: "How do I decide if I'm selfish? How do I differentiate between self-care and narcissism? I've been denying myself love and care for so long, and now that I'm focused on respecting myself-listening to my inner child, and taking care of myself, I still feel insecure to rely on myself. I can't tell if I'm narcissistic or if I'm concentrating on my own. It's about knowing how to see the heart, your inner child, and how to be at least as caring to your inner child as you would be to a real child, you know.

While you may have come to think that narcissism is about enjoying themselves, it is the opposite: that is, narcissistic people are doing everything they can to get others to accept them. We exploit in many forms instead of validating themselves to get others to support them. Since they feel so hollow and vulnerable internally, they are constantly trying to have power over getting the attention and support of others- talking about themselves and themselves, drawing attention in many different ways, being upset and threatening when they don't get what they want, and being dismissive of others. We don't take responsibility for their feelings and needs but drag others to give them what they don't give to themselves.

Women who are on the path of learning to love themselves are open to learning with others in general. We want to learn and grow, so they get excited instead of getting angry when someone points out something about themselves. For narcissists, the opposite is true. Once faced with their self-centered and dishonest actions, they feel attacked and therefore attack back.

The opposites are being self-centered, self-responsible, and self-loving. When we want others to give up on us, we become self-centered and greedy, and when we value ourselves enough to be able to share our happiness with others, we are self-care. Individuals who learn to love themselves and take responsibility for their feelings enjoy sharing their love with others, while narcissistic, self-centered people focus on getting love from others.

You intend to determine whether you are narcissistic or love yourself. You operate from your loving adult self when you intend to love yourself and share your love, and you are connected to your spiritual source of love and truth. You work from your damaged self while your purpose is to receive love from others, completely disconnected from a divine center of compassion and reality.

I'd recommend this to the woman: "Even the idea that you're wondering whether you're arising from self-love or narcissism shows that you're open to learning and that your goal is to know how to esteem yourself. Narcissists never doubt their behavior. You've got to let go of feeling because relying on oneself is selfish. In one degree or another, the injured self in all of us becomes selfish, so learning to love oneself is what ultimately removes the wounded self's narcissism.

Elevate self-love, trust, and empowerment— Proven Tips, Part One — Calm Your Inner Criticism Does your inner critic ever devastate your self-esteem with negative self-talking about your appearance, abilities, or life? Take advantage of validated resources that are sure to help make the inner critic more important than all the gold in Fort Knox as an inspiring inner mentor.

The suggestions in this essay should allow you to evaluate the job description of your internal reviewer. To motivate you to an even higher level of self-respect and self-love, you should retrain your vital inner voice. Because your self-judgments will vanish and your body image and trust will strengthen, the outside community will react to you with more encouragement and positive comments. You're going to faceless "difficult people." It will seem much safer to have discussions that you once thought would be tough. Ready to begin?

Note that what we avoid remains, rather than criticizing the inner critic or trying to get rid of it. Instead of combating within you the pessimistic word, say "Hi" to it in a cool, non-judgmental manner. You will achieve tremendous independence when you become your own critic's impartial observer. Instead of punishing yourself by flailing around at a detractor that bounces here and there with a performance artist's athleticism, make a direct statement, "Thank you for sharing your point of view. Now it's time for a new idea." When the inner enemy is heard, he won't yell for your attention anymore. It's probably going to take a long snooze.

Now, by linking your critical voice, you will grow more self-respect and self-love. Every chance is a gem. Because you are clever, you are reading this book. You know you should change anything you don't like about your life. This ensures you can work through any existing negative comments that annoy you quickly and easily. Most of these important statements are based on unparalleled convictions. Become an investigator with a mind-clutter. Work through the disarray and determine what's real, "I should change this component of how I look in the world, but I'm satisfied with this other dimension of my appearance. Since I'm the only person in the world I'll still stay with, I'm the only one I need to satisfy."

Stop comparing yourself to other individuals, particularly superficial, idealized body standards portrayed by the media and Hollywood. Gain freedom by realizing how good you are just like you are. Your body type, personality, and purpose of life have been personalized to YOU. Your perceptions are adapted to the caring creative force that dwells within each of your body's cells. Through perfect performance, your future unfolds. You're met with the right opportunities that you need to learn and grow while you're providing the amazing talents your special DNA has planned for you. Start with one part of yourself you've criticized, such as "I'm overweight" or "I'm too small." Ask yourself a question, "What's the easiest and fastest way to embrace me as I am right now?" You'll reach your self-improvement objectives even quicker if you acknowledge your current situation. When you ask this question at night, useful answers will be given by your dreams. During the day, before you ask your question, cautiously classify ideas when they appear and study them to find helpful trends. When self-judgment arises, ask the key question, "What is the easiest and fastest way to accept me as I am now?" You will be thankful for the guidance you receive by capturing the experiences and then analyzing them.

What would you do now if you were 100% in love with yourself and your future, even if you were as flawed as the rest of us?

By having a human experience, we are all learning and growing. Acceptance to oneself... Live freely as Your Authentic Self would bring about deep personal strength and independence. Relationships and connections are going to be much easier as the universe reflects us the degree of our self-love so we can learn and grow.

Self-esteem is not self-love?

You're trapped in this gloomy self-denial area. You argue that at anything you are fine. The biggest problem is that you reject it so strongly that you can all too quickly persuade yourself of depression and anxiety.

Low self-esteem can be drilled into a child when either the parents ignore him or her, or take notice of their achievements, while harshly criticizing them for any mistakes they may make. The child feels there's no point in trying, and even if they do good, nothing will ever come out of it, so it's futile to excel.

Of course, it is not just the parents who can develop this most unwelcome function. Families are always, and often wrongly, an easy target.

One of the worst crimes of all when, I was a child was, a conceit. That's why the contributions seemed to be downplayed so often.

But it's not self-esteem, nor is it self-love. It's neither pride nor envy. The Scriptures tell us that pride and vanity are deadly sins, and the apparent reason is that we and God cannot love ourselves. You don't leave room for other people or things if you're full of yourself.

On the other end of the scale, for example, if you are a talented artist and somebody is staring at one of your works. Let's assume this guy, when it comes to art, knows what they're talking about and they're saying how good they think it's. You, with your complete lack of self-esteem, turn around and say,' Well, that's kind of you, but it's not very good.' It's not just an angry response, it's insulting as well. You tell this person, in truth, that he or she has no clue what they're talking about!

"That's kind of you doing that. Yeah, I'm pleased with how it worked out," it's perfectly acceptable. You don't sound your own horn; however, you appreciate your ability as well as the expertise of the other guy.

Lack of self-esteem holds us in Do Nothing's lonely place. It can keep us from doing things that others love, so our hopes and goals can be ruined. So, is caring with self-esteem? Yes. So, what's it exactly? Here are five points of self-esteem.

1. An honest appreciation of what we can do.

2. Realizing our values and abilities honestly.

3. Being fully aware of our capabilities as well as shortcomings.

4. Comprehension about our weaknesses.

5. Not being too concerned about what other people might think of us.

I guess this last is the most important thing. Not only can we be held back by ignorance of the viewpoints of other men, but these beliefs are generally unspoken. That's why I thought I wrote. Just look at how our imagination, in so many other ways, can keep us from achieving Healing Trauma and Stress Starts with Self-Love Your heart, mind, body, and spirit all need security and compassion. Therefore, in the cycle of healing depression and reducing stress, self-love is so necessary.

Your spiritual development and recovery will be hindered without healthy and caring support and guidance and self-love.

Your nervous system needs security to unlock trapped survival energy so you can enjoy life's pleasures with a cool, vigilant mind and stress-free body at last.

When you begin with some degree of self-love and self-acceptance, you're in a better place to allow someone else to support you overcome your pain and reduce your life stress.

Here's an important truth when it comes to true inner healing: true inner healing takes a lot of courage from you because with the emotional wounds you will have to trust someone else.

For the strength you have built to try and overcome the pain and tension in life, please applaud yourself right now. You're on the way to a lot of happiness and joy. You deserve a life free of fear and anxiety.

Is it time for you to restore the nervous system entirely, because in many cases you are now guilty of over-reacting or shutting down fully, and you don't want to function like this any longer?

If so, just plan to respect yourself right now.

When looking in the mirror every morning when you brush your teeth, you can begin to increase your self-love and say to yourself, "I esteem you." You can also decide to stop criticizing yourself. I realize it's easy for me to say that and it's difficult to do that, but at least I intend to start putting yourself down now. Harmful attitudes create negative feelings, which in the nervous system causes anxiety. Give yourself some freedom from your practiced conditioning, most definitely as a teenager, and learn new healthy habits of self-acceptance and self-love.

On the road to trauma healing and stress reduction, your self-love will accelerate your recovery and ensure a life full of joy and love that is your birthright. These feelings are supposed to go away while fear and anxiety are part of life. Such emotions don't go anywhere for you, so they sometimes get worse over time. The depression isn't good either for you.

Anxiety disorders are the most common mental illness in the US, and you can now, once and for all, resolve this epidemic with all the modern stress recovery methods. Trauma is no doubt a lifetime prison sentence. It's time to celebrate and encourage yourself through your self-love and recover 100% of your trauma. When you offer yourself this wonderful gift, the stress level will drop to a healthy level.

From Pain (Suicidal) To Self-love

Suicide is a permanent solution to a temporary problem, and this is what helps us to grow and become stronger people. Nothing is worth taking a lifetime, particularly another man or woman. If someone has that influence on you, you don't have to continue with them in your life. Only suck it up, walk away, take care of you, and be the person you can be!

I was in that position too. I looked like I was sick from a divorce. The gut-wrenching I already know, I-want to-crawl-in - a-hole-and-die agony! It was nearly paralyzing at times. It wasn't until some years had gone by and I could take a step back, that I started to see more distinctly how I played an enormous part in the split. Why? Because I saw someone who didn't take care of themselves the way they should have been and I took a good hard look at myself.

There was a lack of self-love in my life at the time. So self-inflicted damage is not perceived to be self-love! It was difficult to see anything lovable about myself through the haze of pain. But I knew I had to learn to love me if I ever had a healthy relationship. I will continue to draw unhealthy people into my existence if I were sick. All I wanted to do was get smarter and more self-confident because a strong person is much more desirable than a weak person. So it has to continue with me, otherwise, I don't have anything to do with a new relationship.

Love yourself, be true to yourself, and prioritize your well-being. Spiritual, physical, social, them and intellectual focus on yourself. Set goals and carry through at all times. Make positive comments for yourself. Surround yourself with people positive and uplifting. Do for yourself something good. For someone else, do something nice. The list continues and begins. There are so many ways to learn how to love and be content with yourself, and a healthy relationship is important.

After all, if we can't even recognize ourselves, how can we consider someone else? When we can't even respect ourselves, how can we expect others to accept us? In establishing a stable, loving relationship, self-love and self-acceptance are crucial first moves.

Note, love starts internally, and only when you achieve self-acceptance and self-love can you express it with someone else.

Simple Practices of Self-Love to Love Yourself More

In this book I give you 3 Simple Practices of Self-Love to Love Yourself More: Constant affirmations, contemplation, and guided meditation occur.

Shifting the balance From doing more and squeezing more into your day to do less and be more self-loving As super busy working women you recognize and appreciate the value of more-me-time and self-love yet putting it into practice is daunting, especially if you have spent years, like most women, putting the needs, needs and desires of your family before your well-being.

And with that, there's nothing wrong.

In reality, the determination to provide your family with a clean, caring, and secure home is part of your motivation to aspire relentlessly to "do more and cram more into your day." What I mean that, when you have to put the brakes on, look in the mirror and ask "what about me, what do I want?" and turn the light of love to satisfy your desires and rock your inner core.

In many cases, the better it becomes to view life through the lens of self-love and your happiness without feeling guilty and "selfish" to place yourself first, the more you practice self-love.

At the end of the day, the value of self-love and acceptance is stressed by all spiritual teachings and doctrines.

3 Self-Love Activities To Make You Love Yourself More

#1 — Write Self-Love Quotes, Affirmations, and Inspirations "I am the apple of my eye, the light of motivation I pursue" — Ntathu "Every day I love myself more and more" — Ntathu "The more I respect and appreciate myself, the more I develop within" — Ntathu Build your affirmations or choose the 3 above, write them down. You can sneak your affirmations into your handbag as an extra treat to yourself or write them out on your phone and read them to yourself during the day, especially when you feel anxious. You will immediately relax into your being's more caring side.

#2 Pray. And Show Gratitude For Your Health and Wellness If you're not a Christian, you may be confused by the thought of meditation. I understand that as I went through a phase of challenging "Jesus and all that sacred stuff" as my brother and cousin passed away that brought me to a more meaningful and soulful link with life over the years. Over the years, though, I now appreciate the importance of spending a few minutes in quiet contemplation and prayer.

If you're waiting quietly, I've composed a prayer of thanks that I'm happy to share with you.

Take a moment and utter the prayer below Dear Divine Mother Thank you for the grace that runs from my heart openly, for the love and devotion that I now offer to myself; for the emergence of boundless energy and rivers of goodwill. Thank you Mother Earth for the endless streams of life that float into my mind now endlessly enriching my life and filling me up until I overflow; for the sense of peace and peaceful heart. I am purely awful and hope forevermore streaming creation. Thank you, Holy God, for granting me the reason to value myself.

#3 Meditate. If you're doing meditation, you'll know it's one of the best gifts. There are plenty of meditations out there and you will come across different techniques and insights during your self-love path.

As a novice, studying and acquiring yoga from an experienced teacher is always better.

Here's A Guided Self-Love Meditation For You To Practice After you've spoken your 3 daily affirmations, made your morning teacup, and said your daily Gratitude Prayer, find a quiet space, put your phone on a 3-minute timer to make yourself comfortable, take a few steady breaths in and out of your nose, lower your shoulders and read the following passage to yourself loudly. Sit in silence after you have read it and take a couple more minutes remaining still before re-engaging with your day as the timer stops.

Guided Self-Love Meditation. I breathe in calm, I breathe out love I breathe in warmth, I breathe out pleasure I breathe in forgiveness; I let go of the pain and sorrow I breathe in love and happiness, I let go of the misery I breathe in life and groove in sync with the rhythms of my core Closing Thoughts And Call To Action. I urge you to set aside 15 minutes to follow these clear habits of self-care as you wake up for the next 5 days. When you begin your day, you will feel refreshed, energized, and the best of all cherished and nurtured. I would love to know how you're getting on.

Finding Your Way to Self-Love

It's the mystery we're both posing as we recover and rebuild broken self-esteem. We want to respect ourselves more thoroughly and enjoy ourselves. We certainly know the anguish of creeping into those old feelings of worthlessness. They learn even how we are most "sensitive" and self-critical.

But how do we get to feel of self-love from these wincing, self-denying feelings on earth? How do we value ourselves when we don't so clearly respect ourselves in many ways?

Do not be depressed if you feel this annoyance. It will often seem like "you really can't get there from here" in finding your way to self-love. This obvious impasse is to be anticipated.

And this is why. We must first feel full and nourished to feel happy and feel a positive sense of self. Of course, the issue is that these self-negative feelings discourage us from being satisfied and filled properly.

This is especially true as our sense of self, our self-image, our entire personality falls heavily into these hurt emotions. Since we "tell" ourselves mainly through this injury— as not enough (not adequately great, not sufficiently small, not sufficiently achieved, not sufficiently "complete," etc.)— we rob ourselves of that essential, continuous nourishment that we need to encounter more.

So our double-binding is there. We can't see our worthiness to be filled, and to see our worthiness we can't fill ourselves. So how are we supposed to get here?

Thankfully, the Bridge to Self-Love is an intermediate step, a "condition" that bridges the gap between that self-rejection deficiency state and the normal sense of self-love. It's a place that allows us to keep getting nourished, given the self-negative feelings, so we can restore and reawaken the inherent sense of being all right and necessary.

And the middle position is self-acceptance and respect for oneself. Unlike that mystical, distant land of self-love, it's remarkably easy to find this intermediate place... And incredibly strong.

Self-acceptance and kindness are not about trying to convince yourself that you are good or effective (or whatever) at the moment when your damaged emotions warn you that you are not. And it's not about having to kill yourself and correct what's "wrong" with you so you can fulfill the intense, perfectionist vision. Neither of these responses gives you a lot.

Getting into this middle position requires nothing more than handling oneself in reaction to these painful feelings and stressful times with patience and compassion.

Let's be clear about this. These wounded feelings you don't deny. And you don't doubt it's hard. You simply respond in a different way to these painful feelings.

Serving' You' instead of the Wounded Feelings You're taking a different' role.' You're taking a step backward and realizing that, as intense as these wounded feelings sound, they're just that: wounded feelings. They are feelings that a wounded place creates. They don't give you accurate information about your dignity. They only warn you of a hurt, wounded position.

And you choose to be compassionate, caring then healing with yourself in the first place in reaction to that hurt position.

Note the difference again. You choose to handle yourself with dignity, care, and compassion rather than crumble into these fake, self-negative feelings-instead of believing them, viewing yourself as a corrupt person, and driving yourself even harder. By adding kindness and understanding to this painful place, you react to this painful signal.

Note, it is not about "fixing" yourself to regain your self-esteem. It's about self-FEEDING. Your task is not to please oneself or your life's "wounded" perception. Your task is to fix the wound that is at the heart of it: to feed the poor, judging spot.

And you do this by coming to this position with patience and compassion rather than harshness.

In reality, a sign of your bruised self-esteem is that determination and toughness to repair yourself. A strict response is a continuation of the bite, refusing behavior.

So, if you choose to treat yourself calmly and compassionately instead, you break that self-hardened pattern. Despite terms of what you "know" is wrong with you, when you can step back to continue to be compassionate and embrace yourself, the real sense within you continues to be nourished.

It's waking up. Your positive sense of self becomes stronger and stronger when you pursue this strategy.

And just to be sure about that. Self-acceptance doesn't discourage you from taking positive steps for your growth and progress... Or make the necessary changes in your life. These efforts require you to be particularly supportive, patient, and self-approving. This is the very strength you need to recover, improve, and push on.

An RX for those excruciating moments of self-rejection Needless to say, kindness and empathy probably won't be your main reaction when that sense of worthlessness first raises its ugly head. We're going to want to crumble into these painful emotions at first.

So, when this happens, we just need to pull back a bit and remember that these feelings are not accurate. These are injured feelings that take you to a wounded place. Let the discomfort remind you of yourself to be gentle and healing.

For these difficult moments, give it a drug. And the more these positions become sensitive so unpleasant, the more caring, gentle, and cautious you need to be with yourself. Also, the challenge we encounter in learning to love ourselves is that the particularly painful emotions correlated with damaged self-esteem have the unpleasant capacity to "erase" our sense of self-esteem and self-worth altogether... And, in essence, we can't find love for ourselves.

We have to be prepared for this very "natural" answer to our wound. And consider it with sympathy.

Patience and patience, thankfully, are expressions of kindness. Especially when they are directed at you. And this little move will start to bring you back to you immediately: back to fullness and back to life.

You're enjoying yourself? 3 Symptoms that give you your self-love deficiency

It may seem like a stupid question at first, "Will you esteem yourself?" but it's a very significant question that deserves a true answer. Does it make you smile when you hear this question, or does it make you cringe a little? This would be your first sign of the above issue, based on your response. If you respect yourself, when you are confronted with this problem you should be able to feel good. Check out below the 3 indicators that will alert you whether you lack self-love or not.

First, ask yourself if you believe that self-love is an act of selfishness? Most people believe it's a self-love, or it's selfish.

It's not real. Have you ever heard of the saying, "If you don't respect yourself, nobody else can love you?" That assertion has so much validity because; knowing oneself provides an awareness of how to live.

Second, do you need other people around you to praise? If you are constantly searching for approval, this is also a good indicator of lacking self-love. It's a must to know how to create internal self-love.

Third, do you need to make others happy about yourself feeling happy? If you're trying to make someone happier for yourself only having a little joy than it's time to ask yourself, why? It's okay to enjoy doing things that make others happy, but if it's not in balance with your happiness, it might be another sign that you're lacking self-love.

Don't hesitate if you lack self-love. It's easy to create. The first move is to realize that you need it.

Does your lack of self-love affect your children?

If you know that you lack self-love in the back of your mind, should you worry about how it affects your kids? Absolutely. Absolutely. Children pick up everything in their environment and internalize it. So if you know that you don't have self-love, you can bet that your kids know that too. You can also guarantee that the same lack of self-love emerges for your family.

There's no hesitation! Discover 2 strategies to build self-love inside yourself as well as help your kids develop self-love.

1. Take care of yourself every day. Remember to do simple things like taking vitamins, eating whole foods, and going out on walks to energize your body. When was the last time you prepared on your own and had a candlelight bubble bath? But did something else rejuvenate you?

We often get distracted in the hectic day-to-day everyday life by taking care of our jobs, debts, and families, which contributes to gradually forgetting to take care of yourself. Starting today, do one thing that's healthy for you every day, all you.

We are stronger caretakers for our family and friends when we are no longer drained, depressed, or frustrated. It teaches the kids how to value themselves naturally because they see you loving yourself.

2. Embrace your faults or (short-comings) Let yourself and your kids realize that making mistakes is OK; life is not about being flawless, because there is no perfection. Life is about learning and growing, and only if you look at our failures as a gift can we do this.

It's not hard to learn how to accept yourself, but it requires deliberate reflection and knowing that you're losing it. Learn how to love yourself for your sake, and the sake of your children.

A self-love exercise!

Last year, as I visited Jack Canfield's Breakthrough to Triumph in Scottsdale, Az, I first heard about this practice. As one of the co-creators of the mega-popular Chicken Soup for the Soul show, most of you will be acquainted with Jack Canfield. Jack is amazing, so if you ever have the chance to see him at a conference presenting live or current, I urge you to take this opportunity! Jack taught the following exercise of self-love and does it daily himself. This was the one bit of research that we had to do at the meeting any single night. I figured that if someone every day is as successful as Jack Canfield, then I should do it too! Since then, in several popular self-help books, including Louise Hay's You Can Heal Your Life, I have seen variations of this exercise.

The exercise is called The Mirror Exercise, and why. Each night before you go to bed, ideally after you've washed your hair, brushed your teeth, placed on your phi's, etc., seeing a mirror in your house that you'll be able to stand for a few minutes in front of you. If you're married or have a roommate, you're going to want to ask them to give you a few minutes to yourself because you're going to have to do this exercise alone to get maximum results. So, find a mirror in your bathroom or office, and stand alone in front of it.

Only stay there for the first few seconds and look at yourself, deep in your mind. You may never have done this before, so it's going to feel weird or awkward, and you might find yourself turning away from the mirror! Make sure this is natural, then simply turn your gaze back to your eyes and give as much love and acceptance as you can. Look at yourself and see what the outside world looks like. Look at your eyes, skin, forehead, nose, etc., and look at the rest of your body, too, if you're standing in front of a full-length mirror. (If you're brave enough to try this nude workout, go for it! But you don't need to get quick results...) After you've just stared at yourself for a couple of seconds, say "I love you" softly to yourself and then tell your full name. So I'd say to myself, "I love you, Mary Knebel." Remember, you're doing this out loud, and it may give rise to uncomfortable feelings. Do your best to stick with any positive or negative thoughts that come up. They're just feelings and you can accept them and let them be. Then you want to think about things you're proud of yourself to accomplish. These can be big or small stuff, but you're trying to find 5-10 things you've done during the day you can enjoy yourself. Here are a few reasons, "I'm so proud of you eating a healthy meal." "I'm so proud of you completing the report you said you'd complete." "I'm so proud of you reading a bedtime story in front of the bed for the family." The aim is to remember yourself and enjoy the stuff you've done during the day. Again, aim for 5-10 things and remember that you're telling yourself these things loudly!

When you continue to look at yourself in the mirror, love, and compassion pour when much as you can for yourself. Now you want to discover things you love about yourself and remember them. Of starters, "I love you getting such beautiful eyes." "I love you being such a loyal friend." "I love how talented you are." "I love how toned your muscles are." You should focus on things you enjoy about yourself that are either tangible or more connected to who you are as a person. The key is to find stuff about yourself for which you can still love and appreciate yourself.

Eventually, to end this exercise, look a couple more seconds deep in your eyes and then say out loud one more time, "I love you" and then your email. So it would be for me, "I love you, Mary Knebel." Be with any feelings that arise, whether positive or negative and just let them be there. To love yourself is to love all of you, feelings and everything.

And this is it! Like I described before, the first few occasions you do this will probably feel nervous or awkward. I promise, though, that this is natural and that if you continue to practice, you will get over it! Here's the catch: for 40 days you should do this forward, without missing a day. Beginning from Day One and doing the 40 days all over again if you miss a day! This will become a pattern in your subconscious mind after 40 consecutive days, and you will see how much better you feel about yourself and how much more relaxed you are in your clothes. The universe will seem to become an environment for you that is much more caring and welcoming, but in reality, it is your mindset that has changed the world around you. Note, your thoughts are transforming into reality... So the more caring feelings you have in your head, the more the outer world will appreciate you. Give me a sample of this workout and let me know how it's going!

We've heard it said that judgment is false, caring is healthy, and kindness is the way to change. Judgment comes from the male negative, and lack of self-love comes from the female negative. First of all, we must be able to transmute self-judgment into self-love before we can love others. To fall into the role of self-criticism is very easy and to be brutal. This is quite damaging and it is necessary to avoid it.

Write down some harsh opinions you'll make about yourself in your brain for two weeks. For example, "I'm ugly... I have bad hair... bad teeth...nobody likes me... I'm always late... I'm always fat. I'm always fighting... I'm dumb..." If you have any of this kind of conversation, write down all the assumptions you encounter on a piece of paper. This is your "victimizer type" story. You also have a "victim side" who makes certain decisions on an ongoing basis.

The second part of this practice is to go to a room where for at least thirty minutes you will not be bothered. Read your judgment sheet loudly (up and down the list) for about fifteen minutes until the drama has significantly diminished. It vocalizes the (shadow persona) "victimizer self." Experience the "victim selves" in the last fifteen minutes. There are a lot of possible emotions like guilt, terror, rage, and sadness. Only settle down and feel the influence of self-judgment for fifteen minutes. This is often not heard because the criticism comes in one thing at a time as a sub-audible trickle. Now at one point, you've just poured so much stuff on yourself and you sense it. After three times during two weeks, you have completed the victimizer/victim component, then you can take the final step.

For at least four months, this last aspect of this task is to counteract negative beliefs. Write new positive statements similar to every negative statement you've created for yourself. For instance, if you've said, "I'm still late," you might respond, "Because I'm always on time, my life works wonderfully." Every time you hear yourself thinking something derogatory about you, stop saying the same positive statement. Assert that you make the choice to look positively at yourself. Whatever you're concentrating on is getting bigger!

You also have to overcome the shame of previous events. It's helpful to keep in mind the following premise, "I don't regret..... no regrets for anything I've ever done." You can't beat yourself up for what you've already done because these things can't be changed. You have to pardon yourself. Everything won't work as well until you forget all you've ever achieved that you haven't enjoyed. The recovery involves several specific processes. Change your pessimistic belief system as mistakes fall into your consciousness. Be mindful that you are going to make various choices in the future. Today, by making better choices, you will respect that pledge. It's a pledge you're keeping to you. You have to do what you say, and you'll feel better about yourself as you achieve your new goals.

Finally, it's an awareness decision. Without remorse and without continuing to act unintentionally, you can choose to take full responsibility for your actions. You should agree not to compare yourself and others. When you realize that some of them are simply ignorant, you can choose to love people. That's all right. They do not know their issues because they are too blind to properly perceive themselves. Compassion arises from the lack of unrealistic expectations of others. "No expectations, no loss." Knowing that some people just don't know what's righties compassionate. You know they won't be able to understand, so they won't act reasonably (from your point of view). Be careful and have understanding, and you can live in Grace's place.

Soon, you'll be able to stay for days in states of great joy as you accept people where they are. Not having to change things will take away a great deal of internal pressure. Acceptation is a non-resistance condition. It's better to go with the ride and the experience costs you. There's nothing to avoid because everything is there to support you. It takes years to accept this idea, but if you can do it, it helps. By doing this workout, transmute your self-anger into self-love.

Simple Steps to Enhance Your Self-Love Using Self-Hypnosis

Do you look favorably at yourself? Do you know your qualities? Would you spend more time than you do cultivate your skills, allowing you to be like someone else?

For many, a lack of self-love has left a hole in their spirit that can never fill any amount of food or designer clothes. You should continue to indulge in self-loving thoughts and actions, no matter what you have done in the past, and no matter what state you are in at the moment. You can take responsibility for your tender, loving care.

Luckily, to store up on self-love, you don't need to go to the grocery or a shop. Along Aisle 3, self-love is not contained; it cannot be found in frozen foods; it does not stay in the most fanciful designer clothing stores.

The product of a manicure or a new hairdo is not self-love. Inside you, self-love awaits your invitation to the shore. Self-love can hear you call every time you conduct yourself with kindness. Through your caring actions, self-love is fed.

Only when you make it, your self-love grows and blossoms.

Wonderful things happen as you respect and support yourself. You start believing in your skills. You excel because you trust in your ability. You gain the confidence you need to step towards larger and lighter worlds with every small success.

If you appreciate and support yourself, a beautiful upward trajectory happens. It almost sounds like you're raised out of misery and in love cradled. Creating positive changes in your life and attitude are simpler because you respect yourself; it becomes easier to succeed in all the areas that matter the most.

Hypnosis will help you start a self-loving journey that is so rewarding that it sets you on board for your health, joy, and physical fitness. Starting right now, with your affection, you should offer yourself. You can let the light of your affection shine so beautifully with each passing day that you can see plainly what actions to take to suit your body, mind, and spirit.

To boost your trust, self-esteem, and self-love, you should practice self-hypnosis. It is easy and effective for self-hypnosis. You can use a lot of different techniques to hypnotize yourself, but to simplify the process you just need to do the following to get started:

1. In a relaxed position, sit or lie down;

2. Your eyes are closed;

3. Take five to ten long, slow, deep breaths as you imagine that your mind becomes clear and that your body fully relaxes;

4. Take five deeper breaths as you settle deeper and deeper in your body;

5. Reflect on your abilities and qualities;

6. Link useful reminders of your past achievements;

7. Once you know your important goals, fill your mind with positive intentions;

8. Picture the performance for some time as if it had already happened;

9. Take a precious moment to be truly grateful; and

10. Take one to three clearings, calming breaths, open your eyes, and return from a warning, clear, and revitalized self-hypnosis when you're able.

You will find that using these simple steps will help you to strengthen your psyche and experience enhanced self-love immediately.

Including music and nature's grace, self-love for your body, mind, and spirit is calorie-free nourishment. Self-love is an easy-to-pack food; you can take it to work with you; you can share it with your family and friends, and you can eat it all through your life.

You Are Not Broken or Need Fixing, Only Further Self Love and Acceptance

What you need to fix your broken bits are self-love and self-acceptance, so they're made whole again.

What you're feeling is a rising potential that may seem to be missing. You're losing your old self to make room for the new one you're going to emerge.

To persuade you of your worthiness you don't need more posts like this. Although giving reassurance, they are only a reference because when you abandon your former self, your true essence must appear.

Writer and teacher Mike Dooley write: "You don't need to cure or support yourself as much as you need self-love and acceptance. Eventually, as you display genuine love and compassion, old unhelpful habits of thought and behavior start to fade away." The heartbreak, suffering, and frustration you endured served a purpose; to awaken you to your true nature. Regrettably, when it is an existence that leaves the door ajar to light the way for your transition, other people perceive this as being shattered.

"Everything in your life— especially your challenges— is tailor-made to make you see your combat tales. What's in the way is the way!" Mary O'Malley writes in: What's in the Way Is the Way: A Practical Guide to Waking Up to Life.

You may think: if I'm not destroyed, why do I need to be transformed?

It is so that you can feel your being's completeness, which includes: waking to your greater potential, giving and receiving attention, and finding your real self's nature.

To starting with, you've never been split, just undertaking a renewal process. Sometimes, the bits may seem to have fallen apart because you still have to see the whole picture. It's like staring at a jigsaw puzzle bit, unsure of how it's going to come together.

You've been waiting for unrealized potential to emerge. You only need to take the next step and believe that you will be driven to connect with your bigger self.

Be Compassionate with Yourself.

If life sometimes seems chaotic, don't be discouraged. It occurs as you concentrate on the broken pieces rather than seeing how they come together to form the whole.

You are made up of light and dark in a world of duality to complement each other.

You are likely to perceive yourself as broken if you focus on the unintegrated parts. But, as light and dark unite, they are one like the sign of Yin Yang, reflecting opposing and intertwined powers of the opposite.

Matt Kahn states in What Emerges, Loving This: A Love Awakening Which Starts with You: "In embracing what emerges, you discover in the most heart-centered manner the greatest understanding of the Universe. When the heart expands, you can see how any situation and aspect in existence has been developed solely to help you develop on a spiritual level." I encourage you, though, not to focus on your mistakes, but to have compassion for yourself, so that you will continue to grow and develop.

The human spirit is seeking to change, otherwise, you will stay stagnant and trapped. This is what a lot of midlife faces as they lose their identity.

Many people spend their lives trying to fix themselves to become ideal and pleasing to others. But if they aren't handled in the way they're planning, they think they're wrong with something.

I like it scrubbing corrosion off metal thinking the perfect chrome finish will be shown below. Nonetheless, the rust is a natural part of the metal when scrubbing you know. By embracing it, instead of something to be polished away, you come to appreciate it as a unique feature.

"Some of us can embrace people right where they are far better than we can recognize ourselves. We believe like love is meant for someone else, and we never feel it for ourselves," the Buddhist nun Pema Chodron says in: If Things Fall Apart: Heart Advice for Difficult Times.

You're not cracked, but to show your best self, you crack through your shield.

You are letting go of the self-hatred and disempowering thoughts that obscure your true essence by accepting yourself as you are.

As a writer and speaker, I've noticed the same trends that have appeared over the past decade through my writing and speaking. That is the consequence of pain as you deny what is. This notion is nothing new but something that the Buddha reflected on centuries ago. All exist in peace and harmony when we let go of opposition and acknowledge the circumstances of our existence.

Mary O'Malley says: "It's important to understand that when you're fighting it, you transform the discomfort into misery." Depression Precedes Discomfort And Misery

Let me illustrate this idea of releasing frustration through a recent example.

This year in Australia we endured a horrific flu season, with many people falling sick, several needing hospitalizations, and several people passing away sadly. My family members and I succumbed to the flu, but because they ignored their effects they needed longer to recover.

I, on the other hand, gave up completely and stayed in bed without medicine for three days. I slept through the whole thing and let the fever sweat my core. I had lost my energy within three days and feeling considerably better.

At the moment, I recall my naturopath claiming that disease allows the immune system to cultivate infection and virus tolerance. In doing so, it destroys weakened atrophying cells and is purged from the body. What doesn't kill you makes you stronger.

Here the lesson is: resistance leads to fighting.

Pain and suffering are always followed by a battle.

Let go of your opposition and embrace the conditions of life to allow the force of life to pass into you.

You are not ruined, but enjoy yourself just as you are, helping you to unfold the next phase of your life.

Psychotherapist David Richo explains in The Five Things We Cannot Change: And the Joy We Achieve through Embracing It: "Our limitations on self-acceptance are equivalent to the limits on our capacity to enable ourselves. The more we trust in our abilities to reconstitute our broken state, the less we feel the fear that holds us that way. For a cause, the past is there and should not be taken into the present moment, as it disco orates the present moment encounter.

Surrender and believe that life has a purpose for you, similar to the natural water flow that reaches its own pace. Eventually, if you follow the current upstream instead of resisting it, your personal growth will lead you to a wonderful place.

The key is to believe in the process because you won't be deserted by the universe. Perhaps when you're lost in pain and suffering, it may look that way. This is brief, however, and will inevitably recede.

Enable life to repair the broken pieces more than you need without focusing on them.

When the healing and change have taken place, you will have transformed into the individual who has been there all the time; your true self.

Caring for Others - From self-sacrifice to self-love

"Heal yourself first, before helping others."-African proverb I vividly remember the day I told my mother that I was pregnant with my first child. My mother's been overjoyed. This would be her first grandchild, and to her, it meant the world. She encouraged me, and then she said something that shocked me. "Be prepared to give up for this kid at least 10 years of your life." My first reaction was, "Sacrifice 10 Years?!! Well, how about me? How about my future?" Instead, I reached 30, enjoyed my job, and had no expectation of being a stay-at-home mom (although later I stayed home for a couple of years and I would never trade). I believe that my mother always told her the truth. As a mother and wife, that's how she lives her life. Nonetheless, ten or more years of my life's definition of "sacrificing" was such a foreign idea to me that it surprised me intellectually and emotionally. For me, this self-sacrifice parental style feels so "all or nothing." I realized immediately that it's not ideal for my general well-being, even as naive as I was. I remember thinking to myself, "Is this the only way? Why can't I have my daughter, my job, and my life?" Unless you know anything about Chinese culture, you realize that "self-sacrifice" is particularly admirable, even for women in particular. Men are also expected to sacrifice themselves, but typically only for a higher cause, such as family honor, monarch, or government. The bottom line is that most people avoid being viewed at all costs as greedy, and at the hands of others, they place their happiness and self-worth. We conclude that self-sacrifice is a way of showing affection, receiving love from others, and validating their self-worth.

I know that after nearly 20 years of living in the U.S., counseling, and coaching countless people, the Chinese are not the only group that thinks and acts in this way. The truth is, we're all more similar than the other.

I encourage you to pursue Intensive Self-Care, which is an act of self-love, rather than looking outward for care. What is Self-Care Intensive? I describe it to take good physical, financial, emotional, and spiritual care of yourself. It includes (but not limited to) beliefs and behaviors such as loving oneself and accepting oneself unconditionally, respecting oneself, meeting one's own needs, having regular "Me Time" to do things you enjoy, eating a balanced diet, having enough sleep, exercising regularly, having annual physics, enjoying quality relationships (family, friends, colleagues, life coach, mentors) If you are in a caring position in your personal or professional life, it is particularly critical. It's like putting FIRST on your oxygen mask before having someone pull on theirs when the plane reaches midair turbulence.

When you didn't put on your oxygen mask and handed it out, you wouldn't be of much use to your loved ones. Evidence has shown consistently that a host of physical and emotional signs and many major diseases are linked with chronic stress. As a

Nurturer, if you don't make a point of renewing and recharging yourself, you are likely to end up getting stressed out, worn out, or having physical and/or emotional pain. Anyone you care about will hurt you when you do.

As a parent and with roles in teaching, counseling, coaching, schooling, non-profit, small business, etc. over the years. I noticed it was one of the most significant keys to my personal and professional health, life balance, and joy to continue and practice Intensive Self-Care. That's why I want to devote my coaching career to help Nurturers understand the concepts of Intensive Self-Care and integrate the methods of self-care into their daily lives.

So, how are you doing intensive self-care? Take a couple of minutes to answer the following questions. These will help you gain insight and take action regularly and continue cultivating yourself.

Am I satisfying my desires, goals, and values? If not, what can I do to improve my current situation? Write down 1-3 first steps to take this week.

Why do I want to treat myself mentally, emotionally, and spiritually in an ideal world?

In fact, what do I do for my physical, emotional, and spiritual well-being regularly?

What are my self-care habits that are not negotiable?

What can I cut from my calendar (delete or delegate) to make room for ME Time?

What tools do I have (time, energy, people) that might motivate me to practice Intensive Self-Care?

What kind of assistance can I get from my relatives, peers, employers, life coach, or other professional help?

For Self-Love, Let go of Mother, Sister, Daughter position holding you back

The most valuable lesson I've discovered about Life Coaching is "Who I am." I realized that change is constant and I'm continuing my learning curve and evolving as a better person for myself by putting myself in a learning environment. The first thing I learned was to let go of worrying for others to the disadvantage of my well-being.

Girls are brought up to love, defend, and therefore unintentionally neglect the basic obligation of self-care. It is normal for women to feel that they must first take care of others before themselves. This conviction is so deep and powerful that they don't know how to let go of old beliefs that don't match the lifestyles of the 21st century. It's about letting go of having to be all to everyone's positions.

Letting go of the roles of mum, wife, and daughter becomes particularly challenging when we've been performing such positions for a long time. We become so addicted to those positions when we get tired that we no longer know how to participate in other tasks. It is like sacrificing our "identity" to fulfill certain positions. Every position we play today, question ourselves, "Is this what we stand for?" If we're upset, perhaps it's time to rediscover a new "you!" Both individuals have blind spots and behaviors and routines are there. Letting go needs someone to explain what we need to "let go." How can I let go? In particular, what do we need to let go of this "sweet spot" first? After letting go of disempowering behaviors and beliefs, with what can we replace them now?

Sometimes when I try to explain that we first need to value ourselves, certain people immediately grasped it; others are going to say, "Isn't that selfish?" Okay, if you first don't fill your cup and then go on filling in others, the cup can dry up early. There's nothing left to share. Self-love is about your wellness, nutrition, spiritual, emotional, and well-being. Others will be motivated by how you look for yourself and value yourself as you do it. They'll want to do the same as well. The key to happiness is self-love.

My belief is "God helps those who improve themselves." In other words, others are motivated by your way of living as you lead an inspirational existence. First of all, respect yourself. The key to happiness is self-love.

How Women should "Self-Love" their path to personal liberation and honest speech People with whom I talk and mentor told me what I believe is the key to satisfaction and my response is always the same, "self-love." Occasionally I tell chocolate-covered caramel with a touch of sea salt when I'm in a playful mood, but let me remain here on the topic.

It is during these discussions that I can always look into the eyes of a woman and see her focus change simply as she sees me prioritizing self-love above all else. It's like being lost in translation somewhere along the way. From what is being written, "Selfish" is being said... And the sad part is, it makes perfect sense to mislead.

Women are trained from girlhood to be caring and treatment vocal externally. While little boys are allowed to smash their Tonka trucks into the baseboards, the comfort of caring for Dolly is often taught by little girls.. Feed her, adjust her, give her makeup.

Choose one of today's world's 7 plus billion people who haven't got their start from a woman. Also, women who have never given birth for whatever cause are still heavily involved in caring for and maintaining the position of godmother, auntie, mom, niece, tutor, neighbor.

And this is not to say that men are not caretakers and nurturers who are committed, many are, but they do not tend to lose themselves in the role.

The "them first, never mind me" tape that can bog our headspace is harder for women to turn off. In the number of times a day we hear our name called given the reference to "needs" we have the strength, authority, and knowledge to fulfill, we may even go so far as to find value.

Being based on it feels good. That is until there is no other thing.

So, what about recovery?

Sleep's inevitable consequences are even delayed for those who refuse to sleep taking mental notes of the infamous "undone" while still pledging dedication to the potential "hots" that will eventually demand attention.

Listen, it's not your invitation to fatigue. Neither is severity. And if tiny bits of anger starts creeping in through the cracks of that battered woman's symbol on your face, then that's not just more evidence you're not a savior, it's confirmation you need a savior. Let your self-love come to your rescue.

From a turnip, you can't get blood.

If you only have $10 and I'm asking you for $10.10, you're not enough. You might set your sights on saving, gambling, or doing a steady two-minute cartwheel to raise the other dime, but you don't have enough right now. The same is valid when you first seek to do all that caring, supporting, and being there for everyone else with little preparation in place to develop and display self-love.

It's not news. Everyone knows that you can't give away something you don't already have. It's called fraud in many circles, but we act as if we got a pardon from somewhere when it comes to women and our need to meet needs. We haven't.

And so, how does it feel like this self-love anyway? Does it have anything to do with holding the above-mentioned chocolate personal stashes? What about bubble baths every week? Or the owner of a German car? How about our own "true" red bottom shoes coveting?

The marketing and advertising system wants us to believe it, but I disagree strongly.

It's self-love...

Self-love is about equality of feelings. There is no need for other people to acknowledge what a valuable and amazing addition you are to the universe, but to be confident in your understanding of your importance whether or not "they" toot your horn in celebration.

It's about being able to appreciate and enjoy yourself. It's about discovering yourself curious enough to discover the deep knowledge of who feeds your mind, and then respect yourself enough to let it into your life. Knowing what activities will make you feel awesome and warm, and then allowing yourself to mark as many occasions as you can by doing whatever they are.

Self-love respects and acknowledges the wishes, strengths, and abilities of your spirit. Unapologetically.

It takes time to discover what you want to learn so that you remain genuinely interested and invested in what you have called your life. Surely, your judgment is noble and important enough to indulge in the interactions and partnerships that can only progress you into the pleasure of smiling your belly's take-your-breath.

Self-love is about understanding where you are at the moment and an unwavering and genuine appreciation for who you are at all times. It strokes the folds of your tummy fat and likes it because it's there without judgment and gently reminds you that you can (and will) let it go when you're done.

Self-love is a strong self-reflection that, like an alert discerning bodyguard, radiates in your universe. Any person, place, or thing that does not serve your highest good must give up its power and right to hold the space when you have it. Quickly.

So, all this (and more) is self-love, but where does it come from?

Lord, God. Yeah, yeah? I say I hope, I mean... That sounds like religious programming nowadays, but please listen to me because I have an addendum resurrecting this response from cliché graveyards into full-blown life.

And it is a redemption that we need because the fact of self-love is honesty from a relationship with God. It is as alive today as it has ever been, so regeneration is our connection to the world.

The second we make up our minds as women that we are willing to go all in and decide to develop the real deal, Bonafede self-love, is the very second we have to unleash the tradition of addressing God in ancient religious postures. Praying the same old prayers that we have chanted since we were knee-high to a duck is not going to produce the crop that we are after here.

If the goal is self-love...

If self-love is the target, the pose must be true surrender, true readiness to be guided into the depths of the chaos of who we became and why; in whom we permitted ourselves to be transformed while we concentrated on escaping the wilds of a planet that seemed not to matter.

When the target is self-love, we women wail deep prayers like, "God, teach me how I am" and "show me who I am." We pray that way because we realize that self-consideration and redemption is the only path in and out, and we have been squeezed internally for far too long now out of the too little lives.

And then buckle in for your life's ride as this pursuit of self-love is simply not for the weak. Within 1 Corinthians, the popular chapter of love? Okay, get ready to see each of the stuff that true love doesn't do.

Get ready to see yourself puffed up, the restless, quest for your own, and score for you! This process of emotional maturity thing is wild watching it play out!

That's why you have to remember that forgiveness is the biggest step towards love, even self-love.

To receive the light of God in your dark places is all part of His guidance. Jesus hasn't sent a Savior to us because we didn't need one. He sent us a savior because we were doing something!

So trusting in the process of sanctification and remembering that God loves you anyway, has always been the remedy through it all to beat yourself as you grow in self-understanding, acceptance, and love.

God's true love and forgiveness, and Christ's desire for you as a person, is the only thing in existence that is deep and enduring enough to bridge the gap between self-accusation and guilt that is so quickly besetting and self-love that needs to be developed if you want to offer yourself permission to succeed and become what God created you.

But it's not going to happen!

Self-love is not a quality of being that arrives naturally with the knowledge of the Born Again as much as I wish it did. It is the sacred pearl of the Empire, the one of great value to be purposefully found, collected, and maintained above all else.

It is the Good News that I know the Bible is all about: you are set free and empowered to seek, accept, and grow a greater love for yourself without fear of rejection or defeat because of the sacrifice of Jesus.

And as you develop in that passion, it will expose you to the richness of your own honest identity where you and everyone in your love and power circle will gain in the most beneficial ways.

It's not self-love.

Pursue it and wear it proudly as a favorite garment because you will start to see yourself stronger, more purposeful, and more confident, more creative, and bolder, more forgiving, more radiant and freer!

You are going to grow into your God-made selves more and more: God's magnificent mother created you to be!

Steps on how Self Love Overcomes Anxiety

"Fear and Love Cannot Conquer the Same situation," It stuck with me when I first learned the quotation several years ago and encouraged me to fill myself with love when I was scared. Many of us ask the big question, how do we treat ourselves? During these uncertain times, this is so necessary. It's a big question. The key in the universe is to give love to ourselves when so many around us are overflowing with fears.

Here are three strategies to make you respect yourself more: Stop criticizing yourself No one will damage you more by attacking yourself than you do for yourself. Avoid criticizing you is necessary. It's a violent act to condemn yourself because it shakes you up. The emotional harm you are doing to yourself is far more enduring than physical abuse. Tune in and become aware of the negative feedback is the best way to stop self-criticism. We don't know how we continuously crucify ourselves with words such as: "I was too stupid." "Why would I do such a dumb thing?" "I'm not as clever as," "No one likes me to look like that." "I'm too fat," and the list continues on and on. You'll be shocked to relax into your feelings.

Enjoy. The Reflection I have carried an image of myself as a little girl on my nightstand for years. The three-year-old, wide-smiling little girl with a gleam in her eyes tells me every night before I go to sleep to say "I love you." We say that each one of us is a three or four-year-old child who needs reassurance at all times and is constantly calling for attention.

One way to get ready is to look in the mirror, remember to say, "I love you." Every shot you're going to do. Tiger Woods claims he rarely heads over to see an image of himself in a journal, on tv, without saying "I love you" to himself.

Transfer Love to Yourself. Think of someone you love now or in the past if you find it difficult to love yourself. -somebody's a father, a dad, a husband, a friend, or a pet. Take the same feeling and pass it on to yourself.

It instantly dissolves any negativity around us when we are filled with self-love. Most people call that an aura. Whatever people that name the feeling of affection, there is no doubt other people feel love. They're drawn to the warm sound you're emitting even when you're quiet. The secret is to be open and ready to live.

One of the crucial things to remember in the rocky times of today is that love is also required by those around us, particularly those who are gruff and frustrated. Such people make the most of the application. Like many citizens in our country, they are scared of all the negative things they hear in the news and others. Through showing them our affection, we will support them. But we have to note that from our excess we can only send. We must first give love to ourselves.

I discovered that we need the reverse of our lives, however negative emotions we show. If we give away hate, we need love. If you're not trusting, you need confidence. You need to be cool if you're anxious. This is a way to understand our desires and is self-love the way to heal anything that disturbs us. Love will be able to overcome terror. It's the planet's most powerful force.

Welcome Success With self-love and self-acceptance

Are you wondering what self-love is all about finding success in all areas of our lives? The adults were guided to conclude that self-love is vain and conceited.

Loving Jump to Triumph Far from this* Self-love is about healthy self-respect and unconditional acceptance of yourself.

The essence of self-love is to protect the ego, body, and soul.

The right to do what we want and want to do is self-love.

We have to respect each other because if we don't, how can we hope someone else to accept us?

To be loved and loved is human nature.

Self-love is a journey toward a better understanding of our existence and moving against our objectives.

We need all our present strengths and weaknesses to accept ourselves.

As we consider speeding our development the latent expectations of sadness and alienation if we are not aware about the consistency of self-love.

Definite ambitions need to be set throughout life, and this stems from self-confidence and greater self-esteem.

When possible, we need to focus on it, strengthen our values, and fully accept ourselves as we are.

A two-step self-love method is:

1. It is important to scrap all the negative judgment toward ourselves and trust me that this will be the most terrifying thing in the process of accepting ourselves

2. Avoiding defining oneself by other people's prism will help build self-image and truly respect our life.

We will fill life with Self Love Magic and the excess would manifest as Self-love works on the Law of Attraction. It will stimulate all good life stuff for us to prosper our lives as well as our companies.

Self-acceptance and self-love

Introspection is ruminating about self. Looking deeper into us and dwelling on our behavior is the perfect way to enhance our self-esteem and start loving ourselves.

The inner critic is the inner voice of negative self-discussion and judgment. It's the nagging feeling, the unconscious echo that keeps us and others suspicious of ourselves. We need to be less judgmental and critical when we are at Family Business so that we can achieve a harmonious atmosphere that will lead us to a better business.

Once we avoid marching to someone else's drummer wants and needs, we can be less critical of ourselves and strive to be less critical of others if they don't suit what we want or predict. Through the judgment of ourselves and others, the loud voice of the inner critic talks, seeking to castigate. Sometimes our inner critique leaves us with self-doubt feelings, and at other times it allows us to feel negative and critical of others.

When we listen to our internal critics, we listen to the negativity that separates us from our best selves as well as others.

Self-love and acceptance build our best personal and professional selves together. True Self Love helps us to embrace ourselves and our viewpoint towards others is that of personal learning partners on our path.

Love is, of course, a journey that brings us closer to the seed of life and to a position where we can develop, learn, and share the love with others. So, let's suppress both self-criticism and cynicism, concentrating on human values that contribute to personal and professional achievement on the road map.

Let's take some time today (the last day of 2009) and dig out our inner critic's voice and get rid of self-imposed cynicism and judgment. Let's begin 2010 with a message to' Have a Good Day every day! Enjoy the year with the Highest, Greatest, and Best Self-full of self-love and world-love.

The Circular Conundrum of Self-Love

Self-Love means that the very meaning that a person has to love is to hire. But for adult children whose upbringings were full of depression, violence, insecurity, terror, instability, and the constant need to follow survival strategies, this cycle poses a recursive conundrum — namely, that an individual has to give it away to maintain it, yet he cannot give what his earthly parents have failed to do. Besides, they would not be able to receive it adequately, even if he could. Finally, this all-important, intrinsic substance of God was present all the time, as his eternal parent had already endowed him with it.

The first axiom is briefly mentioned in the textbook of the Adult Children of Alcoholics (World Service Organization, 2006, p. 288). "We need to give away what we need to hold," he notes.

Although this sounds inconsistent, it must be noted that love is not a tangible object, such as property, which, if it is wasted or given away, certainly cannot be kept. It is a basic endowment or make-up. It suffers no limitations as both an extension and expression of God. It's relentless. The more it is human offered, the more it spreads by exchanging it with others-or reversing the material flow.

The second, being unable to provide what a person has not been provided to himself, includes an earthly experience stemming from the multitude of childhood events during which certain parents failed to provide that revolutionary "refueling" and extension of infinity. The boy was deflated by his failure of getting it instead of being suffused with this material.

Part of the equation of "self-love" is the body. It means and relies on the assumption that what he has historically embraced as his own has been respectable, important, and lovable. But he has already substituted the real thing with a fake, synthetic replacement because of his need to live and his excuse for the denial of it by his father.

Buried beneath it is the terror, discomfort, and alienation that fueled its creation— a warped self-image that his parents created and mirror-reflected. And buried below that is his inner child in search of safety.

Before he understands that what he has known as his true self has been his reverse, and until he feels safe enough to pull it back out, he is unlikely to be able to tap into any amount of self-love because that self is in disguise and its substitution is nothing more than a hollow, momentarily inflated alternative.

Loving emerges from and is modeled by parents, but the child becomes the target of hate as they unload their negative emotional pressure on him, project and enmesh him with their strength. It's certainly not loved. In reality, it's the opposite diametric.

The kid feels it as anger oozes from his mother. He can't understand it mentally or deny it. He is how he is treated by his mother.

Unlike poison, his ego is slowly eaten away by those chaotic visions, rotting it, and that force will flood through his cells until it becomes his synthetic manifestation.

Immersed in an engulfing cloud of transferring feelings, the child finds it harder and harder to create even a tenuous connection to himself and the affection of which he is created.

Desperately in need of connecting with his parents and gaining their approval and affirmation, he usually comes up empty-a cast fishing line that, when reeled in, has nothing on his hook- and, for all his efforts to infuse them with the affection that he can only receive in return, he always struggles in this tactic, revealing the third conundrum in the cycle of self-love.

"We loved our parents," says the Adult Children of Alcoholics textbook (p. 289), "but our parents couldn't embrace our gift, they didn't love themselves, they couldn't understand what we were trying to give them." Then, by mentioning his weakness, he excuses it and rationalizes their denial.

"We learn to withdraw our affection easily and bury it deep inside," concludes the book (p. 289).

An individual will fill it with something else whenever a hole is generated by eliminating something. According to the textbook, "we created a false self, (which) closed people and things, so we could feel in control but never whole."

However, a deep enough dig, especially after pursuing an extended path of recovery, will reveal what was rarely cultivated by earthly parents of a person, but was inherently provided by his eternal one. This was there all the time, amid vehement denials and complaints, uncovered with each climb through the twelve steps of restoration, the popularity and redemption of the painful and debilitating studies to which he became exposed, and the reclaiming of the actual, inner infant-imbedded self-or the final axiom of the conundrum cycle of self-love.

Self-care, self-love-Two directions to joy

As moms, partners, sisters, friends, workers, writers, magicians (just make sure you're still with me... but we know it's true; clink, clink), we offer so much of ourselves without worrying about it twice. As we come around on Friday, we ask why we're so tired. Or perhaps we just wonder why we're tired. We might be so buried in giving that we are exhausted and left with scarcely enough resources to dedicate ourselves-once all the various things to do are finally done! We have little say over our donation in some ways; it's built into our Genes, it's our biological existence! After all, we are life's contributors and nurtures. Our Genetics, of course, had no idea that we would also have to hold down full-time jobs, mow the lawns, take the three children to school, engage in the PTA, perform the exercise twice a week, go to the grocery store, visit our psychiatrist and walk the family dog at night. We don't need to apologize for being women who give love. That said, we are as valuable in our life as anyone else, and we are intended to be shown reverence, compassion, and goodness, not only by those we so freely give to but also by ourselves realizing that we are deserving and worthy of our own best love.

There are many wonderful ways in which we can respect ourselves. It's a5-minute rest at the end of the day for some of us, a fun meal out, a weekend away, a kiss to/from our family, a good book, a hot bath... you get the idea. These are the things I put in the self-care category (a very important part of our women's lives). We just have some of that sweet little stuff we can do to take care of ourselves, raise our hearts, and give us some energy back... and we're grateful for them. Generally, our children are the same, as are our friends. We should usually incorporate a few small bits of joy in the form of a self-care habit or custom in all our daily routines to keep life flowing smoothly. There are plenty of books on the subject of women's self-care. I say that because most of them are my own! I'm a fan of the self-help book. They're also really good. I got a ton of ideas and new approaches to think about things that motivated me to take better care of myself over the years. So, trust me as a single parent in graduate school in the early years with a part-time job and an overly anxious kid, I wanted all the support I could get.

But there's another less talked about self-care form; I label self-love. You might wonder what the difference between self-care and self-love is. Okay, first of all, they're not each other's exclusive. Each one of them plays an important role in our general well-being, long-term health, and particularly in our self-esteem-which is important when it comes to natural donations.

A fine line between respecting our bodies and honoring our hearts is the contrast between self-care and self-love. We surround ourselves with "stuff" because we enjoy our bodies. As we value our hearts, we reach a deeper aspect of our being by reminding our minds that we are genuinely caring, loving, deserving, and good as we are. We seek ways of finding a greater pleasure of life with self-love rather than a moment of calm apart from it all. Don't get me wrong, from time to time, we all need a moment of peace away from it all. But as we grow in love with ourselves, we eventually find that our current needs give way to something richer and more sustaining; an inner-calm feeling-or if you don't mind the "inner-peace" cliché. Because, when we love ourselves deeply, we are more at peace with everything (including ourselves) more of the time. I remember you're curious how you're going to get there now, right? Well, there are no secret formulas or anything like that... and I can only share my thoughts and experiences with you, of course, but now that I've brought it up and the idea is fresh in your consciousness you have the chance to explore the answers for yourself. Who knows this may be the start of searching for and finding your inner peace for some of you? While you're searching for that in the meantime, how about exchanging some of my thoughts on the matter with you? If you want to get started right away, I'm also going to toss in an exercise at the top.

As a therapist, I have the privilege of working with people who are willing to escape their comfort zone to encourage me, a virtual stranger, to be a witness to their individual development that is always incredible. Now, first and foremost, I'm not a magician. Because of me, my clients don't turn because of their need to recover. In the meantime, I'm just a facilitator, but I digress. Through my research, in certain states of being, I have encountered several individuals who could be identified as stress, anxiety, or just plain misery. Such individuals tend to suffer regardless of how much money they earn, how much affection they get from others, how many gifts they have in their life, how many vacations they have, etc. There's a common connection for many of my clients when it comes to suffering... and that's the cycle of resistance they're engaged in that keeps them from loving themselves and enjoying their lives completely.

Usually, the first step of the resistance process begins with a thought or conviction that we consider it unbearable at some point. Ever notice for whatever reason, you instantly feel angry, irritable, sad, ungrateful, unloved and restless when you are in a certain space of feeling / thought! We are not always conscious of the connection between our thoughts and feelings, but believe me that they exist in some way for most of us. It is very difficult to separate our feelings from our feelings about our feelings when we are in these moments. You will easily see how things get complicated. The problem occurs as we shift around our feelings/thought into a position of self-judgment. We're engaged in a battle of resistance within ourselves when we're in judgment... and guess what? Usually, we get a worse feeling. This struggle takes many forms, but in essence, it is a dedication to anything that stops us from actually expressing our unbearable feelings/thought. In yourself or anyone similar to you, you can know this. For instance, if you feel emotionally uncomfortable, you can spend a lot of time filling your day with meaningless things... taking on more than the usual load. You can catch yourself while you invest, consume, or even sleep; essentially anything that takes you out of your feeling. We do this because we condemn our hearts as we judge ourselves. We undergo pain as we deny ourselves. We become forced to move away from what seems terrible when we encounter pain, thereby perpetuating our self-rejection. This process may be daunting for some people and eventually grow into long-term depression or anxiety disorders.

There are a few important things to consider here: o Feelings are electricity. A sensation can't hurt you in and of itself.

- Our emotions ' energy needs to flow.

- They can become mentally constipated or trapped as they hang on to or avoid the flow of the strength of our emotions. The opposite will happen often and all the time we can become overly sensitive or highly emotional.

- The strength of our emotions is limited in their movement when we are punished, ignored, and/or rejected.

Therefore, on our path of self-love, we have to somehow collect the courage to face ourselves. To enable our feelings to be valid and honored, and to know that we are creating the possibility of joy in the process. We do this by respecting ourselves, our emotions, and our opinions as profoundly as we value others as freely, warmly, and kindly. You will learn a few moves here to support you along the way.

One of my favorite writers is David Richo, a Buddhist counselor who in his book How to Be An Adult created the five A's concept. Love, recognition, respect, love, and authorization are the five A's. When researching energy work in Durango, Colorado a few years ago, during my path of development and self-love, I was deeply familiar with his work. Here's a snapshot of that cycle that you can use in some way that makes you feel better.

Self-love exercise: Consider a problem, a difficult feeling, or situation (past or present) that you notice as a result of which you are struggling with or feeling a certain amount of suffering/discomfort.

1. Make an effort to be aware of this problem. Find a quiet spot to be comfortable; if necessary. Make a mental note or write down on a scale of 1-10 before you get going, how painful or distressing the sensation of' suffering' is right now as a consequence of your emotions, perceptions, or circumstance. (1= the worst, 10= the worst). This is a roadmap that helps you to chart your overall progress in raising your negative feelings.

2. Write down a couple of sentences about the problem if you want (or keep it in mind if it's easier... like if you're in the shower or something.)

3. Take the problem to your mind completely. See that. See that. Sit down with that. Look at it. Give it your full attention for a moment. (The way your child might be cared for when she comes to you in pain.) Care is essentially to be mindful of the present moment; to watch, react, and consider all the emotions at risk.

4. Refrain from making any judgments about it in being with your thought, feeling, or situation. You will gently guide your awareness back to the original feeling, thought, or situation if you notice your mind wandering into the judgmental territory. View[it] as you watch it playing on a movie screen; go past you-just watch the thoughts and feelings as they play along.

5. Now that you're well on your path to fully experience the thinking, emotion, or circumstance, and you've paid it enough consideration, take a few deep breaths in and reach the recognition soft spot. (At first, it may feel tough, but you can just practice by saying, "I embrace myself as I am at this moment; I acknowledge these challenging feelings... etc.) Once you've offered yourself the recognition present, take a couple more steps and see if you can communicate with the gratitude sensation.

6. Look again for a moment as you see your family-think of all the love you have for them-look again at yourself and in the room of recognition of all that you are right now, acknowledge all your talents, shortcomings, longings, and profound human predicament; which maybe your feeling of misery at the moment.

7. Yeah, there's a route. You're perfectly going up. Now bring the feelings of Affection right to the surface with the same intention in mind. Look at the uncomfortable feelings in you to change from fear/shame/guilt/sadness to those you see in a kid that a loving grown-up has just

offered attention to. Here you can even combine your self-care plans-show your care and love in any way that feels right for you. This may just be to mean that you value yourself, or you may just focus on getting life into your heart.

8. Lastly, be in Enable space. With all their happiness and ache, encouraging life and love to be just as they are, without trying to take control. Letting yourself be where you are in emotions, opinions, or situations. Of life's determination. Whole and perfect. You see there's nothing to alter or repair in this room. You're just... breathing the way.

It's not easy to digest or adapt these values to our lives. They're taking time, thinking, and work. What they teach us is that we're all right just the way we're... all our weaknesses and shortcomings... We are opening the door of liberation in this place of unconditional love to view ourselves and our lives with happiness. I hope this was helpful to you in a small way.

The Father-Daughter Relationship's Effects on Self Esteem-From First Love to Self-Love

Can you remember the first boy you loved? Close your eyes and think for a minute about him. What was the name of him? How big have you been? When you first looked in each other's eyes, where were you holding each other's hand? Recall how it feels like being with him. Time was still lingering when you were together. Even when you were among a group of friends, because he was there, you felt special. His very thought was amazing. You were still happy.

What a wonderful sensation! The first kid I fell in love with, I'll never lose. It was the year I turned 13. I was coasting with my mate nearby on my skateboard. That's when I've seen him. Once our paths crossed actually, he was on his motorcycle. What made us all quit, I don't know, but we did. He quickly developed the habit of riding down my street, hoping to find me hanging outside my house or skateboarding across our neighborhood. At the end of the summer, David aged sixteen. This didn't bother me that he was older than any kid I've ever met. I was more curious about how it would be treated by my older brother, as they were the same generation.

David and I spent many days together throughout the season. We spent hours talking. He was unlike most of the boys I met. He was relaxed and knew how to deal with a female. The way he made me feel as he put his arms around me was what stood out most in my memory. I remember that feeling like yesterday. I was so young, yet in love so much. While David may have been the first kid I've ever loved, he wasn't the first man. Consider the first man you've loved. Remember he kept you in his huge, strong arms for the first time? His lips were so soft and so sweet was his hand. His body's warmth against yours has been very comforting. Once you feel so safe, so loving, sleep came easier. Do you remember that? It's been that long ago...

Perhaps you can't remember how you felt, though-you were just a kid. Your father was the first guy you dated. Imagine you as a kid. You have come to this world that needs comfort, water, and contact with people. His arms were the first male arms placed around your baby because your father was missing the moment before you left the womb. This was your first tactile experience with the opposite sex, and the bond between you and your father began to develop even though you were just a baby.

Bonding is a psychological and biological fact, according to the attachment theory, researched thoroughly by Konrad Lorenz. We know for sure that baby ducks, baby monkeys, and human babies are all genetically programmed for attachment in the first few days of their lives immediately after birth. So their nurses (mothers, husbands, housemaids) are also close to the children.

Sadly, not all kids have the same probability of being linked to their mothers, just because they were physically unavailable. Born into the universe, never connecting with your father may sound like you've been trying to fill a void in your life ever since.

Can a young girl be subconsciously driven by the absence of her biological father to find the missing link in other men? Can she still build healthy relationships while her inherent need to connect with him is not met? Wouldn't her mother's mighty affection be enough? Daunting queries that nobody knows for sure about the responses.

Nonetheless, the data provided by studies and real-life experiences in the first version of "Daddy Effects: Why Your

Dad Influenced Who You Are and Who You Love" suggests that young girls feel abandoned, harmed, and discouraged without a father's intervention in these early years. As a consequence, their self-esteem is weak, their self-esteem is questionable, and their intimacy options are all related to pursuing people just like their father (healing wounds) or incredibly negative (eviting avoidance at all costs).

There seems to be a profound desire for a man's love, a father figure they never had as a young child, even with the best maternal figure(s). More investigation shows that when a father's involvement is hostile, a young woman is particularly likely to seek "joy" in a man's arms, whether or not he is ideal for her.

The perspective of the father's daughter teaches us that our father's need to be accepted is a deep emotional urge embedded in our biological and psychological make-up. Because they co-created us, we feel connected to our mothers. Shouldn't they value us and just because of that want to be part of our life? And if they don't, whether they harm or abandon us, doesn't it make sense for us to tailor it? I remember that when my father left, I feel unloved and vulnerable. This took me years to know it wasn't about me. The affection of their father was their first passion for many people. It was their first loss for other citizens. If your father has been unable or unwilling to give you unconditional love, even if he has been cruel, not everything is lost. You don't need to believe your low self-esteem will never change, and because of your father's weak parenting skills, poor judgment, and negative behavior, you will never find a loving partner. You can detach yourself from this situation because you realize you deserve to be cherished.

Your health and the quality of your partnerships depend solely on one element; you-you and your mind's power; you and your inner strength to rise beyond your darkest moments and saddest pulse.

From this day on, turn inward the need for the love and approval of your father and cultivate yourself. Reflect on your positive characteristics. Embrace the spirit in love. You've been burdened, depressed, for long enough influenced, let go of the past. And once in this process of self-healing so self-loving, expand those emotions to those who would greatly appreciate it: your babies, mates, and even your favorite charity.

Challenges of Developing Self-love in women

It can be difficult to develop self-love and self-esteem in increasingly negative world life. Sometimes it may feel that we don't have the power to control our feelings, our climate, or the increasingly negative universe we all reside in. We are living in a society plagued by violence, deprivation, abuse, depression, and diversion. To function successfully within this increasingly modernizing and diminishing social and economic system, we must first understand that we are all armed with all the necessary tools to begin developing a set of simple activities that can ultimately have positive effects on ourselves, our climate, our relationships, and our perspectives through which we view the world.

Self-Empowerment Starts with Self Love Before joining any kind of activity, it is important to start doing the rituals that can enable the subconscious and conscious minds to function together towards the goal of increasing self-love and self-esteem. This is also indicated by many common theories, ideologies, and philosophical doctrines. In reality, loving your life or relationships with others is almost unlikely until you establish a strong sense of self-worth, gratitude, and self-love. While it may often seem that in our current world and state of affairs this can be complicated, it can certainly be done through a few simple principles to grasp.

The Mirror Practice-5 Minutes of Mastery

Several psychologists, religious leaders, effective people, and practitioners in marriages have proposed the influence of the eyes as the "gateway into the spirit." Write about falling in love or connecting effectively with someone else. Talk about how you can act when you gaze into someone else's eyes or when your loved ones look deep into your heart.

So, talk about how many times every day you gaze into a mirror yet don't try to look into your own eyes. The following simple activity will easily be done every day and will have dramatic effects on self-esteem, self-confidence, self-love, and motivational development.

All you need to do is look into a mirror and look deeply into your head-into your own mind-for this simple exercise. This may be daunting at the beginning for some who have been exploited or informed by others that they are useless, inadequate, or have endured certain negative mental conditioning during their lifespan. You absolutely MUST do this for those men. You have to look into your own eyes and pierce your inner mind and soul to begin to tear down the walls of toxic thinking.

You need to develop a sense of love and compassion for yourself as you gaze into your own eyes every morning or evening before bed. You have to accept your shortcomings; you have to look in your own eyes honestly and earnestly the same way you'd look at your lover or someone you cared for deeply.

So, when you gaze into your head, continue complimenting yourself with sincere feedback on all the qualities you might enjoy about yourself. Even if you think there's nothing about yourself that you could love, I'm sure you'll find things about yourself, qualities that are worthy and worthy of appreciation, love, and respect if you thought about it.

The key part of this approach is sincere congratulations that show a real quality, not just hollow compliments like "you're amazing" or "you're beautiful." These have to be congratulations.

If you have a good work ethic, you might say, "I love you because of how you work so diligently to accomplish your tasks." When you support others, you may claim, "I love you the way you leap in and every day try to help others." If you're smart or you feel like you're, you might say, "I love you because of your growing intellect and your great ability to solve problems."

It has a dramatic effect on the preservation of this in your amygdala as you add truthful meaning to a compliment. In life, we often respond to constructive comments and they burnt into our mind more readily by making us feel. If you practice the same concept on yourself, you reinforce your self-esteem and self-love in ways that no external source can ever provide.

The Loving Force of Self Love and Forgiveness

Most individuals have a difficult time expressing self-love. But it can work miracles in your life to feel true self-love. Self-love is not about pride or greed. It's not loving, it's not fear. I'm thinking about great self-respect and reverence. Seeing yourself as a precious human. This is not egotistical. If you respect yourself, the attitude is happier and benefits those around you. Here are some reasons you can't love yourself, see if you accept yourself in any of these areas and how it can influence others around you:

- You scold and judge yourself

- You mistreat your body with unsafe food and drinks

- You misuse your body in any way (smoking, narcotics, lack of exercise, etc...)

- You believe you're not lovable, deserving, or nice enough

- For example, if you suffer from a chronic disease, part of the solution might be to work towards self-love.

Attempt this technique by Louis Hay, one of my favorite authors of self-healing. Pick up a mirror in your house or go to a mirror. Look in your own eyes and say your name, "I love you and embrace you as you are." For some men, this is very challenging. It's OK. It's really good news if you're having a hard time with this. Now you can start looking at the real problem— the real core of why you may not like your life and health to be.

Once you start recognizing that you're attacking yourself (self-talking), just STOP is a good place to start! But first, make a list of all that you think is wrong with you. The bottom line is that most people don't feel they're "healthy enough." They're punishing themselves for having learned to think this somewhere along the way to becoming an adult.

Remember, a conscious mind is a tool that can be used in whatever direction you want to use it. Through telling yourself a new story, you can use your conscious mind to alter some hidden latent negative beliefs towards yourself. Part of self-love is other people's self-forgiveness and forgiving. It's about letting go of pain, remorse, shame, sorrow, anxiety, anger and resentment, and releasing history. I think the answer to almost anything is acceptance and self-love.

There are many strategies and activities to forgive yourself and others as well as the path to self-love, and here's one you can do every day, even embraced by Louise Hay. The sentence "I love myself, and I'll..." is done in your book, you can see that there are many wonderful answers to this question! Here are a few examples:

- *Go out for a stroll.*

- *Eat more balanced, organic food today*

- *do at least one thing that gives me joy today*

- *forgive me or someone else*

- *plan anything*

- *meditate for 15 minutes today*

- *take my supplements*

- *enjoy a tv show that makes me happy*

- *do something positive for someone else today*

- *let go of anxiety, frustration, disappointment*

- *speak to me the way I should love and admire someone else!*

- *Etc... You're having the impression.*

Please positively refer to yourself. You are deserving of fitness, prosperity, love, and happiness. You're proud of being raised! Loving yourself improves your body (and cells) energy and will improve your health and well-being and your future! Eventually, let all this be simple, and don't be critical of not being fine!

Self-healing-Overcoming Self-love challenges

Just reading the phrase almost makes you feel uncomfortable, isn't it? We recognize that we should be kind and respectful of others. Yet you respect yourself? Isn't it... Okay, a little greedy somehow?

That's it. And that's the point. There are times when it can be very, very good to be "selfish." When you are in the middle of a crisis of healing... Try to work your way out and back to rising, sparkling health and wellness like the dickens... That's one of those moments.

Recently one of my daily blog readers sent a big question: "How can there be so many of us who don't accept self-love?" What I got out of her question was a plea for some tips to make self-love more available. We're going to explore a few key tips with that in mind.

Understand the subtle difference between self-love and self-absorption. Self-love is my world means that you care for yourself as if you were a loved one. You build for yourself a healthy and safe atmosphere, take care of your physical, emotional, and spiritual needs, and put yourself in the hands of those who serve the highest benefit. You are healthy and balanced enough from a position of self-love to encourage the grace and light to spill to those around you and share the joy. Contrast that with self-absorption, which means "it's all about you" in your mind. Not healthy, not balanced, not nurturing, and certainly no extra grace for the next-door guy. Let's just go back and forget that we spoke about it.

Know how smart the little people are. You're not the bad guy... For a second, the clinical psychologist part of me takes over. Once babies are born, there is no complete brain growth. Babies can see when something big and important, sometimes traumatic, is happening. They can't put it in context. So when something alarming occurs (as eventually does), a kid thinks they're the issue. That they are either poor, or nasty, or risky, or not worth the bother. Not real! Fill on this idea the spirit: God made you. It wasn't an accident.

Bless and go on with your family of origin. If you were born into a family where breastfeeding wasn't at the top of the agenda, realize that your parents probably educated you with the support they had at their fingertips the best they could. It's common for a young child to view the behavior of their parents as "all about them" (see the tip above), but that's not necessarily true. The acts of your friends affect your mother. If they were too harsh, too busy, too rigid, or too lenient, realize that the same condition would most definitely have been faced by any other person born in your family on the same day. Parenting style is often more about the beliefs and resources of the parents and less about how an individual child is a human being.

Make an independent decision on how the cultural climate can be felt. Many societies utilize criticism and terror as a means of controlling their members ' minds and spirits. Speak of the reports of authoritarian sects based on the fear that you've read. Even in such an extreme situation, you may not have been born, assume that some of the anxiety that might have been purposely put around you had more to do with manipulating you than with the reality of who you are. You're all that. People who use fear are most likely insecure in an attempt to control you. Love yourself enough to move to a place of security and bring to your life more supportive people.

While a short book like this is just an overview, the issue of self-love is vital to your wellbeing and well-being. You're teaching others how to treat you. You're going to walk a rough road until you can treat yourself with generosity and compassion. Help to move to a healthier state, licensed practitioners, psychologists, clergy, and teachers or coaches are available. If you're struggling to reach a point of self-love, find someone you trust on your path to help you.

Bulimia Recovery: 3 Strategies for How to Achieve Self-Love

As a woman, one of my bulimia recoveries turning points were the moves that brought me from self-doubt and self-acceptance to self-love. I assume that we are raised to value ourselves naturally. When we separate ourselves from our true nature and put the standards of society above what we need, we start to de-value ourselves when we begin to compare ourselves with others.

It's not about self-love and conceited. It's about just the way you are embracing and appreciating yourself. You as a human being recognize your value. In those with self-destructive behaviors and addictions, there are regularly low levels of self-esteem, self-confidence, and lack of self-love. It encompasses bulimia, other eating disorders, and other addictions.

I don't believe we're born with an inner critic, but rather over time we're creating one. Several titles have been given over time to this inner critic: Negative Nelly, Ego-self, Mini-Me, Lower Self, Monkey Brain, Demon Within My Head. Whatever you choose to call it, we set up a (mostly negative) survival-oriented defense mechanism to keep us safe and secure.

The inherent need for others to blend in and embrace us allows us to compete with those around us. They consider the idealized size and shape of the community and aspire to transform ourselves to meet the expectations of other citizens. Acceptance of being perfect, outstanding, or amazing-just as we are-does not come naturally, however. And our inner critic will keep us striving to fit in and be accepted so that in the world around us we can "survive."

I agree that one of the pillars of bulimia healing is to strive to become alive first and then separate ourselves from the destructive voice in our mind to focus on compassion and hope from within. Recovery finally came after many attempts to overcome bulimia when I realized that self-love was crucial to my healing. Here are a few questions to help you find out where you are to embrace, respect, and enjoy yourself: Does it make you uncomfortable when you are complimented by strangers or can you take them in step?

Were you stressed or burdened with other people's expectations?

If somebody tells you're sweet, do you believe they're doing that to get something out of you?

Can you dream of your own biggest critic? Do you often compare yourself to others and catch what others want?

Do you have faith in your intuition?

Are you hanging out with optimistic people or are your friends bringing you down or making you feel bad about yourself?

Is it easy for you to forgive yourself if you make an imagined or real mistake?

Was forgiving yourself convenient for you?

Is it very important for you, especially your parents, to work hard to please others?

When you place your desires before those of others, will you think yourself selfish?

If you replied "yes" to any of the above queries, then I would urge you to continue practicing self-love.

There are various ways to go through life. You can choose to see life as challenging and everyone around you can choose to think that what makes you special is what makes you beautiful and smart as well. Without you, the universe wouldn't be the same.

Here are three approaches you should start practicing self-love: if you make a mistake, make it easy on yourself and carry on. Once you start beating yourself, think twice. If you can see the light of what happened and how you made an unintentional mistake. Just as you would give off with compassion to a relative who made a mistake.

Put YOU above your job, your families, your obligations will go a long way to help you understand your needs. You don't value yourself and what you need to be healthy and happy if you put your needs to last. If you have to eat now, get it. If you're going for a walk, do it. This may mean saying no to other people and that's okay. Do nice things for yourself— when was the last time you gave yourself a nice gift or treated yourself to something you enjoy? Lately, if you haven't done anything good for you, it's time. Honor yourself by offering what makes you feel good. Make a list of the 10 most enjoyable things you do at least once a week or once a month. Yeah, why isn't that?!

Self-love isn't something you can expect to achieve in bulimia recovery right away if you've been beating yourself all these years, but with practice, it will grow over time.

Self-love practice is not about being someone you think people are going to like or think others are going to want you. It's about being your true self. If you are caring and kind to yourself and know that you deserve to live a rewarding, happy life not only will you feel better internally, but I agree that everything around you will begin to fit with your new vision.

Self-love - The Ultimate Relationship Advice

Self-love forms the basis of your most important relationship with yourself. The intensity of all other partnerships is precisely the same as that foundation's power. Loving yourself is not just a piece of advice that boosts self-esteem. Truly serving others is the prerequisite. The golden rule suggests "love your neighbor as you love yourself." You're undoubtedly reading it many days, voicing it in different ways, assuming it's about respecting someone. Look a little closer, though, and you will consider the order to value yourself at its very heart.

Self-love's Mistaken Identity: Let's first dissipate any misconceptions about what respecting yourself entails. Self-love is not about being selfish, self-centered, self-centered, or self-centered. So decide if you're nice enough, it's not about contrasting yourself to others. It's not always about putting yourself first. It's not about getting your way at all times. It is not about competing at all times. It's not about "looking about number one only."

Will the Real Self Loving Please Stand Up: To be in appreciation of the wonder of your life is to love yourself? It's about knowing yourself as you are-the pieces of the light and the shadow-and enjoying them all fairly. It's willing to receive as much as you're willing to give and do both in equal measure. It's about understanding and respecting your principles and standards. It's about explaining how to handle you to others by telling them how to treat themselves. It's about yourself being kind. It's about taking care of your skin, body, and mind-all three. It's about knowing that you're worth it, not because of what you've accomplished, what you look like, or what others think of you, but because love is your birthright.

What do you need to know most: Take a moment to think about what you need to learn from others. Whether they love you, admire you, accept you as you are, appreciate you, or forgive you. Take and write a piece of paper. Make sure the selection is finished. You'll notice out what you most expect from others to learn is what you most need to convey about yourself. You should now have a detailed collection of tailor-made optimistic statements. Say them every day, morning and night, and you'll quickly find a sense of self-love and inner peace that you've never had before.

You Can Only Offer That Which You Own: It's a clear statement that you can't give something you don't own, yet so many people love someone intensely without possessing or offering themselves affection. It is little surprise the passion reservoirs are depleted in time and their marriages are faltering. You first have to have love to give love. Thank you for having love. Only then, for the pure joy of knowing them, will you truly love others. Grant yourself the happiness you want to feel, and all the partnerships will be changed in amazing ways.

There is But One Origin of All Love: There is a single, intellectual Consciousness pervading the whole Universe at the same time-all intelligence, all strong, all love, all imaginative, and all present. It's the face of the world. It is Everything Love's Origin. It is Friendship. When you know and understand the Truth that you are one with the One Source of All Love — that love is your very essence— then you will have discovered unconditional self-love and unlimited reserves for all and all. You're going to know that respecting yourself is serving the Same God.

Loving Yourself's Benefits: self-love is a win-win for everyone. It offers you inner happiness, confidence, and peace of mind that is not easily influenced by external events and views. This allows you to make healthier choices and wise decisions from your intimate relationships to your investments throughout all areas of your life. This helps you to enjoy the good fortune of other people instead of asking "why, not me" or even resenting this. This helps you to value others more deeply and to be of greater service to the community as a whole. At the end of the day, the more you love yourself, the more benefits you encounter everyone.

Respecting yourself is, in a nutshell, a precondition for respecting others. Your relationships are just as powerful as your self-love foundation. Remove the conviction that loving oneself is immoral or greedy and substitute it with the Reality that love is your very heart, that your birthright is pure self-love. When you realize that you are one with the One Center of All Love, that you are linked to each aspect, you would recognize that you can not experience true love without loving yourself first. You will have discovered the Truth that the greatest love of all is true self-love.

Your Love Life and Self-Love

Now I'm asking you to look at the current state of your love life, your romantic love life, and your views and feelings about the relationship you're in or–if you don't have an intimate romantic partner at the moment–how you see relationships in general.

I have to make one exception to this chapter: if your partner has recently passed away and you are grieving the loss of the physical presence of this person, please know that your grief will diminish over time. In the meantime, you can still catch any self-love perspective and how you see yourself.

Whether you're in a relationship now or not, how do you see romantic relationships? How do you feel in this relationship if you're in one now?

The thoughts about this partnership and emotions are a direct reflection of your feelings about yourself in this relationship.

When you accept violence, it's because you believe nobody else can respect you. If you're sexually, intellectually, socially, or physically abused, get out of this arrangement is the only way you'll ever accept yourself. I hope with all my heart that today— right now— will be the day you decide to leave, for this will be the beginning of your life filled with self-love and happiness.

If you're scared to be alone and without a friend, it's because no one has told you how to value yourself, respect your emotions, and do what those feelings tell you, so you might feel insecure. More definitely you have been taught to follow what others have asked you to receive acceptance and love from everyone other than yourself.

If this partnership is not really in your best interest, you can be in a relationship and feel completely lost and alone. Having the strength to get out of a traumatic partnership comes with your devotion to yourself and knowing how vital you are; the bravery comes from deliberately deciding to raise yourself out of suffering.

A perfect relationship does not exist, just as there is no such thing as a perfect person. It is the degree of joy or sadness that you feel that shows clearly how you feel about yourself. It's not about what they're doing or about the other guy. In this friendship, it's about how you do.

As I said earlier, it takes complete self-honesty to get to the point where you finally love yourself. If you give yourself plenty of excuses to stay in a relationship where you feel miserable, then you also give yourself plenty of excuses as to why you don't honor your feelings and live your truth. In short, you're self-deceiving. I was also deceiving myself. I used to tolerate a lot because I haven't learned to love myself yet. It's your first move to be truthful with yourself.

The only way you can truly open the door to self-love is to accept the honesty about yourself. Of course, I will discuss with you the remainder of this process, but there are many bases to cover because there are many various areas of life that represent how you feel towards yourself; I have to put them into your conscious awareness and enable you to awaken to the real truth inside you, which is the cornerstone of self-love.

Self-love and self-doubt: complement or conflict?

Seemingly balanced at opposite ends of the spectrum, self-love and self-doubt are contradictory ideas, because at the same time a person cannot esteem himself and question himself. But is it?

Love-or, more specifically-self-love is above the point of life, but it is a sensation and manifestation of what you are as your Creator's continuation and language, not an abstract principle. It originates from above as a path, goes down and passes around you, and then radiates to others if you so desire. Nevertheless, if at your "intersection" it becomes lost, it cannot resume its path to others, including mates, relatives, and even pets, stopping you from having the link in the chain as your own is destroyed. You can't give what you don't have, thus.

For example, how, if you don't know how to do it yourself, can you teach someone to read? Likewise, how can you love someone else until you know how to love yourself first?

But why aren't you? As the term implies, self-love comes from within and extends without, but negligent, dysfunctional, abusive, and/or alcoholic upbringings fail to provide that link from the most important molders and modelers of a child— his parents — when they are themselves examples of broken links in the chain, leaving the child undernourished and undernourished.

Consistently transformed into a negative emotion, which is the opposite of love, he disconnects both from his Higher Power and himself, dissociating himself from these overwhelming emotions until, in a final act of self-abandonment, he drives them and his own heart backward.

Finally, hollow, and with a broken spirit navigating the universe, he is compelled to work with the same weaknesses and deficits as the parent who gave them to him. He is therefore frequently left with little choice but to substitute them with hole-plugging strategies and characteristics that both disguise his breakdown and indicate to those with whom he associates that he is total and competent, like people-pleasing, self-reliance, and an overdeveloped sense of responsibility that can inevitably contribute to freedom and high achievement.

Of course, art their heart is apprehension, distrust, remorse, embarrassment, low self-esteem, a chamber of negative emotions, and doubt.

Self-love compares with self-doubt. But what is it exactly? By its word, an individual doubts when he thinks he is something less than or less than what he was made to be. Or has he been? Could a God who is perfect himself have been made to be flawed? Interestingly, he could find the answer in the affirmative— if he sees his abusive parent as his physical maker, who re-enacts him in his face.

While for most of his life he may have been unaware that the person he regularly sees in the mirror is his parents, it may only be later when he recognizes that he has become the parent's duplicate. He gave him what he had, and his negative attributes in particular, but in the end, this was the equivalent of giving him what he had not.

Self-doubt, at least from its point of view, was most likely the result of the gradual transition of his father, through periods of weak or non-existent limits, of his negative feelings, doubts, and shortcomings, until they became his own, and inability to recognize and accept his accomplishments.

During your childhood, you rest your life on the foundation that your parents build for you, and when theirs are weak, you are given crumbling pieces that cannot be held together without the glue of love. You can't, to some degree.

It may be like seeing a series of dominoes collapse to list the suspicions of such an individual. For starters, he doubts that he is healthy. He believes he can have faith. He's vulnerable and he can't trust. He thinks he's as dignified as others. He thinks they're welcoming him. He doubts his abilities because they are not always accepted by people because they don't always accept him. He fears whether his degree of status will ever be exceeded. He doubts being able to love himself. And he denies as an addition that he might value someone. However, as the years go by, he suspects that he will no longer want any of these things.

What is he here if he's inferior to others and unjust, may he ask? Perhaps, possibly, to ultimately prove to himself that he is not his earthly parent's face, but his spiritual one's picture. And this is when self-love so self-doubt ceases to be incompatible and compatible when that awareness and reconnection regain the esteem displaced by his skepticism.

Conclusion

Many of us were told that self-love means self-absorption, narcissism, egoism, and other misleading adjectives that made the word almost evil. Typically, at a young age, this definition is developed in the mind. The term "selfish" is used as a coercive tactic in some communities and organizations to intimidate others in the line. For centuries, thus, the term "selfish" has been handed down and holds great power.

If we speak of the self-love definition, we first have to understand that self-love is not linked to selfishness. Yes, the more a person feels self-love, the more he or she expresses strength, kindness, and selflessness. In other terms, a win-win state of mind is self-love.

You have a deep regard for yourself when you live in a state of self-love that goes beyond the conditions of life. You are rooted in the fact that you deserve to be on this earth and that you need to contribute something meaningful. You took stock of your abilities, vulnerability, skills, interests, goals, aspirations, and considered yourself a unique combination of qualities that was fascinating.

Self-love equals self-esteem. For example, as a student, you can have high self-esteem and low self-esteem as a rugby player. As an employee, you may feel completely comfortable but be terrified by public speaking. You may feel great about your singing ability, but when writing a report, you have low self-esteem. In a certain environment, when your self-esteem is weak, you usually avoid the behavior and try to fill your day with tasks that represent your areas of trust.

Nevertheless, when you have created and nurtured the self-love trait, it can motivate you to drive yourself beyond your present ability.

Let me offer my own experience as an example. I attended a summer camp in Missouri when I was twelve. As campers, we had a regular outdoor activity program that included swimming and diving. I had been asked to lead my section in the diving competition before the end of the camping term. Because my self-esteem in this area was low, I declined immediately and somebody else was asked to take my place.

I was glad that I didn't have to go through the pain of what I felt was a certain loss. I didn't give it a lot of thought until the match day.

The girl who took my position did a good job, but I was struck by the fact that she wasn't a diver stronger than I was. I knew I had sold myself short at this point. It has become a Life lesson. I certainly would have succeeded if I had gained enough self-love at the tender age of twelve to encourage myself to enjoy the experience for the enjoyment itself.

You love and accept all areas of your life when you have self-love. You have a realistic assessment of your skills, but this is no way that impacts your passion and self-respect as a human being. You have an intrinsic relation to your origins that cannot be affected by external circumstances.

CPSIA information can be obtained
at www.ICGtesting.com
Printed in the USA
BVHW040733290721
613168BV00014B/333